PROGRAMMING IN VB .NET

PROGRAMMING IN VB .NET

(Exclusive Guide for Curious Learners)

By

V. CHRISTY
St. Xavier's Polytechnic College
Seydunganallur, Tuticorin Dist.
Tamil Nadu

UNIVERSITY SCIENCE PRESS
(An Imprint of Laxmi Publications Pvt. Ltd.)

BANGALORE • CHENNAI • COCHIN • GUWAHATI • HYDERABAD
JALANDHAR • KOLKATA • LUCKNOW • MUMBAI • RANCHI • NEW DELHI
INDIA • USA • GHANA • KENYA

PROGRAMMING IN VB .NET

Printed and bound in India
Typeset at Kalyani Computer Services
First Edition: 2015
UPV-9610-250-PROGRAMMING IN VB .NET-CHR
ISBN 978-93-80856-94-0

Published in India by

UNIVERSITY SCIENCE PRESS
(An Imprint of Laxmi Publications Pvt. Ltd.)
113, GOLDEN HOUSE, DARYAGANJ,
NEW DELHI - 110002, INDIA
Telephone : 91-11-4353 2500, 4353 2501
Fax : 91-11-2325 2572, 4353 2528
www.laxmipublications.com info@laxmipublications.com

Branches

✆	Bangalore	080-26 75 69 30	
✆	Chennai	044-24 34 47 26,	24 35 95 07
✆	Cochin	0484-237 70 04,	405 13 03
✆	Guwahati	0361-254 36 69,	251 38 81
✆	Hyderabad	040-27 55 53 83,	27 55 53 93
✆	Jalandhar	0181-222 12 72	
✆	Kolkata	033-22 27 43 84	
✆	Lucknow	0522-220 99 16	
✆	Mumbai	022-24 91 54 15,	24 92 78 69
✆	Ranchi	0651-220 44 64	

C—
Printed at: Repro Knowledgecast Limited, Thane

Dedicated to the
Lord Jesus Christ

Contents

Pages

PART I : .NET FRAMEWORK

PART II : CONSOLE APPLICATION

PART III : WINDOWS APPLICATION

FOREWORD

I have gone through this book written by Selvi V.Karthika. The author had undergone, ME Computer Science & Engineering in Anna University after AMIE Degree of Institution of Engineers (India), Kolkata. Her interest in Computer Science and Engineering had made her to write a book on this subject "Programming in VB .NET".

I am very much impressed with her attempt. This Book will be useful for the Engineering student who wants to learn from the fundamentals of programming in VB .Net.

It is very common to find people from the teaching faculty writing books on such specialized subject, and it is perhaps quite unthinkable for a lecturer with a short span of 4 years experience to write on complex computer subjects like this. It is for this reason I want to congratulate Ms V. Karthika for her excellent work.

It is more commendable as her own major experience has taken in the field of Computer Science & Engineering. But then it is precisely the reason perhaps, why she is able to explain things so clearly from a different perspective. I want to compliment her for her efforts and I wish her success in all her endeavour.

—Er. T. Velayuthan

B.E. (Mech), FIE., C. Eng(I)., PGDBA., PGDHRD.,

Principal

St. Xavier's Polytechnic College

Seydunganallur – 628809

Tuticorin Dist., Tamil Nadu

PREFACE

With the Grace and Blessings of **Jesus Christ,** I feel immensely happy to publish this book "Programming in VB .NET"

Every concept in this book has been explained with number of examples in simple manner. This book has been written for the curious learners of VB.Net in the field of Engineering and Arts & Science and also for the faculty.

Since the day of my learning VB .NET, I have been searching for a book with more examples. But I could not find that dream book. Bearing this in my mind, I have taken every effort to bring this book with as many examples as possible.

I believe that this book will be useful for the very beginners to become programming experts. Feed back from the readers are invited. This will help me to shape this book further in the future.

—AUTHOR

ACKNOWLEDGEMENTS

In this great accomplishment of publishing this book, I praise Jesus Christ for His omnipresence in all walks of my life and deeds.

I express my heartiest thanks with deep love to my father S. Vinayakamoorthy for his sacrifice in all possible ways.

I affectionately thank my mother V. Sundarammal for her sincere prayers to attain success in my efforts.

I sincerely thank Thiru. T. Velayuthan, B.E. (Mech.), FIE., C. Eng.(I)., PGDBA., PGDHRD., Principal, St.Xavier's Polytechnic College, Seydunganallur for his appreciation and guidance.

I also thank Mr. R. Venkatesh M.A., B.Ed., Senior Lecturer in English for the guidance. He has given in the formation of this book.

Last but not the least, I humbly offer my sincere thanks to Rev. Pr. J.P. Kamaraj, B.Th., M.Div., who much prayed for my successful accomplishment of this book.

—AUTHOR

PART I

.NET FRAMEWORK

To attain today's need in the field of computer, Microsoft has developed a solution which has been the dream of computer enthusiasts of modern trend. Yes. .NET Framework has brought our dreams to belief. It provides a Common environment to all type of programmers to work together. Developing of Business packages, System programs, Web applications all come under one common roof .NET Framework.

CHAPTER

1

.NET FRAMEWORK OVERVIEW

1.1 .NET FRAMEWORK

The .NET Framework provides a rich programming Framework for building Win32 client and Web applications. From here we are able to build components and to interact with COM components, .NET Framework services, external type libraries, and many operating system services.

We are free to access the operations and resources based on policy and a set of configurable rules to determine which permits to grant to code, based on the code's domain, user and assembly. We can pass objects by value or by reference between distributed applications

.NET allows us to use the COM+ Services including transactions, object pooling and queued components. In .NET we are able to access the Active Directory from managed code.

It Supports globalization and localization of resources and act as a Programming interface to many of the protocols found on the network such as HTTP, DNS, TCP and UDP.

.NET Framework Design Goals

- *Availability:* Availability is the amount of time the application is available for use.
- *Manageability:* Manageability includes the processes such as Initial deployment, configuration tuning, frequent health checks and occasional troubleshooting.
- *Performance:* Performance includes transaction throughput, network throughput, and disk access and application response time.
- *Reliability:* Reliability is an application's ability to operate failure free.
- *Scalability:* Capacity to add resources to an application to produce an equivalent increase in service capacity.
- *Securability:* Ability to provide security to an application and its data.

Features of .NET

Multilanguage Support

The .NET Framework supports multiple Languages. This allows us to write code in desired Language.

Code Reusability

We can create own classes that can be accessed by Third-party applications.

Automatic Resource Management

The .NET Framework automatically manages resources, such as files, memory, network connections and database resources. The Common Language Runtime (CLR) component of .NET Framework makes automatic resource management possible.

XML Web Services

These services allows to access code through the Web by using any device. By using .NET Framework, we can easily transform a standard application into an XML Web service.

ADO.NET

ADO.NET based on XML is used to access data on the Web.

ASP.NET

ASP.NET supports advanced compilation and catching features that helps to improve the performance of ASP applications

SOAP

It is a simple and XML based protocol used for exchanging structured and type information on the web. SOAP forms the standard protocol for all communication between processes.

Cross-Language Integration

.NET Framework allows code written in different languages to be integrated with one another.

1.2 .NET FRAMEWORK ARCHITECTURE

The .NET Framework includes the necessary classes, namespaces and assemblies to create Web services. The .NET Framework includes two components. These components are:

- CLR (Common Language Runtime)
- .NET Framework class library

CLR–Common Language Runtime

CLR is the runtime engine provided by the .NET Framework. It manages the execution of code and provides services that simplify the development of applications. It provides an infrastructure to execute applications and allows them to interact with other parts of the .NET Framework. The runtime provides services, such as cross-language integration, code access security, object lifetime management and debugging and profiling support.

Features Provided by CLR

Language Integration

The CLR component of the .NET Framework allows languages to be integrated with one another. For example, it is possible to create a class in C++ that derives from a class created in

Visual Basic. The .NET Framework can enable this because it defines a type system common to all .NET languages.

Code Reusability

CLR also supports code reusability. Here we can create our own components that can be accessed by third party applications.

Automatic Resource Management

CLR is responsible for automatic resource management in the .NET Framework. It manages resources such as files, memory and database resources by automatically tracking resource usage and eliminating resource leaks. This avoids the most common application bugs.

Type Safety

The .NET CLR ensures type safety of your code. Type safety implies that allocated objects are always accessed in compatible ways.

Rich Debugging Support

CLR supports debugging applications that support cross – language interoperability and integration. The runtime also provides features to easily locate bugs in the applications.

Easy Deployment of Application

The .NET Framework has simplified the process of installing, displaying and uninstalling applications.

MSIL (Microsoft Intermediate Language). When a source file is created using .NET Framework, the compiler generates code, called MSIL. MSIL is a set of instructions in which the .NET Framework programs are compiled. MSIL does not depend on the processor on which it is executed. MSIL includes instructions to load, store, initialize and call methods for objects. It allows integration of applications written in different languages.

JIT (Just In Time). MSIL instructions cannot be executed directly by CPU. Therefore, CLR must first compile MSIL instructions into native CPU instructions. CLR does not convert all the applications MSIL code to CPU instructions at load time; instead, it compiles the MSIL instructions as the functions are called. This is known as **JIT compiling.** The component of CLR that is responsible for performing JIT compiling is known as the **JIT compiler.** CLR provides two JIT compilers namely Normal JIT compiler and an Economy JIT compiler. The **Normal JIT compiler** works in a manner similar to normal, unmanaged C/C++ compiler. It examines MSIL and optimizes the resulting native code. The **Economy JIT compiler** simply replaces each MSIL instruction with its native code counterpart.

Metadata. The compiler embeds metadata into every EXE or DLL file, which makes it possible to convert the file into native code using JIT. .NET metadata is a collection of information that exists in the EXE or DLL file in binary form. The metadata contains declaration for every type and its members. It enables the fast and accurate development of code.

Class Library in .NET Framework

Another component of the .NET Framework, the .NET Framework class library consists of a collection of object-oriented and reusable classes that can be used to develop Windows and Web applications. The .NET Framework class Library consists of base classes, data classes, XML classes, XML web service classes, Web Forms classes and Window Forms classes. Table 1.1 shows the .NET Framework Class Library.

Table 1.1 .NET Framework Class Library

Class Type	*Functionality*
Base classes	Provide basic or standard functionality, such as input/ output, string manipulation, security management, network communications, thread management and text management
Data classes	Allow persistent data management; include SQL classes to manipulate persistent data stores through SQL interface.
XML classes	Allow manipulation of XML data, and XML searching and translations
XML Web service classes	Allow creation of lightweight distributed components that can work despite firewalls and network address translation (NAT) software
Web Forms classes	Allow development of Web applications
Windows Forms classes	Allow development of Windows applications

1.3 NAMESPACES

A namespace is a logical naming scheme for types that have related functionality. The .NET framework uses a hierarchical naming scheme for grouping types into logical categories of related functionality. The contents of various namespaces are listed here in the Table 1.2.

Table 1.2 Namespaces in the .NET Framework

Namespace	*Contents*
System	Contains the basic types that are commonly used by almost all the applications
Sytem.Collection	Contains types that helps to manage collections of objects
System.Data	Contains basic types for database management
System.Globalization	Contains types that allow National Language Support(NLS)

System.IO	Contains types that are used for performing I/O operations on data stream
System.Net	Contains types that enable communication in a network
System.Reflection	Contains types that allow the examination of metadata
System.Runtime.Remoting	Contains types that provide support for managed remote objects
System.Security	Contains types that provide security features
System.Web.UI.WebControls	Contains types that provide rich user interface controls for web-based applications
System.WinForms	Contains types that provide rich user interface controls for Windows applications

PART II

CONSOLE APPLICATION

Object Oriented Programming (OOP) concepts are used to develop real time applications. VB .NET provides a Graphical User Interface (GUI) Environment to develop Object Oriented Programming (OOP). These applications can be created by activating the **Console Application** template from the **new project** window.

CHAPTER

2

INTRODUCTION TO VB .NET

The Visual Studio .NET Integrated Development Environment (IDE) provides a common interface for developing various kinds of projects for the .NET Framework. Visual Studio .NET supports languages such as Visual Basic, Visual C++ and C#.

2.1 VISUAL BASIC .NET

Visual Basic .NET is the result of a significant language enhancement of Visual Basic for the .NET Framework. Visual Basic .NET or VB .NET is easier to use and more powerful for access to system resources.

VB .NET supports **inheritance**, which means we can derive a class from another class known as base class. The derived class inherits all the methods and properties of the base class. In the derived class, you can either use the existing code of the base class or overriding the existing code.

VB .NET supports **Garbage collection**, which automatically releases memory for reuse by destroying objects that are no longer in use.

Visual Basic .NET supports **overloading**, that enables to define multiple methods with same name but with a different set of arguments.

It supports **Multithreading**, can handle multiple tasks simultaneously. And also **structured Exception handling** , which identify and remove errors at runtime.

Components of Visual Studio .NET IDE

The Solution Explorer Window

By using Solution Explorer window, we can easily access the project. It lists the solution name, the project name and all the forms and modules that are used in the project.

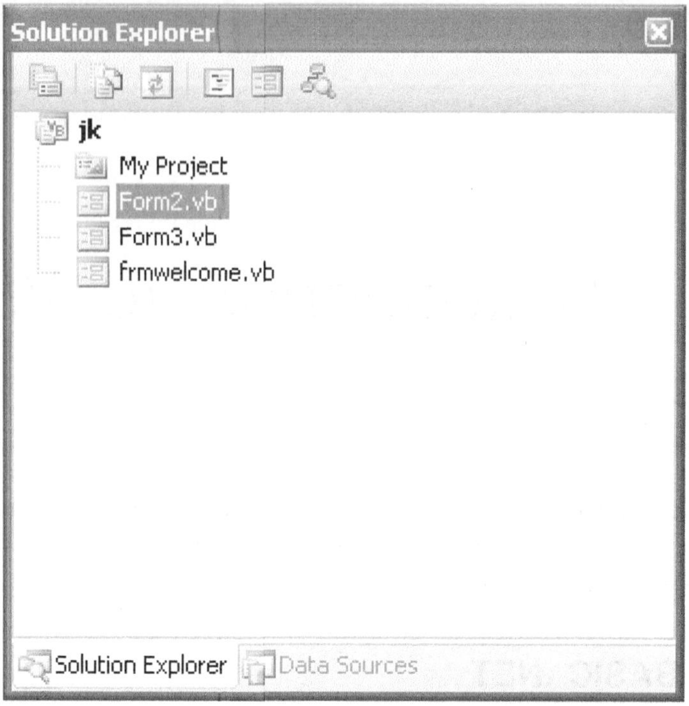

Fig. 2.1 *The Solution Explorer Window*

The Output Window

This window displays the current status of the running program, and displays errors if any after compilation.

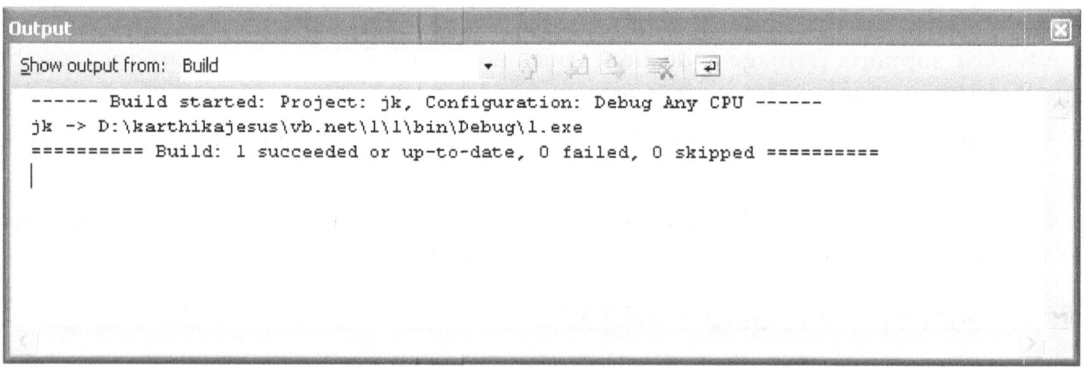

Fig. 2.2 *The Output Window*

The Properties Window

The properties window displays the properties that are associated with an object.

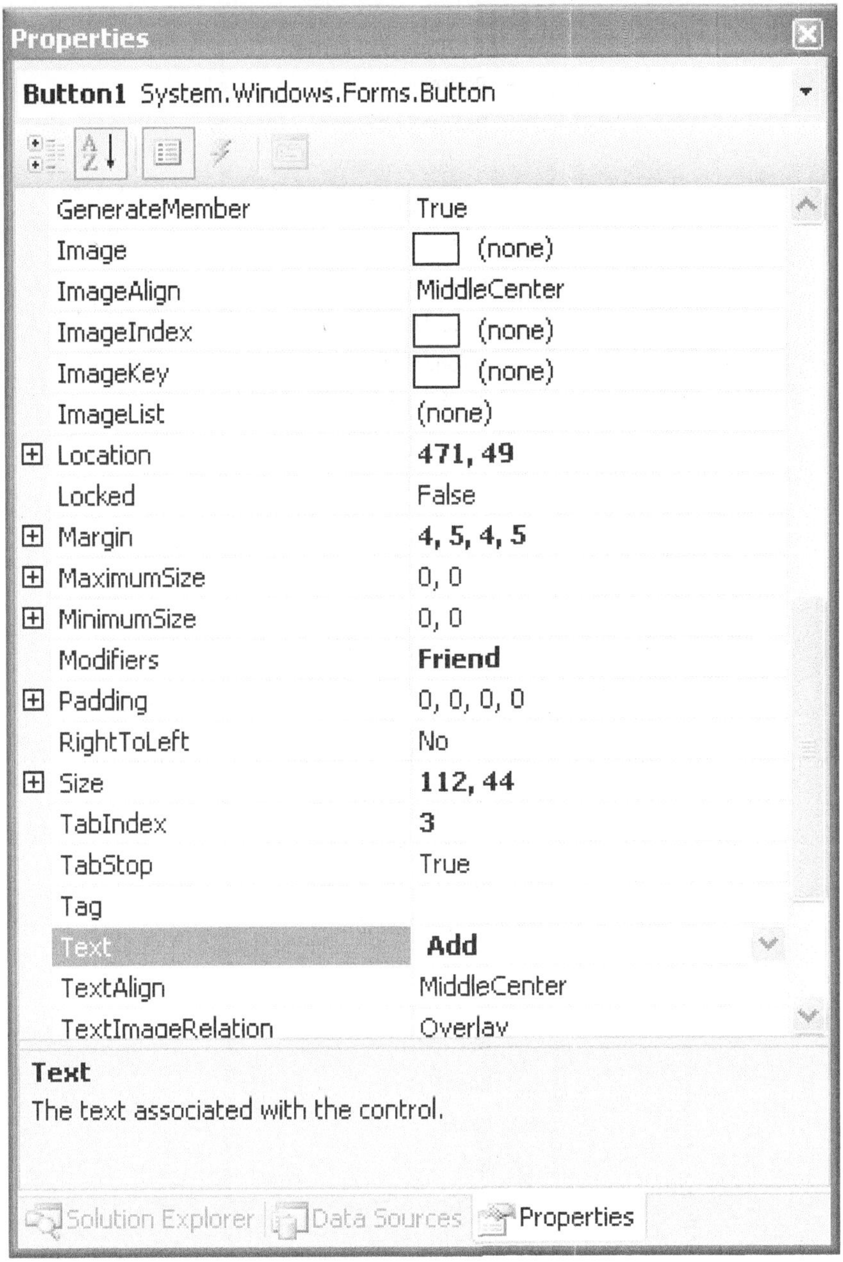

Fig. 2.3 *The Properties Window*

The Toolbox

The Toolbox displays a variety of components such as Data, Component, Windows Form, Clipboard Ring and General.

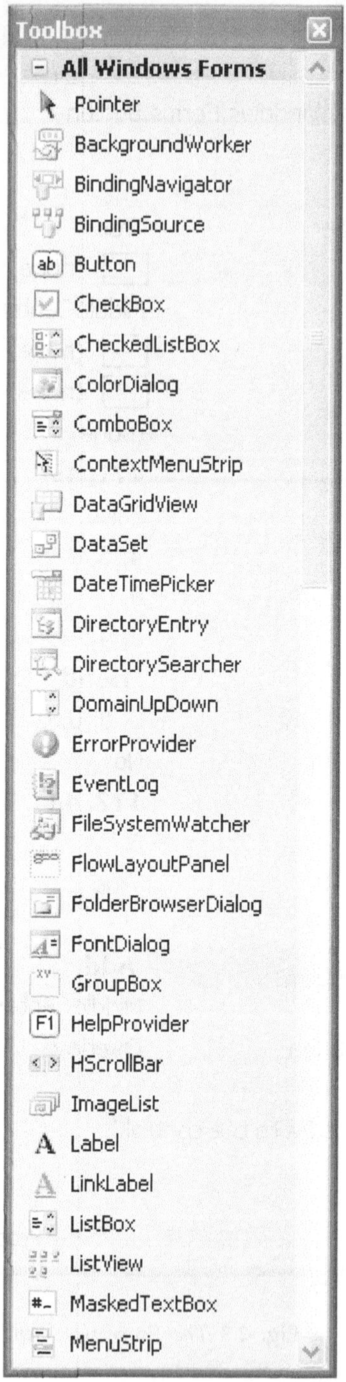

Fig. 2.4 *The Toolbox*

The Task List Window

The Task List window displays a list of errors along with the file and line number of the error.

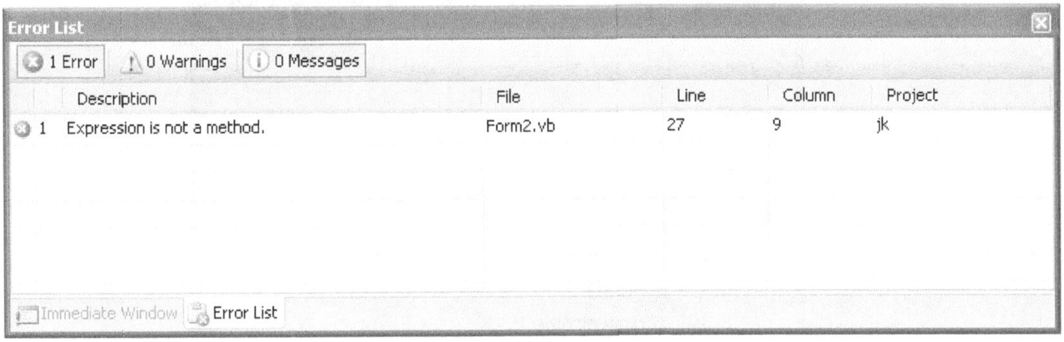

Fig. 2.5 *The Task List Window*

The Server Explorer Window

The Server Explorer window is used to handle various administrative tasks such as monitoring the performance of other machines on a network and locating and connecting to the various servers on the network.

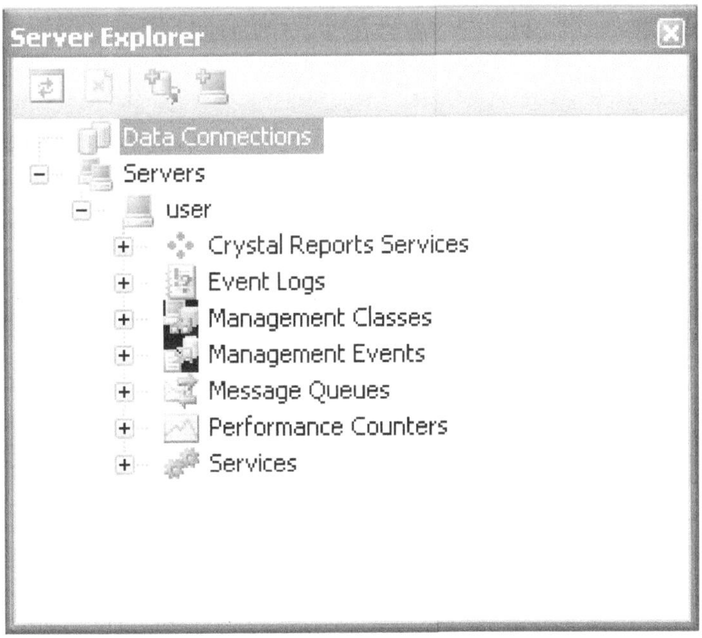

Fig. 2.6 *The Server Explorer Window*

The Class View Window

The class view window displays the classes, methods and properties associated with a particular file or project. They are displayed in a hierarchical tree-view.

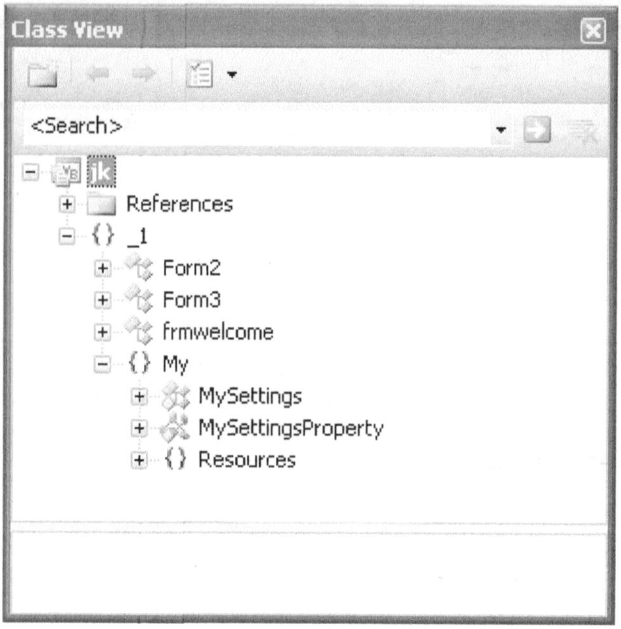

Fig. 2.7 *The Class View Window*

Getting Started

Now it is the time to get in Microsoft Visual Studio. For this, open the Microsoft Visual studio. Net Application. The start page appears as follows:

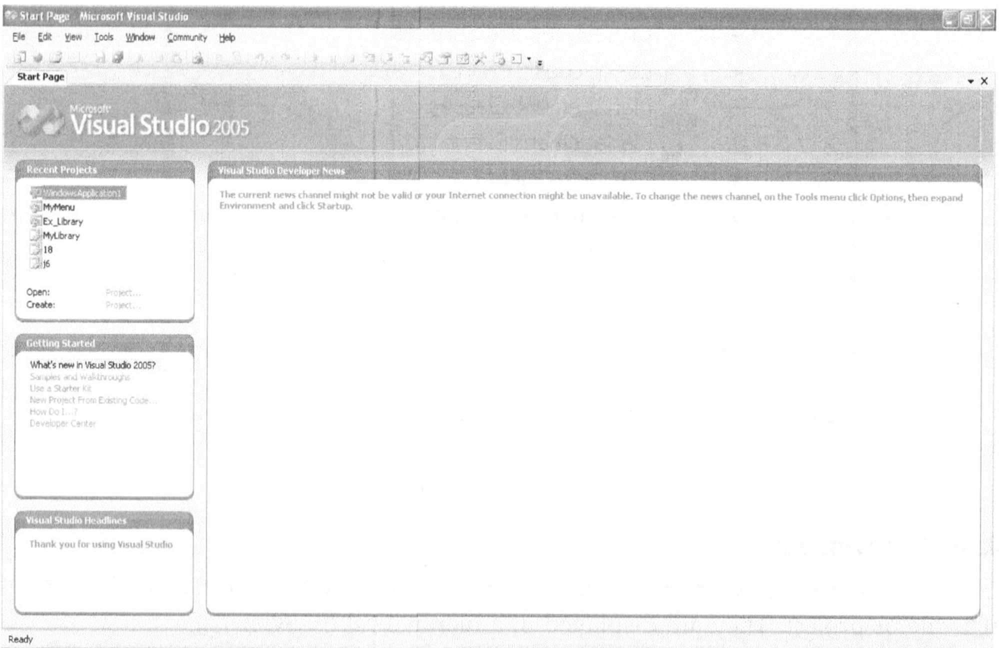

Fig. 2.8 *The Start Page*

From the start page, we open a new project for console application.

Open a New Project for Console Application

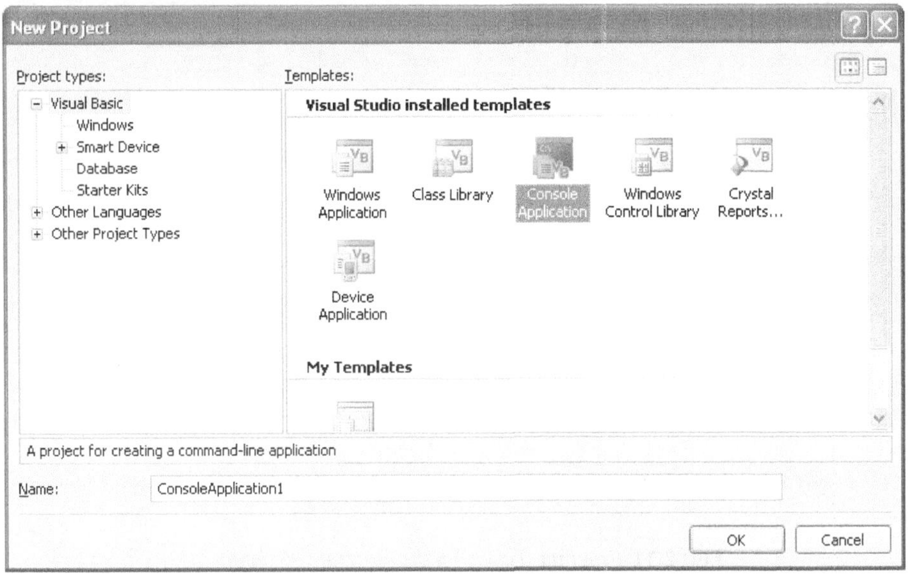

Fig. 2.9 *Opening a New Project for Console Application*

Specify the name for the console application and select **OK** button. Now the actual program window for console application appears as follows:

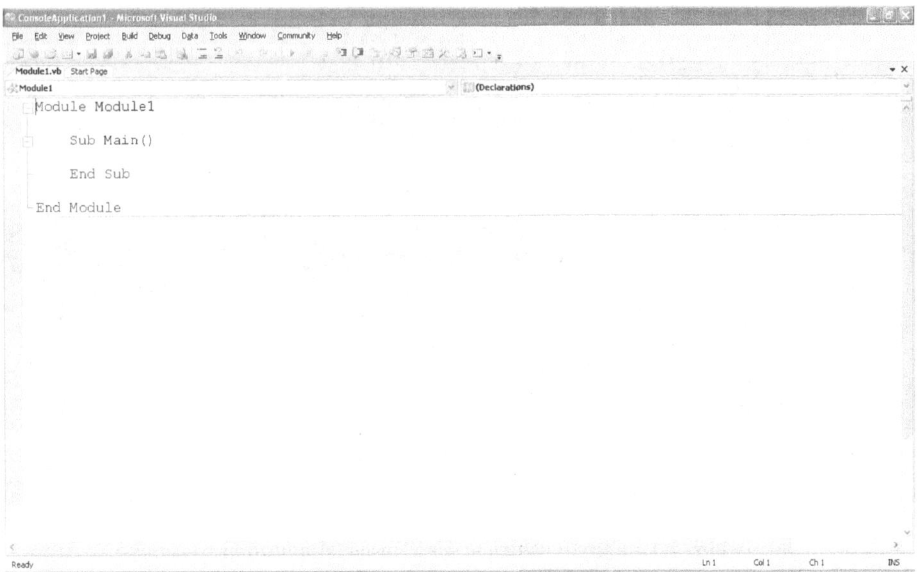

Fig. 2.10 *Program Window for Console Application*

In the program window, type our first program.

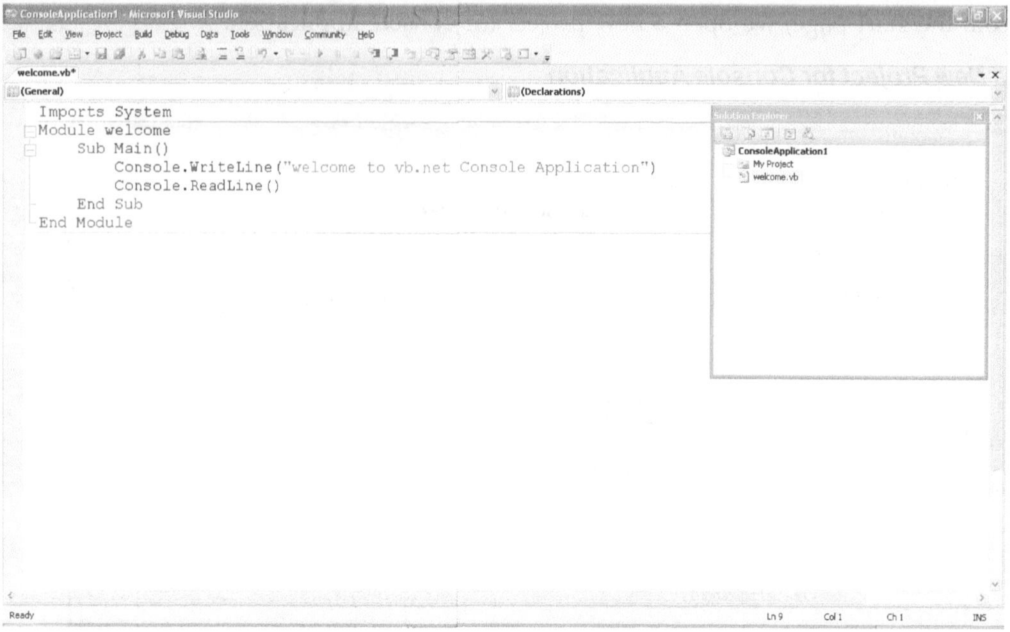

Fig. 2.11 *Program Typed in the Program Window*

Now, run our project by selecting **Start Debugging** option from **Debug** menu or Press **F5** The output windows shown here

Fig. 2.12 *Output Window for Console Application*

2.2 PROGRAMMING ESSENTIALS

Here, we will deal the concepts required to develop a **Console Applications.**

When we create the **Console Application**, it automatically adds the necessary files and folders to the project. They are:

AssemblyInfo.VB This file contains all the information about the assembly of the application.

Module1.VB This file contains Sub **Main()** which act as the entry point for the application

References This folder contains references to the .NET Framework namespaces such as **System, System.Data** and **System.XML**

The .NET Framework class Library provides the **Console** class, which can be used in Console applications to accept input and display output to user. The Console class represents a standard input, output and error streams. Some of the methods are:

Read() Reads the next character from the standard input stream.

ReadLine() Reads a line of characters from the standard input stream.

Write() Writes the specified data to the standard output stream.

WriteLine() Writes the specified data followed by a new line to the standard output stream.

Data Type

Data Type refers that the type or nature of data. For example, suppose we deal the siblings of a person it must be integer information. To specify the temperature of our room it must be expressed as fractional value. VB .NET supports following Data types Table 2.1.

Table 2.1 Data Types in VB .NET

Data Type	*Size in Byte*	*.NET Representation*	*Description*
Byte	1	Byte	Unsigned byte
Sbyte	1	SByte	signed byte
Short	2	Int16	signed short
Ushort	2	UInt16	Unsigned short
Integer	4	Int32	Signed integer
UInteger	4	UInt32	Unsigned integer
Long	8	Int64	Signed big integer
ULong	8	UInt64	Unsigned big integer
Single	4	Single	Floating point number
Double	8	Double	Double precision floating point number
Decimal	16	Decimal	Fixed precision number
String	-	String	String of variable length

Char	2	Char	Unicode character
Boolean	1	Boolean	True or False
DateTime	8	Date	Date and time
Object	4	Object	Any type can be stored in a variable of type object

Constant

It is a quantity whose value does not change during the execution of program.

Variables

It is a quantity whose value changes during the execution of program.

Considerable points when forming a variable is:

1. Variable can be of any length
2. First character must be a letter
3. Both uppercase and lowercase and digits are permitted
4. Special characters are not permitted(except _[underscore])
5. They Should not be a keyword.

Valid Examples	a, first_variable, sum1	
Invalid Examples	root r	Space not Allowed
	1sum	First character must not be a digit

Displaying a String

This program displays a string stored in a string variable.

Program

```
Module ModuleDisplay
    Sub Main()
        Dim s As String
    s = "A Lazy person is as bad as someone who is destructive"
        Console.WriteLine(s)
        Console.ReadLine()
    End Sub
End Module
```

Output

```
A Lazy person is as bad as someone who is destructive
```

Operators

An operator may be defined as a passive symbol employed over a variables or constants and provide the result depending upon the manipulation. VB .NET supports,

1. Arithmetic operators
2. Relational operators
3. Logical operators

Arithmetic Operators

The following table specifies the arithmetic operators

Table 2.2 Arithmetic Operators

Operator	*Description*
+	Addition
–	Subtraction
*	Multiplication
/	Division
\	Integer division (gives quotient)
Mod	Modulo operation (gives remainder)

Simple Calculation

This program demonstrates the arithmetic operators.

Program

```
Imports System
Module calculation
       Sub Main()
              Dim a, b As Integer
              Console.WriteLine("Enter the first number")
              a = Integer.Parse(Console.ReadLine())
              Console.WriteLine("Enter the second number")
              b = Integer.Parse(Console.ReadLine())
              Console.WriteLine("The sum is {0}", a + b)
              Console.WriteLine("The difference is {0}", a - b)
              Console.WriteLine("The product is {0}", a * b)
              Console.WriteLine("The quotient  is {0}", a / b)
              Console.WriteLine("The quotient in integer division is
{0}", a \ b)
              Console.WriteLine("The remainder is {0}", a Mod b)
              Console.ReadLine()
       End Sub
End Module
```

Output

```
Enter the first number
50
Enter the second number
20
The sum is 70
The difference is 30
The product is 1000
The quotient is 2.5
The quotient in integer division is 2
The remainder is 10
```

Relational Operators

The following table describes the relational operators

Table 2.3 Relational Operators

Operator	*Description*
<	Less than
>	Greater than
<=	Less than or equal to
>=	Greater than or equal to
=	Equal to
<>	Not equal to

Relation between Numbers

This program shows the relation between two numbers

Program

```
Module Relation
      Sub Main()
            Dim status As Boolean
            Dim a, b As Integer
            Console.WriteLine("Enter the value of a and b")
            a = Int32.Parse(Console.ReadLine())
            b = Int32.Parse(Console.ReadLine())
            status = a < b
         Console.WriteLine("{0}  <   {1}     {2}", a, b, status)
         Console.WriteLine("{0}  >   {1}     {2}", a, b, a > b)
```

```
        Console.WriteLine("{0} >= {1}      {2}", a, b, a >= b)
        Console.WriteLine("{0} <= {1}      {2}", a, b, a <= b)
        Console.WriteLine("{0} =  {1}      {2}", a, b, a = b)
        Console.WriteLine("{0} <> {1}      {2}", a, b, a <> b)
        Console.ReadLine()
    End Sub
End Module
```

Output

```
Enter the value of a and b
10
5
10 <  5         False
10 >  5         True
10 >= 5         True
10 <= 5         False
10 =  5         False
10 <> 5         True
```

Logical Operators

The following table describes the logical operators

Table 2.4 Logical Operators

Operator	*Description*
AND	Logical AND
OR	Logical OR
NOT	Logical NOT

The following table describes the operations of logical operator.

Table 2.5 Logical Operations

Exp1	*Exp2*	*Exp1 AND Exp2*	*Exp1 OR Exp2*	*NOT Exp1*
F	F	F	F	T
F	T	F	T	T
T	F	F	T	F
T	T	T	T	F

Logical Manipulations

This program inputs integer values and processing them in binary fashion and display the result in integer form.

Program

```
Module Logical_manip
        Sub Main()
                Dim a, b As Integer
                a = 6         'Binary equivalent of 6 is 110
                b = 3         'Binary equivalent of 3 is 011

               Console.WriteLine("{0} Or {1}    = {2}", a, b, a Or b)
                '110 Or 011 = 111
                'decimal equivalent of 111 is 7

               Console.WriteLine("{0} And {1}   = {2}", a, b, a And b)
                '110 And 011 = 010
                'decimal equivalent of 010 is 2

                Console.WriteLine("Not {0}       = {1}", b, Not b)
                'not 011 = -100
                'decimal equivalent of 101 is -1
                Console.ReadLine()

        End Sub
End Module
```

Output

```
6 Or 3   = 7
6 And 3  = 2
Not 3    = -4
```

2.3 BOXING AND UNBOXING

Boxing refers the casting of primitive data to object and unboxing refers the casting of object to primitive data.

Program

```
Module Bo_Unbox
        Sub main()
```

```
        Dim a, b As Integer
        Dim obj As Object
        a = 10
        obj = a 'boxing
        Console.WriteLine("Object : {0}", obj)
      Console.WriteLine("object to string  :{0}", obj.ToString)
        b = Int(obj)        'unboxing
        Console.WriteLine("object to Integer : {0}", b)
        Console.ReadLine()
    End Sub
End Module
```

Output

```
Object : 10
object to string  : 10
object to Integer : 10
```

CHAPTER

3

CONTROL STRUCTURES

This chapter deals the Control structures in VB .NET. Control structures are used to transfer the control from one part of the program to another. Using Control structures we can redirect the flow of execution.

3.1 IF STATEMENT

This statement executes the statements depending upon the given condition. If the condition is true it execute true block statements, otherwise it executes false block statements. The general format is

```
if   (condition)  then
true-block  statements

else

false-block  statements

end  if
```

Largest of Two Inputs

This program inputs two integer numbers and the largest number of them will be an output.

Program

```
Imports  System
Module  lar2
      Sub  Main()
            Dim  a,  b  As  Integer
            Console.WriteLine("Enter  two  numbers  ")
```

```
            a = Integer.Parse(Console.ReadLine())
            b = Integer.Parse(Console.ReadLine())
            If a > b Then
                Console.WriteLine(" {0} is largest number", a)
            Else
                Console.WriteLine(" {0} is largest number", b)
            End If
            Console.ReadLine()
        End Sub
End Module
```

Output

```
Enter two numbers
78
90
 90 is largest number
```

Largest of Three Inputs

This program inputs three integer numbers and the largest number of them will be an output.

Program

```
Module larg3
        Sub Main()
            Dim a, b, c As Integer
            Console.WriteLine("Enter the Numbers")
            a = Integer.Parse(Console.ReadLine())
            b = Integer.Parse(Console.ReadLine())
            c = Integer.Parse(Console.ReadLine())
            If (a > b And a > c) Then
                Console.WriteLine("{0}  is large", a)
            Else
                If (b > c) Then
                    Console.WriteLine("{0}  is large", b)
                Else
                    Console.WriteLine("{0}  is large", c)
                End If
```

```
                End If
                Console.ReadLine()
        End Sub
End Module
```

Output

```
Enter the Numbers
7
9
4
9  is large
```

3.2 ELSE IF STATEMENT

This statement checks multiple condition and executes the statements corresponds to the true condition. The general format is,

```
if (condition) then

  statements block 1

else if (condition2) then

statements block 2

.

.

else if (condition n) then

statements block n

else

default statement

end if
```

Grade Calculation

This program calculates the grade depending upon the mark input.

Program

```
Imports System
```

```
Module elseladder
      Sub Main()
            Dim m As Integer
            Console.WriteLine("Enter the mark")
            m = Integer.Parse(Console.ReadLine())
            If (m >= 90) Then
                  Console.WriteLine("Grade A")
            ElseIf (m >= 70) Then
                  Console.WriteLine("Grade B")
            ElseIf (m >= 50) Then
                  Console.WriteLine("Grade C")
            Else
                  Console.WriteLine("Grade F")

            End If
            Console.ReadLine()
      End Sub
End Module
```

Output

```
Enter the mark
98
Grade A
```

Temperature Condition

This program inputs the temperature and displays the text message depends upon your input.

Program

```
Module Temp
      Sub main()
            Dim temp As Double
            Console.WriteLine("Enter the temperature you feel...")
            temp = Double.Parse(Console.ReadLine())
            If (temp > 42) Then
              Console.WriteLine("Coconut water is good for you...")
            ElseIf (temp > 38) Then
                  Console.WriteLine("Palm water is OK ")
```

```
            ElseIf (temp > 32) Then
                Console.WriteLine("Cool water is enough...")
            Else
                Console.WriteLine("Hot milk is best!")
            End If
            Console.ReadLine()
        End Sub
End Module
```

Output

```
Enter the temperature you feel...
40
Palm water is OK
```

3.3 SELECT CASE

It also used to check multiple conditions. The expression is evaluated first. Depending upon the value it executes different block of statement. The general format is

Select case(variable)

Case value 1

statement block 1;

Case value 2

statement block 2;

.....

.....

Case value n

statement block n;

case else

default statement

End select

Calc Function

This program implements the simple calculator functions. Depending upon the input choice given the corresponding function is executed.

Program

```
Imports System
```

```
Module Exselect
      Sub Main()
            Dim a, b As Integer
            Dim c As Char
            Console.WriteLine("Enter the numbers")
            a = Integer.Parse(Console.ReadLine())
            b = Integer.Parse(Console.ReadLine())
            Console.WriteLine(" +   addition")
            Console.WriteLine(" -   subtraction")
            Console.WriteLine(" *   multiplication")
            Console.WriteLine(" /   division")
            Console.WriteLine("Enter your choice")
            c = Console.ReadLine()
            Select Case (c)
                  Case "+"
                Console.WriteLine("The sum is  {0}", a + b)
                  Case "-"
              Console.WriteLine("The difference is  {0}", a - b)
                  Case "*"
                  Console.WriteLine("The product is  {0}", a * b)
                  Case "/"
                 Console.WriteLine("The quotient is  {0}", a / b)
            End Select
            Console.ReadLine()
      End Sub
End Module
```

Output

```
Enter the numbers
4
5
 +   addition
 -   subtraction
 *   multiplication
 /   divison
```

```
Enter your choice
+
The sum is  9
```

Device Category

This program inputs a device code and displays the category of the device you selected.

Program

```
Imports System
Module Device_Selecttion
      Sub main()
            Dim ch As Char
           Console.WriteLine("Select any one of the following item
by inputting the first character")
            Console.WriteLine("Note : case senstive")
            Console.WriteLine("mouse")
            Console.WriteLine("CD")
            Console.WriteLine("trackball")
            Console.WriteLine("joystick")
            Console.WriteLine("MICR")
            Console.WriteLine("barcode reader")
            Console.WriteLine("OCR")
            Console.WriteLine("printer")
            Console.WriteLine("DVD")
            Console.WriteLine("Touch Screen")
            Console.WriteLine("Plotter")
            Console.WriteLine("keyboard")
            Console.WriteLine()
            Console.Write("Type your choice : ")
            ch = Char.Parse(Console.ReadLine())
            Select Case (ch)
                  Case "m"
                  Case "k"
                  Case "j"
                  Case "t"
                  Case "M"
```

```
                Case "b"
                Case "O"
        Console.WriteLine("your selection belong to Input device")
                Case "P"
                Case "p"
        Console.WriteLine("Your selection belong to Output device")
                Case "D"
                Case "C"
                Case "T"
         Console.WriteLine("your selection belongs to I/O device")
                Case Else
                    Console.WriteLine("Your input is wrong")
            End Select
            Console.ReadLine()
        End Sub
End Module
```

Output

```
Select any one of the following item by inputting the first
character
Note: case senstive
mouse
CD
trackball
joystick
MICR
barcode reader
OCR
printer
DVD
Touch Screen
Plotter
Keyboard
Type your choice : T
your selection belongs to I/O device
```

CHAPTER 4

LOOP STRUCTURES

In this chapter we discuss the looping structures which refer to the statements that allow the execution of statements for number of times based on some conditions.

4.1 WHILE STATEMENT

This executes the statements within the body of the loop as long as the condition is true. If the condition is not true, body of the loop will not be executed at least once. The general format is

```
while(condition)

Body of the loop

End while
```

Multiples of Three

This program displays the multiples of three.

Program

```
Module Exwhile
      Sub Main()
            Dim i, n As Integer
            Console.WriteLine("Enter the limit")
            n = Integer.Parse(Console.ReadLine())
            i = 3
            Console.WriteLine("multiple of 3 upto {0}", n)
            While (i <= n)
                  Console.WriteLine(i)
```

```
                i = i + 3
            End While
            Console.ReadLine()
        End Sub
End Module
```

Output

```
Enter the limit
10
multiple of 3 upto 10
3
6
9
```

Multiplication Table

This program displays the multiplication table.

Program

```
Module MultiplicationTable
        Sub main()
            Dim i, j, n As Integer
            Console.WriteLine("Enter the Limit")
            n = Int32.Parse(Console.ReadLine())
            i = 1
            j = 1
            Console.WriteLine("Multiplication Table")
            Console.WriteLine("...........")
            While (i <= n)
                Console.Write("{0}", i)
                i = i + 1
            End While
            Console.WriteLine()
            i = 1
            While (i < n)
                Console.Write("{0}", i)
                j = 1
```

```
                While (j < n)
                    j = j + 1
                    Console.Write("{0} ", i * j)
                End While
                Console.WriteLine()
                i = i + 1
            End While
            Console.ReadLine()
        End Sub
End Module
```

Output

```
Enter the Limit
5
Multiplication Table
............
1    2    3    4    5
1    2    3    4    5
2    4    6    8    10
3    6    9    12   15
4    8    12   16   20
```

4.2 DO WHILE STATEMENT

This executes the statements within the body of the loop as long as the condition is true. Regardless of condition status, the body of the loop will be executed at least once. The general format is

```
Do   while(condition)

Body of the loop

Loop
```

Multiples of Five

It displays the multiples of five.

Program

```
Module Exdo
    Sub Main()
```

```
            Dim i, n As Integer
            Console.WriteLine("Enter the number")
            n = Integer.Parse(Console.ReadLine())
            i = 5
            Console.WriteLine("Multiples of Five")
            Do While (i <= n)
                  Console.WriteLine(i)
                  i = i + 5
            Loop
            Console.ReadLine()
      End Sub
End Module
```

Output

```
Enter the number
50
Multiples of Five
5
10
15
20
25
30
35
40
45
50
```

Difference Table

This program displays the difference table.

Program

```
Module DiffTable
  Sub main()
    Dim i, j, n As Integer
    Console.WriteLine("Enter the Limit")
    n = Int32.Parse(Console.ReadLine())
```

```
            i = 0
            j = 1
            Console.WriteLine("Difference Table")
            Console.WriteLine("..........")
            While (i < n)
             Console.Write("{0}", i)
             i = i + 1
            End While
            Console.WriteLine()
            i = 1
            Do While (i < n)
             Console.Write("{0}", i)
             j = 1
             Do While (j < n)
                Console.Write("{0}", i - j)
                j = j + 1
              Loop
              Console.WriteLine()
             i = i + 1
            Loop
            Console.ReadLine()
        End Sub

End Module
```

Output

```
Enter the Limit
5
Difference Table
..........
0     1     2     3     4
1     0    -1    -2    -3
2     1     0    -1    -2
3     2     1     0    -1
4     3     2     1     0
```

4.3 DO UNTIL STATEMENT

This executes the statements within the body of the loop as long as the condition is false. The general format is

```
Do until(condition)
Body of the Loop
Loop
```

Multiple of Two

This program display the multiples of 2.

```
Module dountil
   Sub Main()
     Dim i, n As Integer
     Console.WriteLine("Enter the limit")
     n = Integer.Parse(Console.ReadLine())
     i = 2
     Console.WriteLine("Multiple of 2 upto {0} ...", n)
     Do Until (i > n)
       Console.WriteLine(i)
       i = i + 2
     Loop
     Console.ReadLine()
   End Sub
End Module
```

Output

```
Enter the limit
10
Multiple of 2 upto 10...
2
4
6
8
10
```

Addition Table

This program displays the addition table.

```
Module additiontable
   Sub main()
      Dim i, j, n As Integer
      Console.WriteLine("Enter the Limit")
      n = Int32.Parse(Console.ReadLine())
      i = 0
      j = 1
      Console.WriteLine("Addition Table")
      Console.WriteLine(".........")
      Do Until (i > n)
        Console.Write("{0}", i)
        i = i + 1
      Loop
      Console.WriteLine()
      i = 1
      Do Until (i > n)
        Console.Write("{0}", i)
        j = 1
        Do Until (j > n)
          Console.Write("{0}", i + j)
          j = j + 1
      Loop
      Console.WriteLine()
      i = i + 1
   Loop
     Console.ReadLine()
      End Sub
End Module
```

Output

```
Enter the Limit
5
Addition Table
...........
0       1       2       3       4       5
1       2       3       4       5       6
```

```
2    3    4    5    6    7
3    4    5    6    7    8
4    5    6    7    8    9
5    6    7    8    9    10
```

4.4 FOR STATEMENT

For statement allows the initialization, condition checking and control variable setting (increment or decrement) in same line. Statements within the body of the loop are executed as long as the condition is true. If the condition is not true, body of the loop will not be executed at least once. The general format is

```
for   var = initial_value to Finalvalue step incre/dec
            Body of the loop
Next
```

Displaying a String

This program displays the string number of times as specified.

Program

```
Module Exfor
      Sub Main()
            Dim i, n As Integer
            Console.WriteLine("Enter the number")
            n = Integer.Parse(Console.ReadLine())
            For i = 1 To n
                  Console.WriteLine("King of Kings")
            Next
            Console.ReadLine()
      End Sub
End Module
```

Output

```
Enter the number
5
King of Kings
King of Kings
King of Kings
King of Kings
King of Kings
```

CHAPTER

5

ARRAYS AND STRUCTURES

A situation arises to process the age of all students in a class, if we use separate variable for each student it is tedious to manage all variables. In this situation we use array that store all values in a common name and each value is referred by a subscript value. In General Array stores homogeneous values

5.1 ONE DIMENSIONAL ARRAY ELEMENTS

A list of items grouped in a single variable with only one index is called one-dimensional array. For example, the one dimensional array named Age with dimension n can be referred as Age(0), Age(1),…Age(n-1). The array elements are stored in consecutive memory locations as follows:

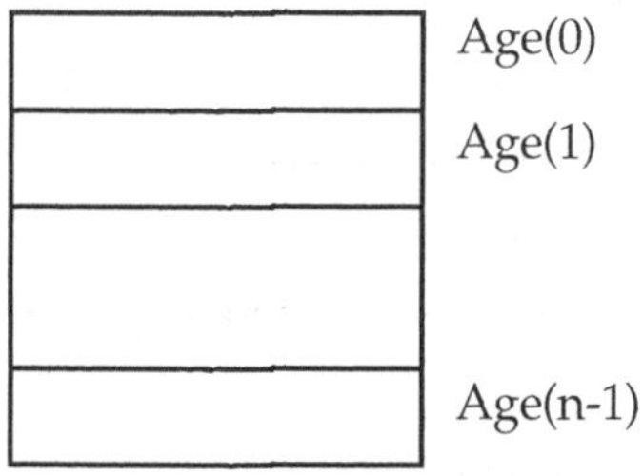

The index of an array must be an integer. In this book, I use the array element location from 1, this leads no problem. It is just for convenience.

Array declaration had the general format

```
Dim Arrayname(size) As Datatype
```

Example:

Dim A(10) as Integer

The above statement allocates 10 consecutive memory locations for storing integer values and named it as A.

Displaying Array Elements in Reverse

This program inputs numbers and stores them in an array and displays the elements in reverse order

Program

```
Module ExArray
      Sub Main()
            Dim a(15), i, n As Integer
            Console.WriteLine("Enter the total number of elements")
            n = Integer.Parse(Console.ReadLine())         'input the
total number of item
            Console.WriteLine("Enter the numbers one by one")
            For i = 1 To n
                  a(i) = Integer.Parse(Console.ReadLine())' input
the elements one by one
            Next
            Console.WriteLine("Elements in reverse order")
            For i = n To 1 Step -1          'displays the elements
in reverse
                  Console.WriteLine(a(i))
            Next
            Console.ReadLine()
      End Sub
End Module
```

Output

```
Enter the total number of elements
5
Enter the numbers one by one
23
45
67
8
9
Elements in reverse order
9
8
67
45
23
```

5.2 TWO DIMENSIONAL ARRAY

An array with two dimensions is called two dimensional array. It takes the general form as

Dim Arrayname(row_size,column_size) As Datatye

Here maximum of row_size*column_size elements can be stored

Example

```
Dim A(2,2) as Integer
```

It creates an array 'A' with two rows and two columns

A(0,0)	A(0,1)
A(1,0)	A(1,1)

Transpose of a Matrix

Transpose of a matrix is obtained by interchanging the row into column and column into row of an input matrix.

Program

```
Module ExArray2d
        Sub Main()
                Dim a(3, 3), i, j, n As Integer
                Console.WriteLine("Enter the order of square matrix")
                n = Integer.Parse(Console.ReadLine())
                Console.WriteLine("Enter the elements")
                For i = 1 To n
                        For j = 1 To n
                                a(i, j) = Integer.Parse(Console.ReadLine())
                        Next
                Next
                Console.WriteLine("Given Matrix")
                For i = 1 To n
                        For j = 1 To n
                                Console.Write(a(i, j) & "     ")
                        Next
                        Console.WriteLine()
                Next
                Console.WriteLine("Transpose of a given Matrix")
                For i = 1 To n
```

```
                For j = 1 To n
                    Console.Write(a(j, i) & "      ")
                Next
                Console.WriteLine()
            Next
            Console.ReadLine()
        End Sub
End Module
```

Output

```
Enter the order of square matrix
3
Enter the elements
1
0
0
0
1
0
0
0
1
Given Matrix
1     0     0
0     1     0
0     0     1
Transpose of a given Matrix
1     0     0
0     1     0
0     0     1
```

5.3 STRUCTURES

Structure is a user defined data type which stores the heterogeneous data values. A single name can store more than one type of values instead of array can store single type of values. The individual data items in the structure are called fields or members. It takes the general form as

```
Structure tagname
  Dim   field-1 as Datatype
        ….
  Dim   field-n as Datatype

Function function-name as return type
     Statements
End Function

End Structure
```

Structure variable or reference for a structure can be created as follows

```
Dim structure_variable as tagname

Members can be accessed as follows
Structure_variable.field-1
Structure_variable.field-n
Structure_variable.function-name
```

Employee Record

This program stores the employee details in a structure and process them.

Program

```
Module Exstruct
    Structure stu_rec
        Dim name As String
        Dim reg As Long
        Dim gender As Char
      End Structure
      Sub Main()
        Dim S As stu_rec          ' Structure variable created
        S.name = "Karthikajesus" 'access the structure field
        S.reg = 1408531001
        S.gender = "F"
        Console.WriteLine("Name              : {0}", S.name)
        Console.WriteLine("Register No       : {0}", S.reg)
        Console.WriteLine("Gender            : {0}", S.gender)
        Console.ReadLine()
```

```
    End Sub
End Module
```

Output

```
Name            : Karthikajesus
Register No     : 1408531001
Gender          : F
```

Nested Structure

It is possible to define the structure as an element of another structure. This is called nested structure or structure within structure.

Employee Record with Date of Joining

In this program we define a structure **doj** as an element to the another structure **Employee**

Program

```
Module nes_stru
   Structure Employee
      Dim name As String
      Dim design As String
      Structure doj       'structure within structure
         Dim yy, mm, dd As Integer
     End Structure
  End Structure
  Sub Main()
   Dim emp As Employee   'reference  created
   Dim d As Employee.doj ' reference created for structure within
structure
    emp.name = "Karthikajesus"
    emp.design = "Lecturer"
    d.yy = 2005
    d.mm = 2
    d.dd = 10
    Console.WriteLine("Name              :{0}", emp.name)
    Console.WriteLine("Designation       :{0}", emp.design)
    Console.WriteLine("Date of joinig    :{0}/{1}/{2}",d.dd,d.mm, d.yy)
    Console.ReadLine()
```

```
  End Sub
End Module
```

Output

```
Name             :  Karthikajesus
Designation      :  Lecturer
Date of joinig   :  10/2/2005
```

Function within the Structure

Defining the function as an element of structure is called function within structure.

Student Record

Here the function **total()** is defined in the structure **stu_rec**

Program

```
Module fun_within_stru
      Structure stu_rec
            Dim name As String
            Dim m1, m2 As Integer
            Function total() As Integer
                  Return m1 + m2
            End Function
      End Structure
      Sub Main()
            Dim S As stu_rec
            S.name = "Muthuli"
            S.m1 = 99
            S.m2 = 98
            Console.WriteLine("Name   : {0}", S.name)
            Console.WriteLine("Mark1  : {0}", S.m1)
            Console.WriteLine("mark2  : {0}", S.m2)
            Console.WriteLine("Total  : {0}", S.total)
            Console.ReadLine()
      End Sub
End Module
```

Output

```
Name   :  Muthuli
```

```
Mark1  :  99
mark2  :  98
Total  :  197
```

Array of Structure

Array of structure is defined as a group of data of different data types stored in a single name. Here a structure is created to store the details of a student. Suppose if we want to store the details of more than one student then, we have created array of structure.

Program

```
Module ExstructArr
   Structure stu_rec
      Dim name As String
      Dim reg As Long
      Dim gender As Char
   End Structure
   Sub Main()
      Dim S(5) As stu_rec
      Dim n, i As Integer
      Console.WriteLine("Enter the total number of student")
      n = Integer.Parse(Console.ReadLine())
      For i = 1 To n
         Console.WriteLine("Enter details of student No {0}", i)
         Console.Write(" Name             : ")
         S(i).name = Console.ReadLine()
         Console.Write(" Reg No           : ")
         S(i).reg = Long.Parse(Console.ReadLine())
         Console.Write(" Gender           : ")
         S(i).gender = Char.Parse(Console.ReadLine())
      Next
      Console.WriteLine("Student Details ")
      Console.WriteLine("S.No     Name          RegNo        Gender")
      For i = 1 To n
      Console.WriteLine("{0}     {1}     {2}     {3}", i, S(i).name,
S(i).reg, S(i).gender)
   Next
```

```
    Console.ReadLine()
  End Sub
End Module
```

Output

```
Enter the total number of student
4
Enter details of student No 1
 Name      : Muthulingam
 Reg No    : 101
 Gender    : m
Enter details of student No 2
 Name     : Gurusankar
 Reg No  : 102
 Gender  : m
Enter details of student No 3
 Name     : Jansirani
 Reg No  : 103
 Gender  : f
Enter details of student No 4
 Name      : Pandiarajan
 Reg No    : 104
 Gender    : m
Student Details
```

S.No	Name	Reg No	Gender
1	Muthulingam	101	m
2	Gurusankar	102	m
3	Jansirani	103	f
4	Pandiarajan	104	m

CHAPTER

6

FUNCTIONS AND PROCEDURES

6.1 FUNCTIONS

Function is defined as a set of code which does a specific task. These functions can be called any number of times as required. There are two types of functions, namely

1. built – in function
2. user defined function

The former one, built-in function is a system function which are written and stored on the namespaces and can be called anywhere in our program. For example, Math.Pow is a built – in function.

The later one is a function which was defined by the user and can be used in our programs. The user defined function definition takes the general format

```
[accessibility] Function function-name (arguments) as return-type

 Body of function

End function
```

Accessibility can be Public, Protected, Friend, Protected Friend or Private. **Public** refers that the function had no restriction on accessibility and can be accessed from any part of our class. **Private** refers that the function is accessible only with in the declaration context. The keyword **Protected** refers that the function is accessible only from within own class or from a derived class. The keyword **Friend** refers that the function is accessible within the program that contains their declaration and from anywhere else in the same assembly. The keyword **Protected Friend** refers that the function referred from the same assembly as well as the derived classes.

Function-name is nothing but a name given to the function. The return type defines the type of value return by the function.

The calling of function takes the general form as follows

```
Function-name(arguments)
```

There are two ways to return the value to calling program.

By using function name

In this way when the **End Function** statement is executed, it returns the value whatever in the function name.

By using return statement

In this way, the value in the return statement is returned. More than one return statement is allowed in the same function.

Functions Return Value by its Name

Here this program calculates the factorial value and that is returned using function name **Fact**

Program

```
Imports System
Module fun1
        Sub main()
                Dim n, fa As Integer
                Console.WriteLine("Enter the value of n")
                n = Integer.Parse(Console.ReadLine())
                fa = Fact(n)                        'Function calling
                Console.WriteLine("The Factorial is {0}", fa)
                Console.ReadLine()
        End Sub
        Public Function Fact(ByVal x) As Integer 'Function defined
                Dim f As Integer = 1
                Dim i As Integer
                For i = 1 To x
                    f = f * i
                Next
            fact = f 'factorial value returned by the function name
        End Function
End Module
```

Output

```
Enter the value of n
5
The Factorial is 120
```

Function with Return Statement

Here largest of two number is calculated and return the result by **return** statement.

Program

```
Module ExWithReturn
      'function with return
      Sub Main()
            Dim a, b As Integer
            Console.WriteLine("Enter two numbers")
            a = Integer.Parse(Console.ReadLine())
            b = Integer.Parse(Console.ReadLine())
            Console.WriteLine("Largest no is {0}", big(a, b))
            Console.ReadLine()
      End Sub
      Public Function big(ByVal x, ByVal y) As Integer 'argument
passed by value
            If (x > y) Then
                  Return x
            Else
                  Return y
            End If
      End Function
End Module
```

Output

```
Enter two numbers
4
5
Largest no is 5
```

Call by Value

Usually, to call a function from program, the argument values of program are passed to the arguments of function. The changes of arguments that take place inside the function will not affect the same in the program. This type of execution generally referred as **call by value**.

Program

```
Module ExCallByVal
      Sub main()
```

```
            Dim i, n1, n2 As Integer
            Console.WriteLine("Enter the range")
            n1 = Integer.Parse(Console.ReadLine())
            n2 = Integer.Parse(Console.ReadLine())
            Console.WriteLine()
            Console.WriteLine("N Square Cube SquareRoot")
            Console.WriteLine()
            For i = n1 To n2
                Console.WriteLine("{0} {1} {2} {3}", i, square(i),
cube(i), squareroot(i))
            Next
            Console.ReadLine()
        End Sub
        Public Function square(ByVal x) As Integer
            square = x * x
        End Function
        Public Function squareroot(ByVal x) As Double
            squareroot = Math.Sqrt(x)
        End Function
        Public Function cube(ByVal x) As Integer
            cube = x * x * x
        End Function
    End Module
```

Output

```
Enter the range
4
9

N       Square      Cube        SquareRoot

4       16          64          2
5       25          125         2       .23606797749979
6       36          216         2       .44948974278318
7       49          343         2       .64575131106459
8       64          512         2       .82842712474619
9       81          729         3
```

Call by Reference

When a function is called by reference, the changes inside the function affect the values of the calling program. This is because of accessing the argument value in the calling function directly.

Program

```
Module ExCallByRef
        'call by reference
        Sub Main()
                Dim x, res As Integer
                Console.WriteLine("Enter the number")
                x = Integer.Parse(Console.ReadLine())
                Console.WriteLine("Before going to function")
                Console.WriteLine("x = {0}", x)
                res = square(x)
                Console.WriteLine("After coming to main...")
                Console.WriteLine("Square of the given number is {0}",
                res)
      Console.WriteLine("x = {0}", x)
                Console.ReadLine()
        End Sub
     Public Function square(ByRef x)     'argument passed by reference
                square = x * x
                x = x + 10       'this incremented value will reflect
on Main()
        End Function
End Module
```

Output

```
Enter the number
10
Before going to function
 x = 10
After coming to main...
Square of the given number is  100
 x = 20
```

Function with Array

Here we pass the array as the argument to the function. Largest of an array element is return by the function.

Program

```
Module Funarray
        Sub Main()
                Dim a(15), i, n, big As Integer
                Console.WriteLine("Enter the total number of elements")
                n = Integer.Parse(Console.ReadLine())
                Console.WriteLine("Enter the numbers one by one")
                For i = 1 To n
                  a(i) = Integer.Parse(Console.ReadLine())
                Next
                big = max(a, n)             'array passed as argument
                Console.WriteLine("The Largest number is  {0}", big)
                Console.ReadLine()
        End Sub
        Function max(ByVal a() As Integer, ByVal n As Integer) As
Integer
                Dim m, i As Integer
                m = a(1)
                For i = 2 To n
                        If (m < a(i)) Then
                                m = a(i)
                        End If
                Next
                max = m
        End Function
End Module
```

Output

```
Enter the total number of elements
4
Enter the numbers one by one
78
```

```
67
45
99
The Largest number is  99
```

Function Overloading

The process of defining more than function with same name and different parameter list is called function overloading. When a function is invoked, the compiler matches the function by comparing function name, number of arguments and order of arguments and then executes the corresponding function.

Here we have two functions named **min()** with different type of arguments

Program

```
Module Exoverload
      Sub Main()
            Dim a, b, c As Integer
            Dim n1, n2, n3 As Single
            Console.WriteLine("Enter two integer numbers")
            a = Integer.Parse(Console.ReadLine())
            b = Integer.Parse(Console.ReadLine())
            c = min(a, b)' Function with integer argument invoked
            Console.WriteLine("The Smallest number is  {0}", c)
            Console.WriteLine()
            Console.WriteLine("Enter two real numbers")
            n1 = Single.Parse(Console.ReadLine())
            n2 = Single.Parse(Console.ReadLine())
            n3 = min(n1, n2) 'Function with single argument invoked
            Console.WriteLine("The Smallest number is  {0}", n3)
            Console.ReadLine()
      End Sub

'Function min() with two integer arguments
    Overloads Function min(ByVal x As Integer, ByVal y As Integer)
As Integer
            If (x < y) Then
                  Return x
            Else
```

```
                Return y
            End If
        End Function

    'Function min() with two single arguments
        Overloads Function min(ByVal x As Single, ByVal y As Single)
As Single
            If (x < y) Then
                Return x
            Else
                Return y
            End If
        End Function
    End Module
```

Output

```
Enter two integer numbers
8
9
The Smallest number is  8

Enter two real numbers
5.6
9.7
The Smallest number is  5.6
```

6.2 SUB PROCEDURE

The procedure is defined as a set of code that does some specific task and does not return any value to the calling function. These procedures can be called any number of times as required. It takes the general format as follows,

[accessibility] ***Sub*** *procedure-name (arguments)*

Statements within the procedure

End Sub

Accessibility can be Public, Protected, Friend, Protected Friend or Private. Procedure-name is nothing but a name given to the procedure.

The calling of procedure takes the general form as follows

```
Call procedure-name(arguments)
```

Almighty Names

The following program code demonstrates the defining and calling of sub procedure

Program

```
Module Name
      Sub Main()
    Dim AlmightyNames() As String = {"Who was", "Who is", "Who is to
come", "Wounder", "Beerlahairoi", "Elshaddai"}
            Dim i As String
            For Each i In AlmightyNames
                  Console.WriteLine(i)
                  Call myprocedure()       'calling of sub procedure
            Next
            Console.ReadLine()
      End Sub
      Sub myprocedure()             'sub procedure defined
            Console.WriteLine()
            Console.WriteLine("<<<<<<>>>>>>>")
            Console.WriteLine()
      End Sub
End Module
```

Output

```
Who was

<<<<<<>>>>>>>

Who is

<<<<<<>>>>>>>

Who is to come

<<<<<<>>>>>>>
```

```
Wounder

<<<<<<>>>>>>>

Beerlahairoi

<<<<<<>>>>>>>

Elshaddai

<<<<<<>>>>>>>
```

Different Procedures in GUI. This program also demonstrates the calling of sub procedure. Run this program under Windows Application (see Part III)

Form Designing

Table 6.1 Calling of Sub Procedure

Control	*Property*	*Value*
Form1	Name	Form1
	Text	Procedure Demo
Button1	Name	CmdDemo
	Text	Click Here

Coding

```
Public Class Form1

        Private Sub CmdDemo_Click(ByVal sender As System.Object, ByVal
e As System.EventArgs) Handles CmdDemo.Click
            MsgBox("Now, You are going to visit different procedure",
MsgBoxStyle.Exclamation, "Button")
                Mumbai()
                Chennai()
                Delhi()
                Veppathur()

        End Sub
        Public Sub Mumbai()
                    MsgBox("Hi You are in Gateway of India",
MsgBoxStyle.Information, "Mumbai")
```

```
        End Sub
        Public Sub Chennai()
                MsgBox("Hello, it is very busy city",
MsgBoxStyle.Information, "Chennai")
        End Sub
        Public Sub Delhi()
        MsgBox("This is our Capital", MsgBoxStyle.Information, "Delhi")
        End Sub
        Public Sub Veppathur()
            MsgBox("Welcome to Veppathur!!!", MsgBoxStyle.Information,
"Veppathur")
        End Sub
    End Class
```

Output

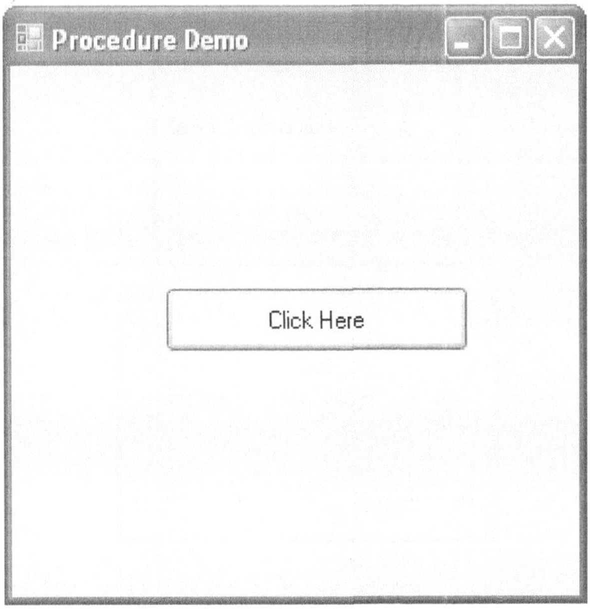

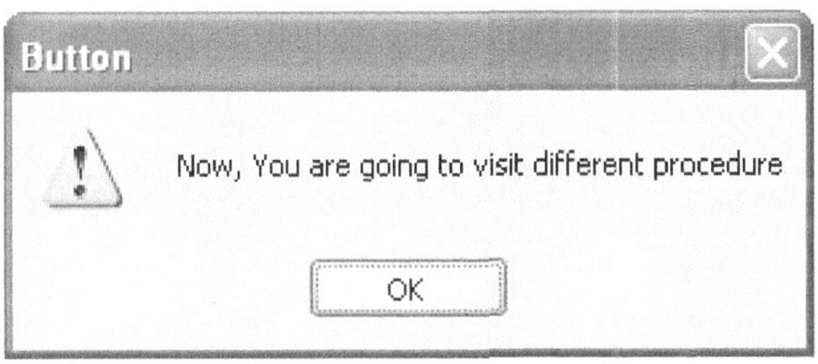

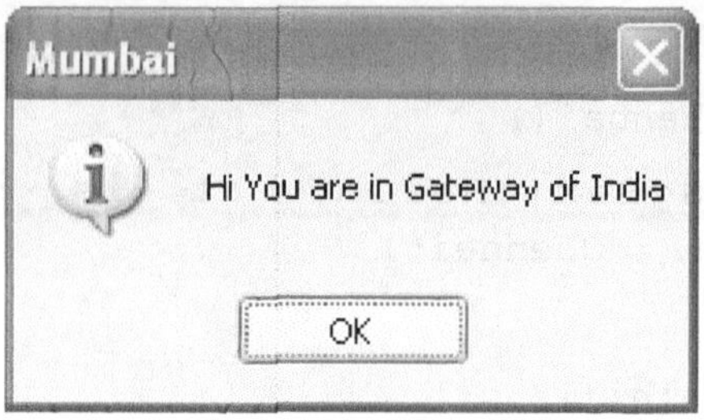
Mumbai
Hi You are in Gateway of India
OK

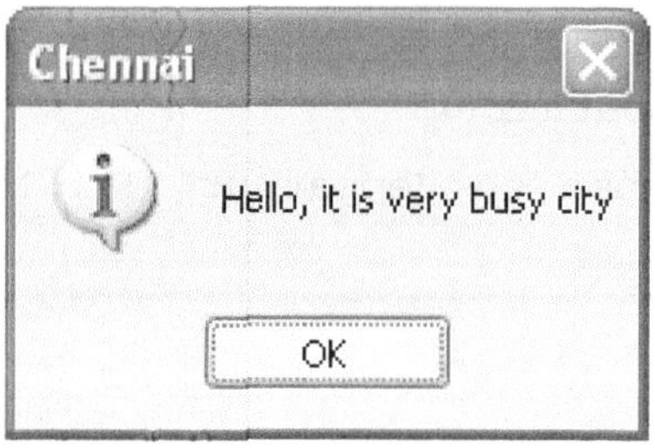
Chennai
Hello, it is very busy city
OK

Delhi
This is our Capital
OK

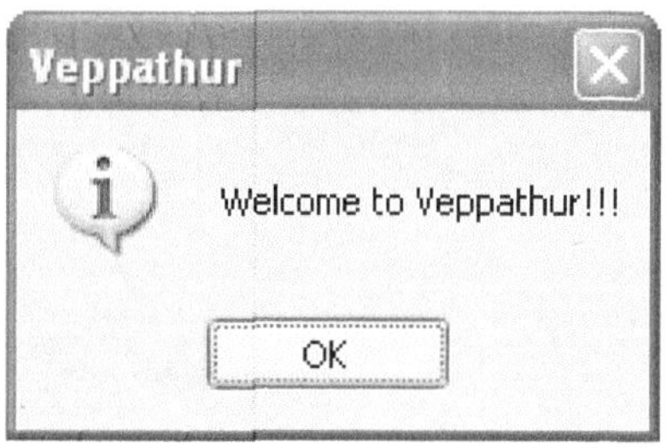
Veppathur
Welcome to Veppathur!!!
OK

CHAPTER

7

OOP CONCEPTS

7.1 CLASS AND OBJECT

Class is a user defined data type that allows different types of member and functions operate on them. The following is the general syntax of class with field and method only. A class may also have property and events as discussed later.

```
[Accessibility] Class Class-name
        [Accessibility] field-1 As data-type
            :
        [Accessibility] field-1 As data-type
[Function function-name1(parameter list) As return-type
            Statements inside the function
            Return   exp
        End Function
Function function-name2(parameter list) As return-type
            Statements inside the function
            Return   exp
        End Function
]
End Class
```

Classes are stored like a template and the creation of object allocates memory spaces to all the instance variables.

Object creation takes the general form

```
Dim obj   As New Class-name
```

After the creation of object, the instance members are accessed as follows

```
obj.field-1
```

```
obj.field-n
obj. function-name2(parameter list)
obj. function-name2(parameter list)
```

Complex Number

This program simply defines the field of the class only. The imaginary and real part of the complex number is input and it displays the same.

Program

```
Public Class Complex                'class definition
      Public im, re As Integer
End Class
Module Module1
      Sub Main()
            Dim C As New Complex          'object created
            Console.WriteLine("Enter the Imaginary part")
            C.im = Integer.Parse(Console.ReadLine())
            Console.WriteLine("Enter the real part")
            C.re = Integer.Parse(Console.ReadLine())
             Console.WriteLine("The Complex number is {0}+i {1}",
C.re, C.im)
            Console.ReadLine()
      End Sub
End Module
```

Output

```
Enter the Imaginary part
4
Enter the real part
5
The Complex number is 5+i 4
```

Simple and Compound Interest

Here the class interest is defined with functions and calculates the simple and compound interest.

Program

```
Public Class Interest
      Dim n As Integer
```

```
        Dim p, r As Double
        Function getdata(ByVal p1 As Double, ByVal n1 As Integer,
ByVal r1 As Double)
            p = p1
            n = n1
            r = r1
            Return 0
        End Function
        Function Simple() As Double
            Return p * n * r / 100
        End Function
        Function Compound() As Double
            Return (p * ((1 + r / 100) ^ n) - p)
        End Function
    End Class
    Module Si_Ci
        Sub main()
            Dim I As New Interest
            Dim si, ci As Double
            I.getdata(1000, 2, 8)
            si = I.Simple()
            ci = I.Compound()
            Console.WriteLine("The Simple Interest is  {0}", si)
            Console.WriteLine("The Compound Interest is {0}", ci)
            Console.ReadLine()
        End Sub
    End Module
```

Output

```
The Simple Interest is  160
The Compound Interest is 166.4
```

7.2 CONSTRUCTOR

A constructor is a special method that initializes the instance variables of an object. The constructors are called at the time of object creation. In VB.Net **New()** method is used as constructor.

Rectangle with new

Program

```
Module constru 1
Class Rectangle
      Dim length, breath As Single
      Sub New(ByVal a As Single, ByVal b As Single)
            length = a
            breath = b
      End Sub
      Function display()
            Console.WriteLine("Length = {0}", length)
            Console.WriteLine("breath = {0}", breath)
            Console.WriteLine("Area = {0}", length * breath)
            Return 0
      End Function
End Class
Module Constru
      Sub Main()
            Dim R As New Rectangle(2.0, 3.0)
            R.display()
            Console.ReadLine()
      End Sub
End Module
```

Output

```
Length = 2
breath = 3
Area = 6
```

Rectangle without New()

This program manipulates constructor without using **New ()** method

Program

```
Module Constru1
      Class Rectangle
            Dim length, breath As Single
           Function Rectangle(ByVal a As Single, ByVal b As Single)
                  length = a
```

```
            breath = b
            Return 0
        End Function

        Function Display()
            Console.WriteLine("Length = {0}", length)
            Console.WriteLine("breath = {0}", breath)
            Console.WriteLine("Area = {0}", length * breath)
            Return 0
        End Function
    End Class
    Sub Main()
        Dim R As New Rectangle
        R.Rectangle(21.0, 3.0)
        R.Display()
        Console.ReadLine()
    End Sub
End Module
```

Output

```
Length = 2
breath = 5
Area = 10
```

System Information

This constructor displays the system information

Program

```
Module Module1
    Class Computer
        Dim model As String
        Dim clk_speed As Decimal
        Dim RAM As Integer
        Public Sub New()
            model = "Presario CQ40"
            clk_speed = 2.0
            RAM = 2
```

```
            End Sub
            Public Sub Display()
            Console.WriteLine("Model          : {0}", model)
            Console.WriteLine("Clock Speed   : {0} GHz", clk_speed)
            Console.WriteLine("RAM capacity : {0} GB", RAM)
            End Sub
        End Class
        Sub Main()
            Dim C As New Computer
            C.Display()
            Console.ReadLine()
        End Sub
    End Module
```

Output

```
Model          : Presario CQ40
Clock Speed    : 2 GHz
RAM capacity   : 2 GB
```

7.3 INHERITANCE

Inheritance is the process of creating new classes from the existing classes. The new classes are called sub class or derived class and the existing classes are called super class or base class.

Advantages

- New classes can be derived from the existing classes without modification
- It saves time and memory

The general structure for deriving one class from another is

```
Public class BaseClass
Sataements in BaseClass
End class

Public class DerivedClass
        Inherits BaseClass
Statements in Derivedclass

End Class
```

Property in Class

A property is a member of a class that combines a field with the methods that access it. A property consists of a name along with **get** and **set** accessors. The accessors used to get and set the value of a variable. The benifit of a property is that its name can be used in expressions and assignments,the get and set accessors are automatically invoked. The general format is

```
Property propert-name() As return-type
            Get
                  Return Field
            End Get
            Set(ByVal value As data-type)
                 Field = value
            End Set
      End Property
```

Note: *return-type* and *data-type* must be same. *Field* is the instance member of class associated with this property

Traditional Student – Staff Info

Here the base class **Student** is inherited by the derived class **Staff.** The property value of this class is accessed.

Program

```
Public Class Student          'base class
      Dim id As Integer
      Dim na As String
      Property idn() As Integer        'property idn defined
            Get
                  Return id
            End Get
            Set(ByVal value As Integer)
                  id = value
            End Set
      End Property
      Property name() As String        'property name defined
            Get
                  Return na
            End Get
```

```
            Set(ByVal value As String)
                na = value
            End Set
        End Property
    End Class
    Public Class Staff
        Inherits Student
        Dim des As String
        Property design() As String          'property design defined
            Get
                Return des
            End Get
            Set(ByVal value As String)
                des = value
            End Set
        End Property
    End Class
    Module Module1
        Sub Main()
            Dim S As New Student
            S.idn = 14085319
            S.name = "Muthuli"
            Console.WriteLine("***Base class Information***")
            Console.WriteLine("Student ID   : {0}", S.idn)
            Console.WriteLine("Student Name : {0}", S.name)
            Console.WriteLine()
            Dim Sta As New Staff
            Sta.idn = 33555203
            Sta.name = "Karthikajesus"
            Sta.design = "Lecturer"
            Console.WriteLine("***Derived class Information***")
            Console.WriteLine("Student ID   : {0}", Sta.idn)
            Console.WriteLine("Student Name : {0}", Sta.name)
            Console.WriteLine("Student Name : {0}", Sta.design)
```

```
            Console.ReadLine()
        End Sub
End Module
```

Output

```
***Base class Information***
Student ID    : 14085319
Student Name  : Muthuli

***Derived class Information***
Student ID    : 33555203
Student Name  : Karthikajesus
Student Name  : Lecturer
```

Constructor in Inheritance

This program handles inheritance with constructor. The special method **Mybase.New()** in derived class is used to invoke the base class constructor

Program

```
Class Student            'base class
        Dim regno As Long
        Dim name As String
        Public Sub New(ByVal rn, ByVal na) 'base class constructor

            regno = rn
            name  = na
        End Sub
        Public Sub Disp()

            Console.WriteLine("Register Number : {0}", regno)
            Console.WriteLine("Name            : {0}", name)
        End Sub

End Class
Class Staff                              'derived class
        Inherits Student
        Dim design As String
        Public Sub New(ByVal rn, ByVal na, ByVal desi)  'derived
class constructor
```

```
            MyBase.New(rn, na) 'invokes the base class constructor
            design = desi

        End Sub
        Public Sub Display()
            MyBase.Disp()                'invokes base class Disp()
            Console.WriteLine("Designation : {0}", design)
        End Sub
    End Class

    Module Module1
        Sub Main()
            Console.WriteLine("Student Details")
            Console.WriteLine("..........")
            Dim s As New Student(1002, "Gurusankar") 'invokes base
class constructor
            s.Disp()           'invokes the base class Disp()
            Console.WriteLine()
            Console.WriteLine("Staff Details")
            Console.WriteLine("...........")
          Dim St As New Staff(33555203, "Karthikajesus", "Lecturer")
'invokes the derived class constructor
            St.Display()       'invokes the derived class Display()
            Console.ReadLine()
        End Sub
    End Module
```

Output

```
Student Details
..............................
Register Number    : 1002
Name               : Gurusankar

Staff Details
.............................
Register Number    : 33555203
Name               : Karthikajesus
Designation        : Lecturer
```

Not Inheritable Class

The keyword **NotInheritable** is used to prevent a class from being inherited by another class. Here class **Welcome** is declared as **NotInheritable.** So deriving of class **Welcome** will cause an error. This is one of the Security mechanisms.

Program

```
Public NotInheritable Class Welcome            'base class
      Public Sub print()
            Console.WriteLine("Greetings!!!  from base class")
      End Sub
End Class
Class Welcome1
          Inherits Welcome 'sealed class is inherited. Error occurs!!
      Public Sub disp()
            Console.WriteLine("Greetings!!!  From derived class")
      End Sub
End Class

Module Module1
      Sub Main()
            Dim w As Welcome
            w.print()
            Dim w1 As New Welcome1
            w1.disp()
            Console.ReadLine()
      End Sub
End Module
```

Running the above program will cause the following error

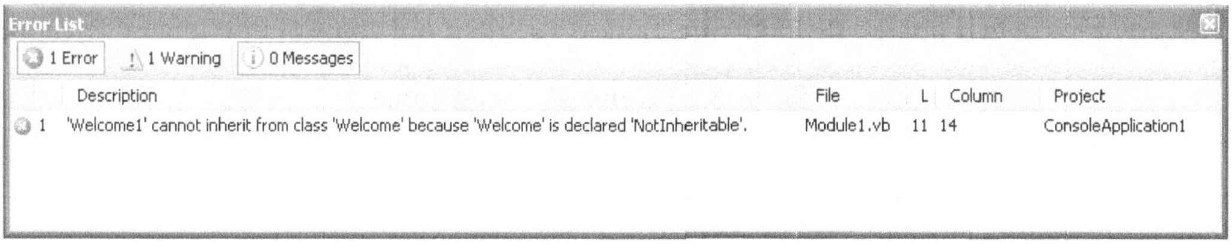

CHAPTER

8

EXCEPTION HANDLING

8.1 EXCEPTION HANDLING

An Exception is an error that occurs at run time. Exception handling is a technique to deal the exceptions. In response to an exception, some action can be taken automatically by CLR. VB .NET allows the user to write program code in order to heal the exception. The general form is

```
Try
        Statements for Try block
Catch Exception_obj As Exception_class
      Statements for catch block
Finally
       Statements for Finally block
End Try
```

The **Try** block contains the code that may doubt to cause error. The **Catch** block contains the code that handles the Exception. The **Finally** blocks contains code that executes after the execution of catch block statements whether if there was an error or not.

Commonly Used Exceptions

The **System.Exception** is the base class for all exception classes. Generally class **Exception** will catch any type of exception. The following Table 8.1.1Listed out some of the General Exceptions

Table 8.1 General Exceptions

Exception	*Meaning*
ArgumentException	This exception is thrown when one of the arguments provided to a method is not valid
ArgumentNullException	This exception is thrown when a null reference is passed to a method that does not accept it as a valid argument.

ArithmeticException	This exception is thrown for errors in an arithmetic, casting, or conversion operation.
DivideByZeroException	This exception is thrown when there is an attempt to divide a integer value by zero
FormatException	This exception is thrown when the format of an argument or variable does not meet the specifications
IndexOutOfRangeException	This exception is thrown when an attempt is made to access an element of an array with an index that is outside the bounds of the array.
NullReferenceException	This exception is thrown when there is an attempt to reference a null object
OverflowException	This exception is thrown when an arithmetic, casting or conversion operation in a checked context results in an overflow

Simple Try Catch

This example program shows the try catch structure which attempt to calling the base class **Exception.**

Program

```
Module try_catch
    Sub Main()
        Dim a, b, c As Integer
        Console.WriteLine("Enter the first number")
        a = Integer.Parse(Console.ReadLine())
        Console.WriteLine("Enter the second number")
        b = Integr.Parse(Console.ReadLine())
        Try
            c = a/b
            Console.WriteLine("The result is  {0}", c)
            Console.Write("Process Complete")
        Catch ex As Exception
         Console.WriteLine("Division not possible due to :")
          Console.WriteLine(ex.Message)
        End Try
        Console.ReadLine()
    End Sub
End Module
```

Output

```
Enter the first number
```

```
6
Enter the second number
0
Division not possible due to:
Arithmetic operation resulted in an overflow.
```

Try Catch with Finally

The following module demonstrate the try catch with finally block.

Program

```
Module Module1
  'try catch with finally
Sub Main()
        Dim n As Integer = 0
        Dim r As Integer
        Try
            Console.WriteLine("Enter a Number")
            n = Integer.Parse(Console.ReadLine())
        Catch fx As FormatException
            Console.WriteLine(fx)
        Finally
            If (n < 0) Then
                Console.WriteLine("<< n takes positive values
                only >>")
            Else
              Console.WriteLine("your input in reverse....")
                While (n <> 0)
                    r = n Mod 10
                    Console.Write(r)
                    n = n \ 10
                End While
            End If
        End Try
        Console.ReadLine()
    End Sub
End Module
```

Output 1:

```
Enter a Number
345
your input in reverse....
543
```

Output 2:

```
Enter a Number
-789
<< n takes positive values only >>
```

Another Example for Finally

This program also demonstrates the **Finally** block which allows values only from 1 to 100 for n.

Program

```
Module trycat_final
    Sub Main()
        Dim n As Integer = 0
        Try
            Console.WriteLine("Enter the number")
            n = Integer.Parse(Console.ReadLine())
        Catch ex As FormatException
            Console.WriteLine(ex.Message)
        Finally
          If (n <= 0 Or n > 100) Then
          Console.WriteLine("Your input must between 1-100")
          Else
          Console.WriteLine("Square of your i/p is {0}", n *n)
          End If
        End Try
        Console.ReadLine()
    End Sub
End Module
```

Output 1:

```
Enter the number
45
Square of your i/p is  2025
```

Output 2:

```
Enter the number
110
Your input must between 1 - 100
```

Multiple Catch

Here multiple catch blocks are constructed to catch the errors.

Program

```
Module Module1
        'Multiple catch
        Sub Main()
                Dim a() As Integer = {10, 20, 30, 40, 50}
                Dim b As Integer
                Try
                        Console.WriteLine("Enter the Location")
                        b = Integer.Parse(Console.ReadLine())
                        Console.WriteLine("The value in the Location {0} is {1}", b, a(b))
                Catch ex As IndexOutOfRangeException
                        Console.WriteLine("Your value is above the Maximum limit")
                        Console.WriteLine(ex)
                Catch ex1 As FormatException
                        Console.WriteLine("Input must be an integer")
                        Console.WriteLine(ex1)
                End Try
                Console.ReadLine()
        End Sub
End Module
```

Output 1:

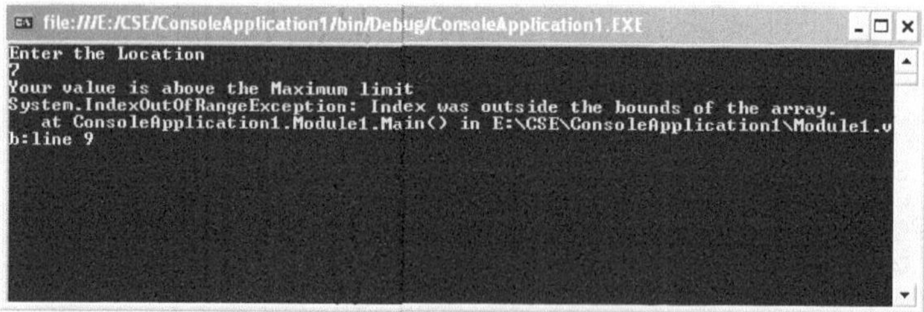

Output 2:

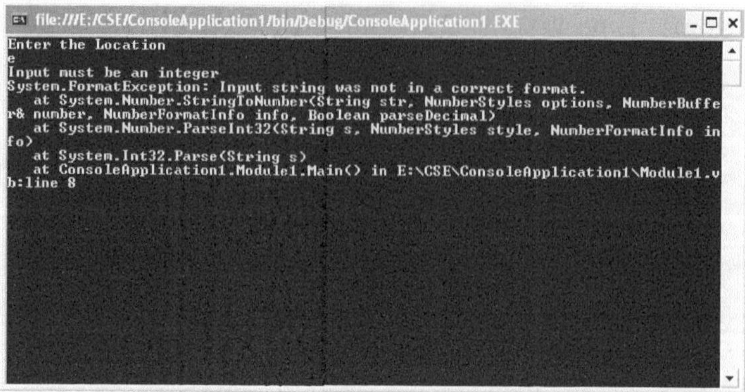

PART III

WINDOWS APPLICATION

VB .NET is a flexible and easiest tool to develop standalone applications. In VB.NET we can create various types of Graphical User Interface applications. These applications can be designed by activating the **Windows Application** template from the **New Project** window.

INTRODUCTION-III

GETTING STARTED

To work with the VB.NET windows applications, select **Windows Application** from **New Project** window as pictured below (Figure III a).

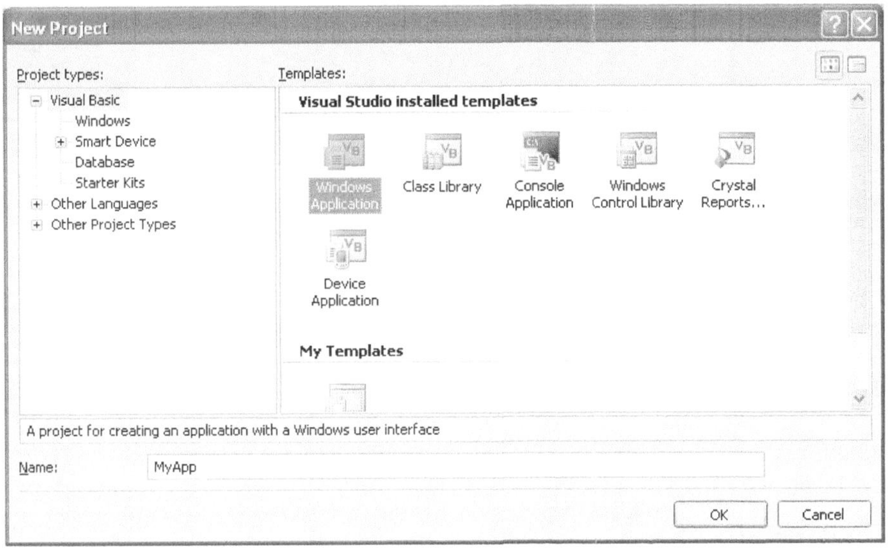

Figure III a. **New Project** window

Whatever is typed in the textbox will be the name of our Windows Application. Here **MyApp** is our Windows Application.

Select OK, it shows the Visual Studio IDE as pictured here (Figure III b)

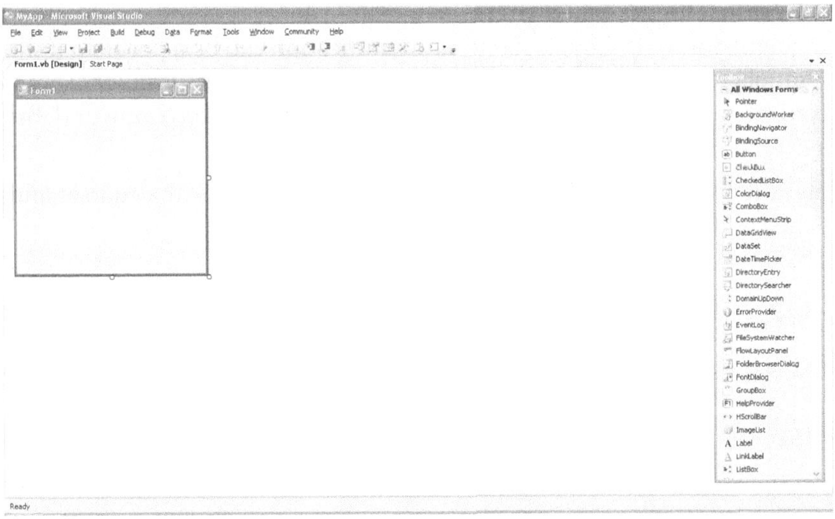

Figure III b. Visual Studio IDE

Place controls on the form, by selecting controls on the **ToolBox** as shown on Figure III c

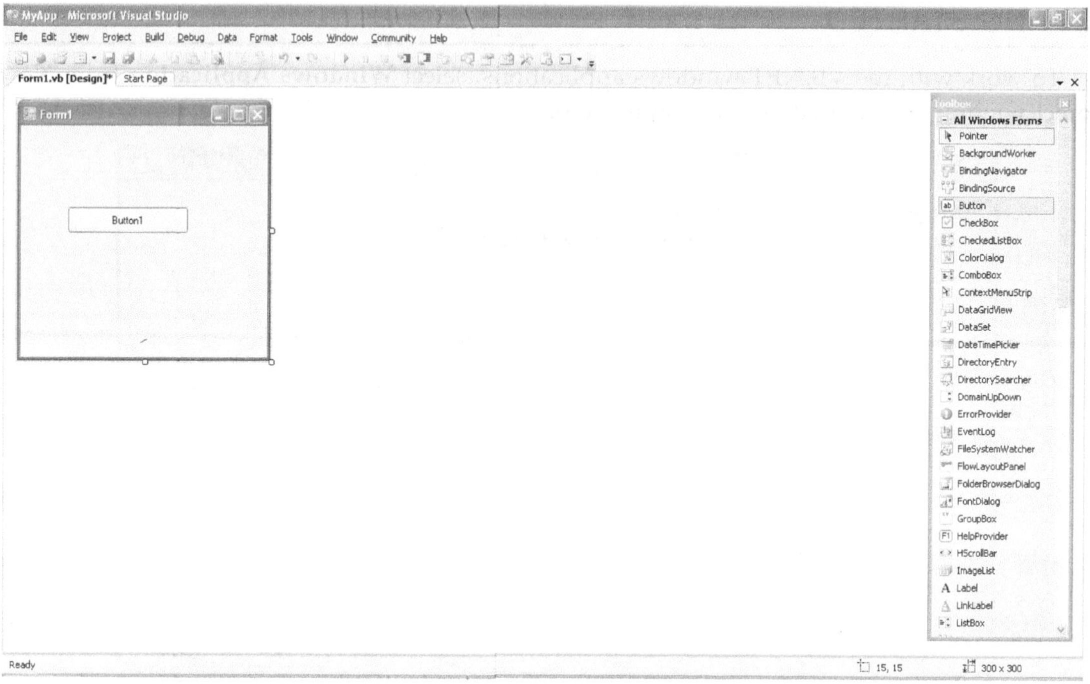

Figure III c Control placed on the form

Right click the control and select **properties** option from the menu or press **F4** , to edit properties window as here and change the **Text** property of button1 to "My First Button".

It is a good practice to give meaningful names to a form and the controls on the form. It becomes easy to identify a control by its name, as identification can be a problem if the application involves a large number of controls. **Form** control name is prefixed with **Frm** for example **FrmLogin** and **TextBox** control name is prefixed with **Txt** for example **TxtUserName** and **Button** control name is prefixed with **cmd** for example **CmdSubmit** etc.

To open the code window, double click the control or right click the control and select **view code.** It shows the code window (Figure III d).

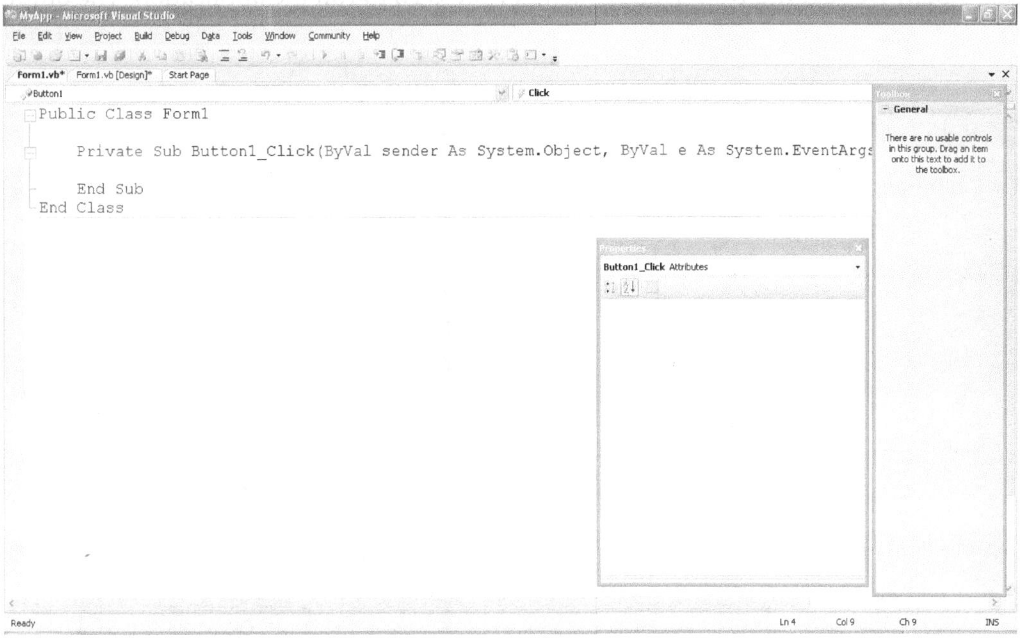

Figure III d Code window

Type the code in the code window as shown below (Figure III e)

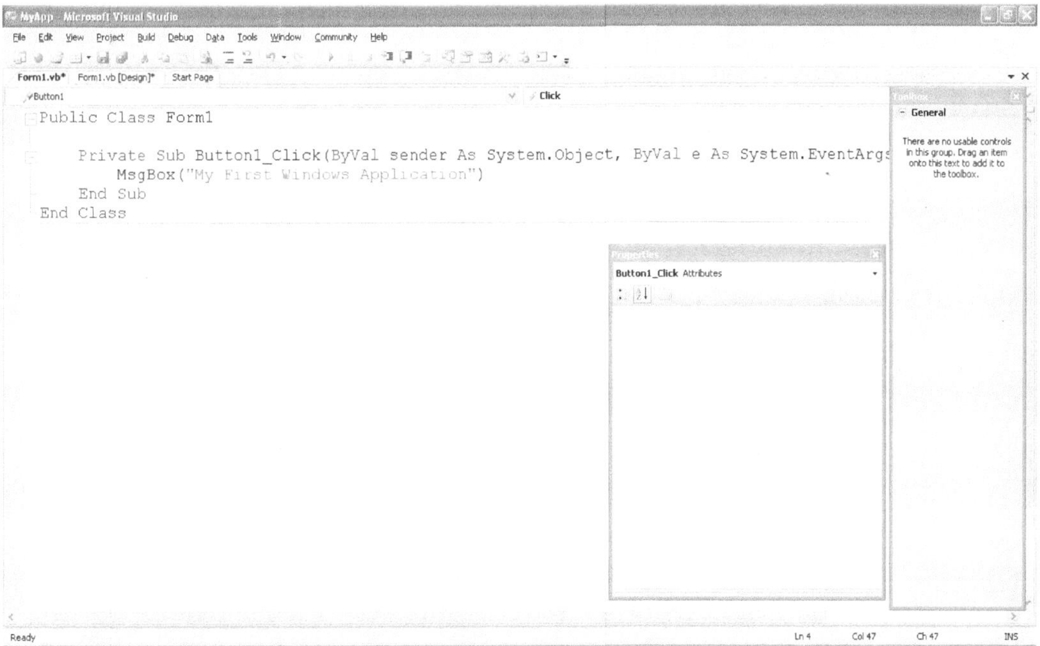

Figure III e Code window

Select **Start Debugging** from **Debug** menu or press **F5** to run the application. The output as follows

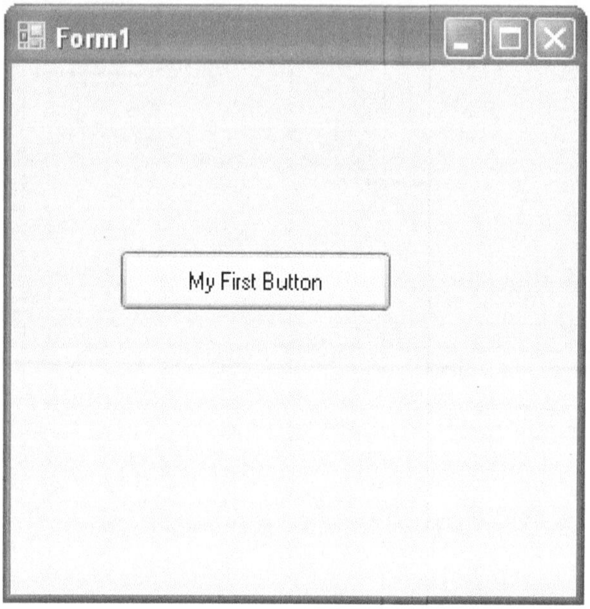

CHAPTER

9

TEXTBOX, BUTTON, LABEL AND LINKLABEL

9.1 LABEL, BUTTON AND LINKLABEL

The Label Control

The **Label** control is used to display the text that cannot be edited by the user directly. The **Text** property of this control is used to set the text to be displayed. The **ForeColour** property is used to set the colour of the text to be displayed.

Welcome Form

These designing displays a text property of label is changed during run time

Form Designing

Table 9.1 Welcome Form

Control	*Property*	*Value*
Label1	Name	LblDisplay
Form1	Text	Demo Form
	Name	Frmwelcome

Coding

```
Public Class frmwelcome
Private Sub Form1_Load(ByVal sender As System.Object, ByVal e As System.EventArgs) Handles MyBase.Load
LblDisplay.Text = "The sweetness of the lips increaseth learning"
        LblDisplay.ForeColor = Color.DarkBlue
    End Sub
End Class
```

Output

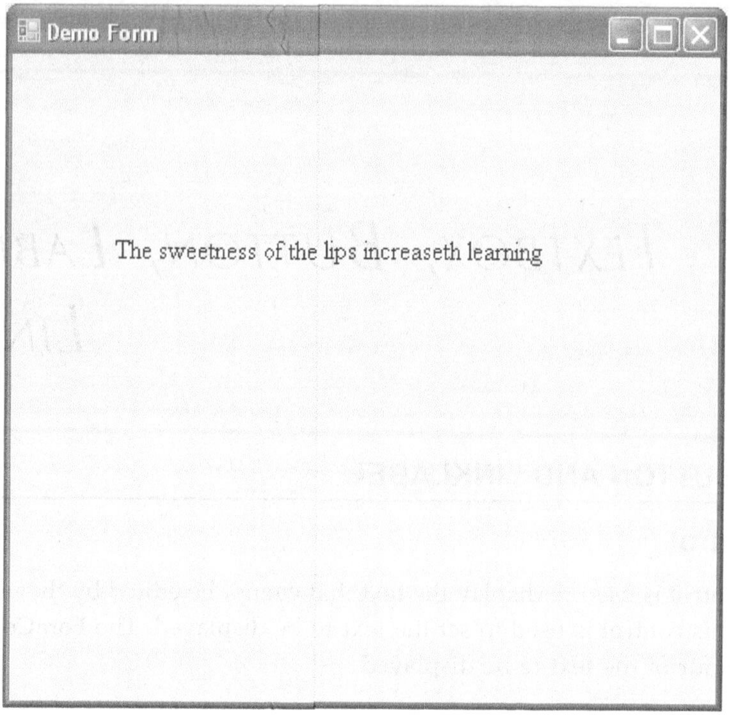

The LinkLabel Control

The **LinkLabel** control is used to display a text as a link. When we click the link, it opens another link or form or file or link. The **LinkColour** property is used to get or set the color of the link to be displayed. The **ActiveLinkColour** property is used to get or set the color used to display the active link. The **DisabledLinkColour** property is used to get or set the color of the disabled link.

The following code is used to link a file in the specified directory.

System.Diagnostics.Process.Start ("D:\karthikajesus\vb.net\jk.txt")

The **Start()** method of the **Process** class resides in the **System.Diagostics** namespace is used to invoke the specified file. The **LinkLabel** control displays the link and when the link is clicked, it shows the file named jk.txt.

Form Designing

Table 9.2 The LinkedLabel Control

Control	*Property*	*Value*
LinkLabel1	Name	LnkLbl
	LinkArea	19,6
	Text	Click here to open jk.txt

Coding

```
Public Class Form1
        Private Sub LnkLbl_LinkClicked(ByVal sender As System.Object,
ByVal e As
        System.Windows.Forms.LinkLabelLinkClickedEventArgs) Handles
LnkLbl.LinkClicked
          System.Diagnostics.Process.Start("D:\karthikajesus\vb.net\jk.txt")
        End Sub
End Class
```

Output

9.2 TEXTBOX

The Textbox Control

The **Textbox** control is used to display a text to a user or accept input from a user. By default, we can enter a maximum of 2048 characters in a **Textbox** control. The **Text** property of this control is used to set the text to be displayed. The **PasswordChar** property allows us to set a single character that act as a placeholder for the characters to be displayed.

Displaying the Text

This designing display the text whatever typed on the textbox

Form Designing

Table 9.3 Displaying the Text

Control	*Property*	*Value*
Button1	Name	CmdOk
	Text	OK
Textbox1	Name	Mytxt

Coding

```
Public Class Form1
    Private Sub CmdOk_Click(ByVal sender As System.Object, ByVal
e As System.EventArgs) Handles CmdOk.Click
        MsgBox(Mytxt.Text)
    End Sub
End Class
```

Output

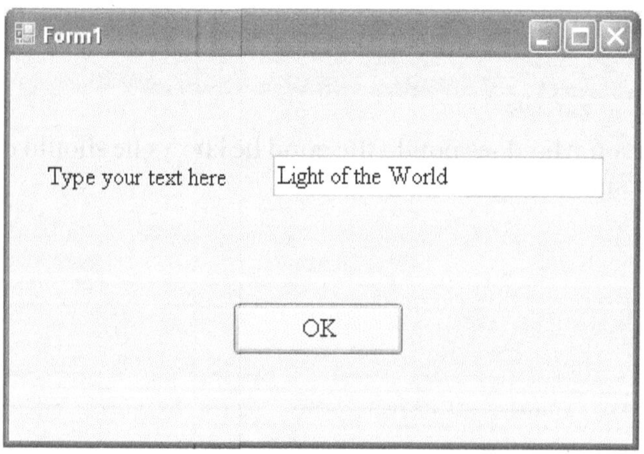

Mouse Button Demo

This program detects the button pressed. The output displayed in the textbox.

Form Designing

Table 9.4 Mouse Button Demo

Control	*Property*	*Value*
Button1	Name	CmdDemo
	Text	Mouse Button Demo
TextBox1	Name	TxtDisplay

Coding

```
Public Class Form1
  Private Sub CmdDemo_MouseDown(ByVal sender As Object, ByVal e As
        System.Windows.Forms.MouseEventArgs) Handles
CmdDemo.MouseDown
     If Control.MouseButtons = Windows.Forms.MouseButtons.Left Then
           TxtDisplay.Text = "Left Button Pressed"
        End If
     If Control.MouseButtons = Windows.Forms.MouseButtons.Right Then
           TxtDisplay.Text = "Right button Pressed"
        End If
     If Control.MouseButtons = Windows.Forms.MouseButtons.Middle Then
           TxtDisplay.Text = "Middle button pressed"
        End If
   End Sub
End Class
```

Output

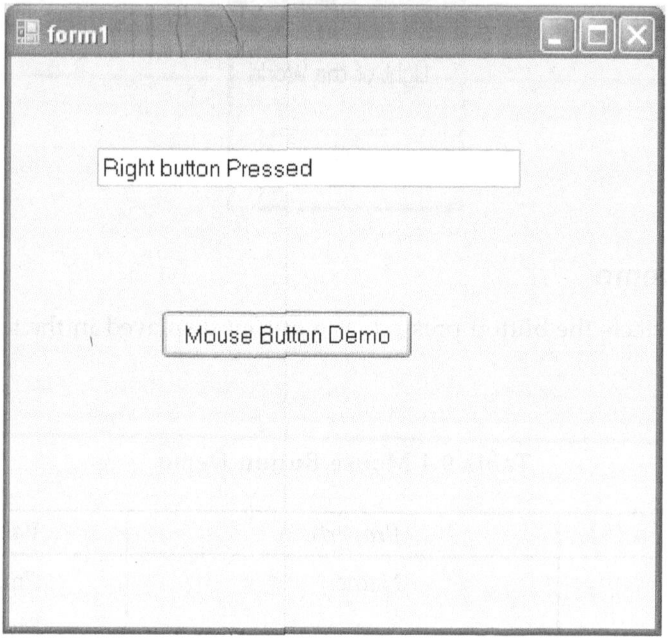

Displaying Mouse Position

This program displays the mouse position. The output displayed in the textbox.

Form Designing

Table 9.5 Authorization Form

Control	*Property*	*Value*
Label1	Text	Mouse moved at
TextBox1	Name	TxtDisplay

Coding

```
Public Class Form1
        Private Sub Form1_MouseMove(ByVal sender As Object, ByVal e
As
                   System.Windows.Forms.MouseEventArgs) Handles
Me.MouseMove
  TxtDisplay.Text = e.X & "," & e.Y
        End Sub
End Class
```

Output

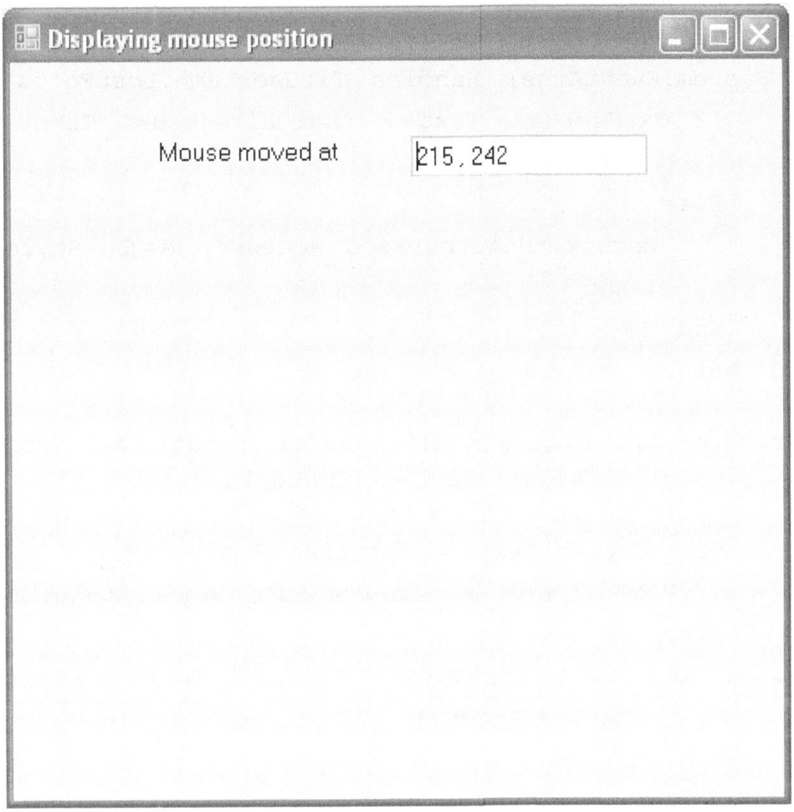

Authorization Form

This form checks the user validity. It takes username and password as input and check with the pre described values.

Form Designing

Table 9.6 Authorization Form

Control	*Property*	*Value*
Button1	Name	CmdLogin
	Text	Login
Textbox1	Name	TxtUserName
TextBox2	Name	TxtPwd
	passwordchar	*
Form1	Text	Login form

Coding

```
Public Class Form1
    Private Sub TxtUserName_LostFocus(ByVal sender As Object, ByVal e As System.EventArgs) Handles TxtUserName.LostFocus
        If TxtUserName.Text = "Karthikajesus" Then
            TxtPwd.Focus()
        Else
            MsgBox("UnAuthorized Access", MsgBoxStyle.Critical)
            End
        End If
    End Sub

    Private Sub CmdLogin_Click(ByVal sender As System.Object, ByVal e As System.EventArgs) Handles CmdLogin.Click

        If  TxtPwd.Text = "praise" Then
            MsgBox("Welcome to Domain", MsgBoxStyle.Exclamation)
        Else
    MsgBox("incorrect Password", MsgBoxStyle.Information)
            TxtPwd.Focus()
        End If
    End Sub
End Class
```

Output

Login
UnAuthorized Access
OK

Login Form
UserName
Karthikajesus
Pass Word
****
Login

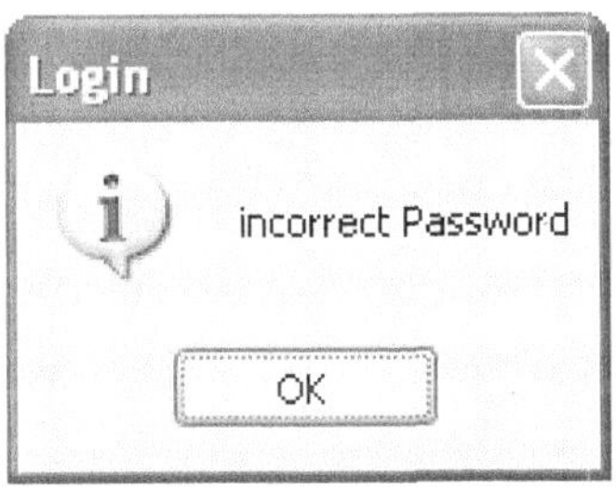
Login
incorrect Password
OK

Login Form
UserName
Karthikajesus
Pass Word
****
Login

Login
Welcome to Domain
OK

CHAPTER

10

LISTBOX, SCROLL BARS, CHECKBOX AND RADIO BUTTON

10.1 THE LISTBOX CONTROL

The **ListBox** control is used to display a list of items to a user. The user can select and process particular item at runtime. The items are included in the ListBox either at design time or runtime.

To include the items to the ListBox1 at design time select the button displayed on the **Item** property on the **Properties window** as shown here Fig. 10.1.

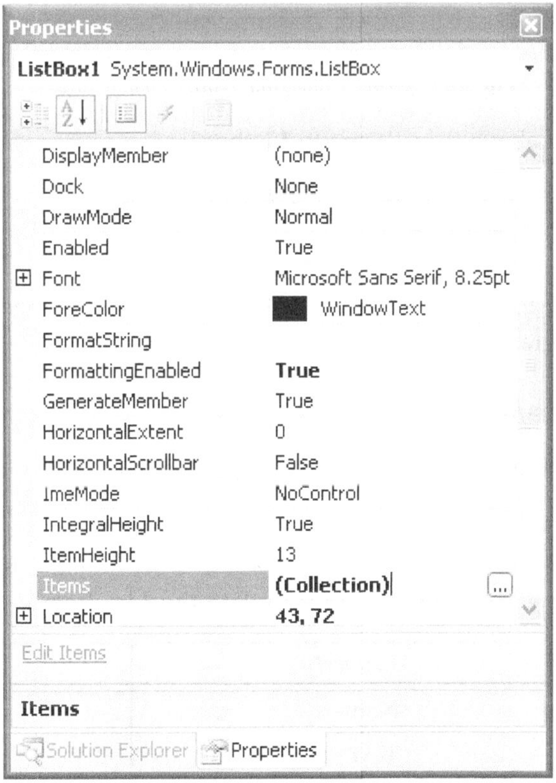

Fig. 10.1 *Properties Window of ListBox*

This opens the **String Collection Editor** Dialog box. Here we type the items one by one and select **OK** button to confirm as in Fig. 10.2.

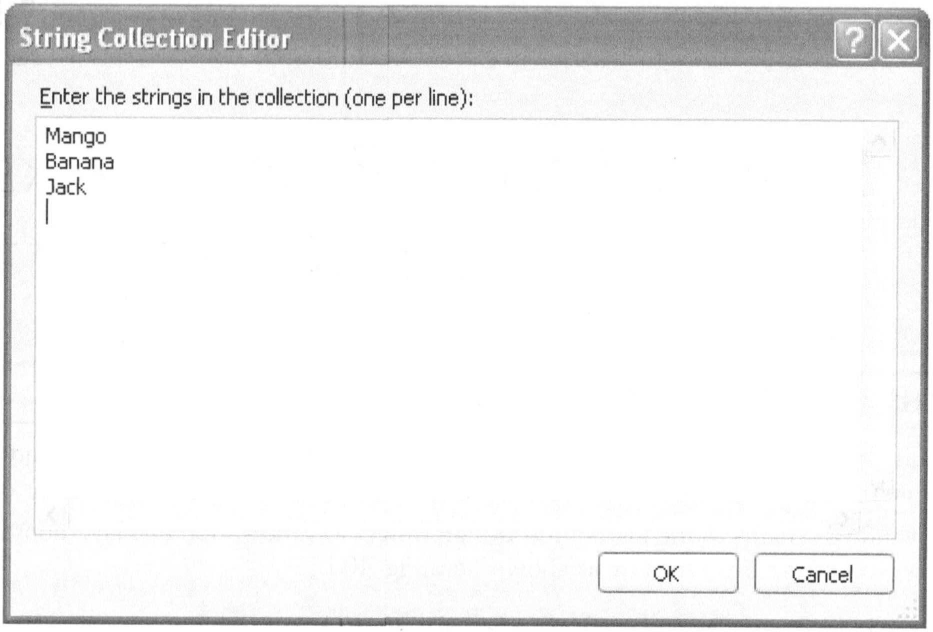

Fig. 10.2 *String Collection Editor Dialog Box*

This will include the above three items to **Listbox1**.

```
Another way, Listen the following code
      ListBox1.Items.Add("Mango")
```

The method **Add()** of the **Items** collection will add the string Mango to **ListBox1** at runtime ie while running the program.

Manipulate the List Item

This program manipulates the list items through the **click** event of button control.

Form Designing

Table 10.1 Manipulate the List Item

Control	*Property*	*Value*
Button1	Name	CmdAdd
	Text	Add
Button2	Name	CmdRmv
	Text	Remove

Button3	Name	CmdClr
	Text	Clear
Button4	Name	CmdCnt
	Text	Count
TextBox1	Name	TxtInput
ListBox1	Name	ListBox1

Coding

```
Public Class Form2

Private Sub CmdAdd _Click(ByVal sender As System.Object, ByVal e As System.EventArgs) Handles CmdAdd.Click
            'add the text of textbox to listbox
            ListBox1.Items.Add(TxtInput.Text)
        End Sub

Private Sub CmdRmv _Click(ByVal sender As System.Object, ByVal e As System.EventArgs) Handles CmdRmv.Click
            'Remove the selected listbox item
            ListBox1.Items.Remove(ListBox1.SelectedItem)
        End Sub

Private Sub CmdClr_Click(ByVal sender As System.Object, ByVal e As System.EventArgs) Handles CmdClr.Click
            'clear the listbox and textbox
            ListBox1.Items.Clear()
            TxtInput.Text = ""
        End Sub
Private Sub CmdCnt_Click(ByVal sender As System.Object, ByVal e As System.EventArgs)Handles CmdCnt.Click
            'Displays the number of items in the listbox
            MsgBox("There are" & ListBox1.Items.Count & "items")
        End Sub
End Class
```

Output

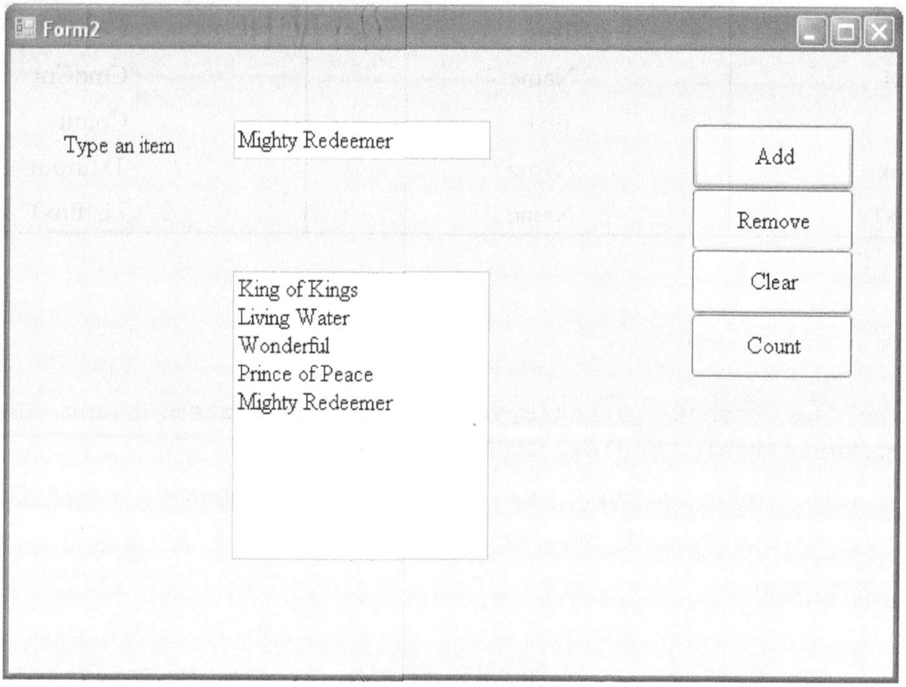

Some More Manipulations

Here the list items are moved from one box to another.

Form Designing

Table 10.2 Some More Manipulations

Control	*Property*	*Value*
Button1	Name	CmdLS
	Text	<
Button2	Name	CmdRS
	Text	>
Button3	Name	CmdLA
	Text	<<

Button4	Name	CmdRA
	Text	>>
ListBox1	Name	ListBox1
ListBox2	Name	ListBox2
Form1	Name	FrmLst

Coding

```
Public Class FrmLst
    Private Sub FrmLst_Load(ByVal sender As System.Object, ByVal e As System.EventArgs) Handles MyBase.Load
            ListBox1.Items.Add("AAA")
            ListBox1.Items.Add("BBB")
            ListBox1.Items.Add("CCC")
            ListBox1.Items.Add("DDD")
            ListBox2.Items.Add("111")
            ListBox2.Items.Add("222")
            ListBox2.Items.Add("333")
            ListBox2.Items.Add("444")
        End Sub

    Private Sub CmdLS_Click(ByVal sender As System.Object, ByVal e As System.EventArgs) Handles CmdLS.Click
            'add the selected item of listbox2 to listbox1
            ListBox1.Items.Add(ListBox2.SelectedItem)
        End Sub

    Private Sub CmdRS _Click(ByVal sender As System.Object, ByVal e As System.EventArgs) Handles CmdRS.Click
            'add the selected item of listbox1 to listbox2
            ListBox2.Items.Add(ListBox1.SelectedItem)
        End Sub

    Private Sub CmdLA_Click(ByVal sender As System.Object, ByVal e As System.EventArgs) Handles CmdLA.Click
            'add the all available items of listbox2 to listbox1
            Dim i As Integer
```

```
        For i = 0 To ListBox2.Items.Count - 1
            ListBox1.Items.Add(ListBox2.Items.Item(i))
        Next
    End Sub

    Private Sub CmdRA _Click(ByVal sender As System.Object, ByVal
e As System.EventArgs) Handles CmdRA.Click
        'add the all available items of listbox1 to listbox2
        Dim i As Integer
        For i = 0 To ListBox1.Items.Count - 1
            ListBox2.Items.Add(ListBox1.Items.Item(i))
        Next
    End Sub
End Class
```

Output

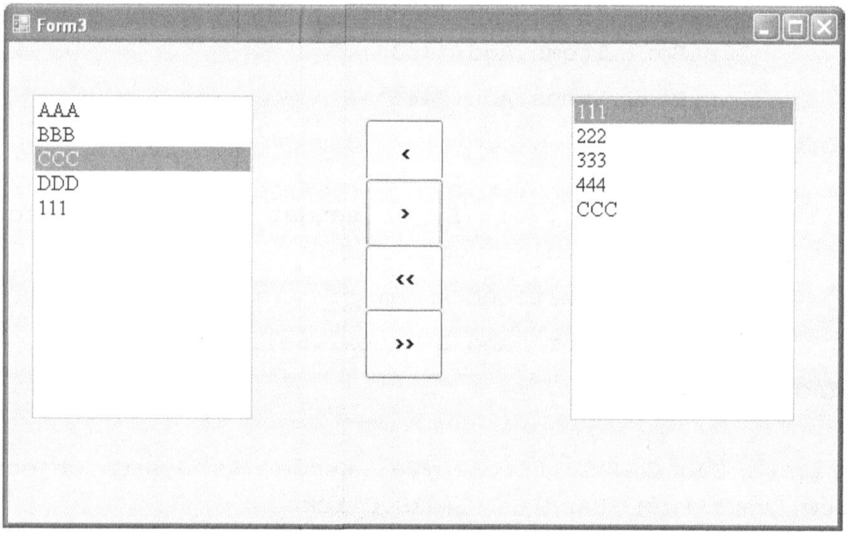

10.2 SCROLL BAR

The ScrollBar controls are used to provide easy navigation through a long list of items or a large amount of information by scrolling either horizontally or vertically within an application or control. Scroll bars are a common element of the Windows interface. The **Value** property (default value is 0) is an integer value corresponding to the position of the scroll box in the scroll bar. The property **Minimum** represents the left-most position (for horizontal scroll bars) or the top position (for vertical scroll bars). Similarly the property **Maximum** represents the right-most or bottom position.

Displaying of Scroll Value

This program displays the current value of scrollbar on textbox by using **scroll** event.

Form Designing

Table 10.3 Displaying of Scroll Value

Control	*Property*	*Value*
Label1	Text	Scroll bar value is
TextBox1	Name	TxtValue
HScrollBar1	Maximum	100
	Minimum	10

Coding

```
Public Class Form1
    Private Sub HScrollBar1_Scroll(ByVal sender As System.Object,
ByVal e As System.Windows.Forms.ScrollEventArgs) Handles
HScrollBar1.Scroll
TxtValue.Text = HScrollBar1.Value
    End Sub
End Class
```

Output

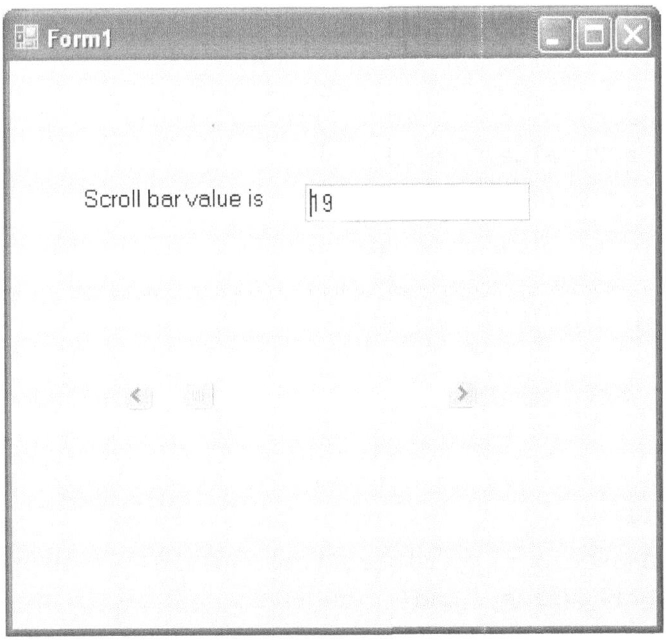

Form in Different Colours

This program changes the backcolour of the form by scrolling the scrollbars. The **BackColour** property of the **Form** control represents the Back Colour of the form. **FromArgb()** function of **Colour** class takes three argument such as the Red, Green, Blue values to produce a System Colour. **Rnd()** function generate different values from 0 to 1 randomly during execution.

Form Designing

Table 10.4 Form in Different Colours

Control	*Property*	*Value*
HScrollBar1	Maximum	255
	Minimum	0
HScrollBar2	Maximum	255
	Minimum	0
HScrollBar3	Maximum	255
	Minimum	0

Coding

```
Public Class Form1

Private Sub HScrollBar1_Scroll(ByVal sender As System.Object, ByVal
e As
            System.Windows.Forms.ScrollEventArgs) Handles
HScrollBar1.Scroll
            Me.BackColour = Colour.FromArgb(Rnd() * HScrollBar1.Value,
Rnd() * HScrollBar2.Value, Rnd() *
      HscrollBar3. value)
      'Me.BackColour represents the BackColour of the current running
form
         End Sub

    Private Sub HScrollBar2_Scroll(ByVal sender As System.Object,
ByVal e As
                  System.Windows.Forms.ScrollEventArgs) Handles
HScrollBar2.Scroll
            Me.BackColour = Colour.FromArgb(Rnd() * HScrollBar1.Value,
Rnd() * HScrollBar2.Value, Rnd() *
     HScrollBar3.Value)
```

```
        End Sub

        Private Sub HScrollBar3_Scroll(ByVal sender As System.Object,
ByVal e As
                    System.Windows.Forms.ScrollEventArgs) Handles
HScrollBar3.Scroll
            Me.BackColour = Colour.FromArgb(Rnd() * HScrollBar1.Value,
Rnd() * HScrollBar2.Value, Rnd() *
                                            HScrollBar3.Value)
        End Sub

    End Class
```

Output

Resizing of Form

This program changes the form size at run time by **click** event of the button. **WindowState** property of the form determines the form size. The constant such as **FormWindowState.Minimized** represents the size value for the **Form** control.

Form Designing

Table 10.5 Resizing Form

Control	*Property*	*Value*
Button1	Name	CmdMin
	Text	Minimum
Button2	Name	CmdMax
	Text	Maximum
Button3	Name	CmdNor
	Text	Normal
Button4	Name	CmdCls
	Text	Close

Coding

```
Public Class Form1
Private Sub CmdMin _Click(ByVal sender As System.Object, ByVal e As System.EventArgs) Handles CmdMin.Click
        Me.WindowState = FormWindowState.Minimized
    End Sub

    Private Sub CmdMax _Click(ByVal sender As System.Object, ByVal e As System.EventArgs) Handles CmdMax.Click
        Me.WindowState = FormWindowState.Maximized
  'Me.WindowState represents WindowState of  the current running form
    End Sub

    Private Sub CmdNor _Click(ByVal sender As System.Object, ByVal e As System.EventArgs) Handles CmdNor.Click
        Me.WindowState = FormWindowState.Normal
    End Sub
Private Sub CmdCls _Click(ByVal sender As Object, ByVal e As System.EventArgs) Handles CmdCls.Click
        End
    End Sub
End Class
```

Output

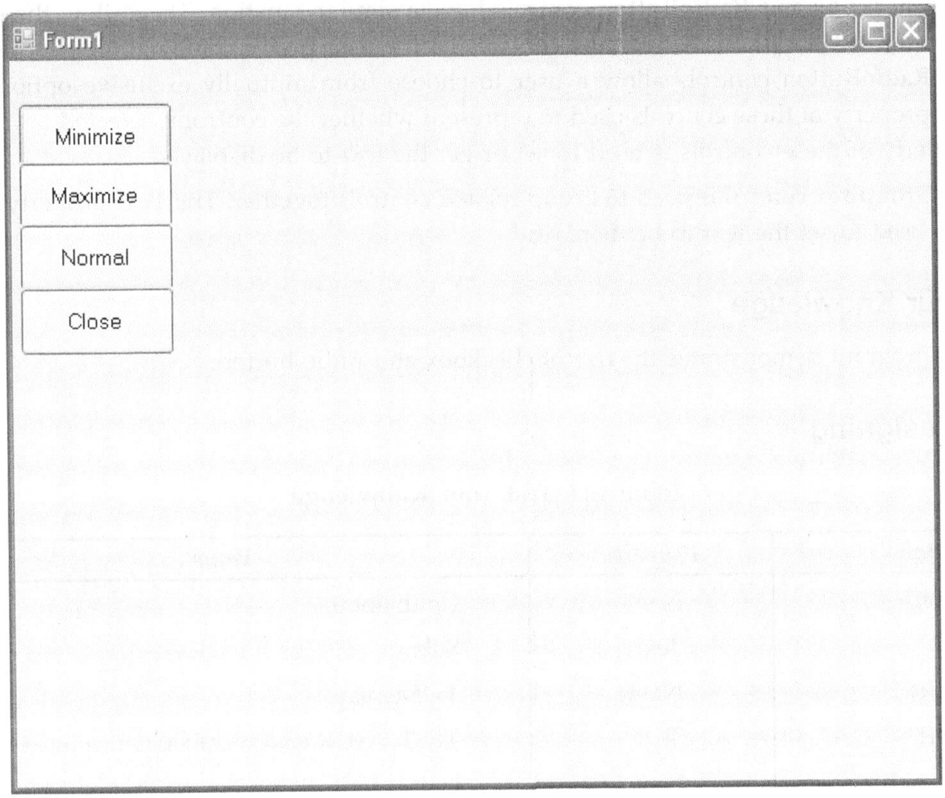
Form1
Minimize
Maximize
Normal
Close

Form1
Minimize
Maximize
Normal
Close

10.3 CHECK BOX AND RADIO BUTTON

The **CheckBox** and **RadioButton** controls have a similar function. They allow the user to choose from a list of options. **CheckBox** controls let the user pick a combination of options. In contrast, **RadioButton** controls allow a user to choose from mutually exclusive options. The **Checked** property of these controls used to represent whether the control is selected or not. The **Text** property of these controls is used to set or get the text to be displayed.

The **GroupBox** control is used to group related controls together. The **Text** property of this control is used to set the text to be displayed.

Test Your Knowledge

This program demonstrates the use of checkbox and radio button.

Form Designing

Table 10.6 Test Your Knowledge

Control	*Property*	*Value*
Button1	Name	CmdSubmit
	Text	Submit
TextBox1	Name	TxtDisplay
Label1	Text	TEST YOUR KNOWLEDGE
	Font	[select font dialog box to change font size]
Label2	Text	A-Excellent B-Good C-Poor
Label3	Text	Which of the following are GUI?
Label4	Text	Mouse falls in the category of?
Label5	Text	Your Grade is
CheckBox1	Text	DOS
CheckBox2	Text	VB.NET
CheckBox3	Text	UNIX
CheckBox4	Text	Windows vista
RadioButton1	Text	I/O
RadioButton2	Text	O/P
RadioButton3	Text	I/O
RadioButton4	Text	None of these

Coding

```
Public Class Form1
```

```
    Private Sub CmdSubmit _Click(ByVal sender As System.Object, ByVal
e As System.EventArgs) Handles CmdSubmit.Click
            Dim grade As String = "C"
            If CheckBox1.Checked = False And CheckBox2.Checked =
True And CheckBox3.Checked = False And CheckBox4.Checked = True Then
                grade = "B"
            End If
            If RadioButton1.Checked = True Then
                grade = "A"
            End If
            textbox1.text = grade
        End Sub
    End Class
```

Output

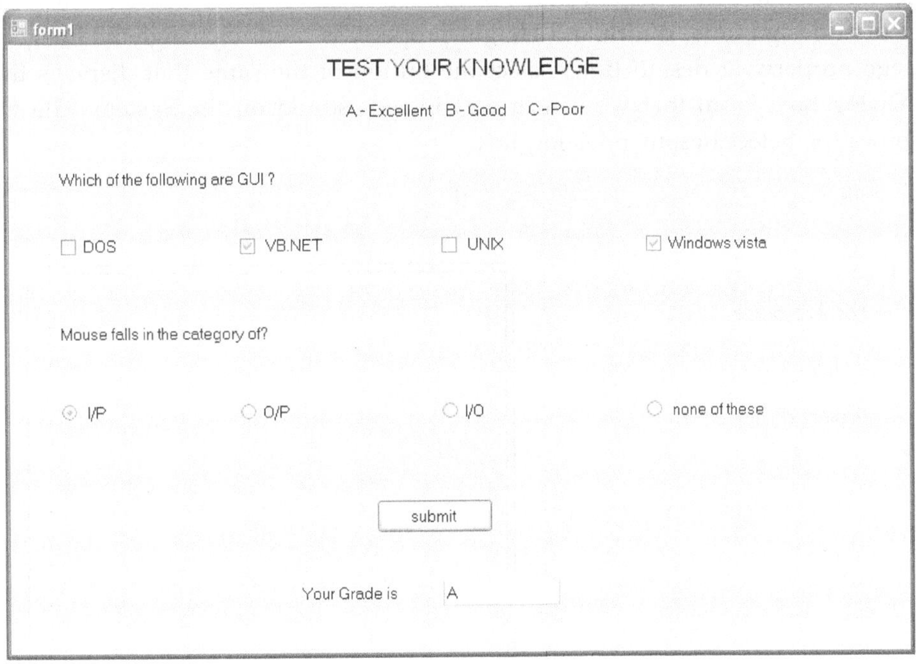

CHAPTER

11

PICTURE BOX, TIMER, MENU STRIP

11.1 PICTURE BOX

The **PictureBox** control is used to display graphics from a bitmap, metafile, icon, JPEG, GIF, or PNG file. The picture that is displayed is determined by the Image property, which can be set at run time or at design time. **Width** and **Height** property is used to change the image size. To set the **Image** property at design time, select the button of the same that displays the **Select Resource** Dialog Box. From that we can import images stored on the System. The following Fig. 11.1 shows the Select Resource Dialog Box.

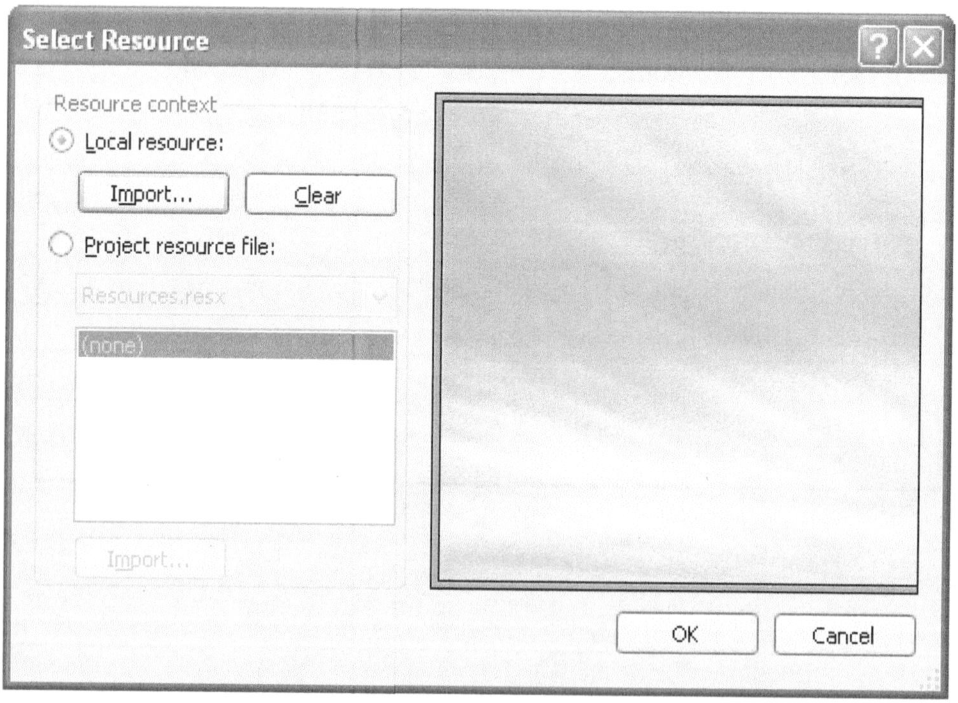

Fig. 11.1 *The Select Resource Dialog Box*

The Image can be included in the **PictureBox** at the runtime also. The following code will include the image at runtime.

```
PictureBox1.Image = Image.FromFile("D:\Karthikajesus\Garden.jpg")
```

Picture Resizing

This program resizes the picture in the **PictureBox** at run time by scrolling the scrollbars.

Form Designing

Table 11.1 Picture Resizing

Control	*Property*	*Value*
PictureBox1	Name	MyPicture
	Image	D:\Karthikajesus\Garden.jpg[select from the Dialog Box]
HScrollBar1	Maximum	750
	Minimum	0
VScrollBar1	Maximum	750
	Minimum	0

Coding

Public Class Form1

```
        Private Sub HScrollBar1_Scroll(ByVal sender As System.Object,
ByVal e As System.Windows.Forms.ScrollEventArgs) Handles
HScrollBar1.Scroll
                MyPicture.Width = HScrollBar1.Value
                MyPicture.Height = VScrollBar1.Value
        End Sub

        Private Sub VScrollBar1_Scroll(ByVal sender As System.Object,
ByVal e As System.Windows.Forms.ScrollEventArgs) Handles
VScrollBar1.Scroll
                MyPicture.Width = HScrollBar1.Value
    MyPicture .Height = VScrollBar1.Value
        End Sub
    End Class
```

Output

Picture Modes

This program changes the mode of the picture at run time by **click** event of Button control.

Form Designing

Table 11.2 Picture Modes

Control	*Property*	*Value*
Button1	Name	CmdStretch
	Text	Stretch
Button2	Name	CmdCenter
	Text	Center
Button3	Name	CmdNor
	Text	Normal

Button4	Name	CmdZoom
	Text	Zoom
PictureBox1	Name	Mypict
	Image	D:\karthikajesus\baby.jpg [Select image from dialog box]

Coding

```
Public Class Form1
        Private Sub CmdStretch _Click(ByVal sender As System.Object,
ByVal e As System.EventArgs) Handles CmdStretch.Click
                Mypict.SizeMode = PictureBoxSizeMode.StretchImage
        End Sub

        Private Sub CmdCenter _Click(ByVal sender As System.Object,
ByVal e As System.EventArgs) Handles CmdCenter.Click
                Mypict.SizeMode = PictureBoxSizeMode.CenterImage
        End Sub

        Private Sub CmdNor _Click(ByVal sender As System.Object,
ByVal e As System.EventArgs) Handles CmdNor.Click
                Mypict.SizeMode = PictureBoxSizeMode.Normal
        End Sub

        Private Sub CmdZoom _Click(ByVal sender As System.Object,
ByVal e As System.EventArgs) Handles CmdZoom.Click
                Mypict.SizeMode = PictureBoxSizeMode.Zoom
        End Sub

End Class
```

Output

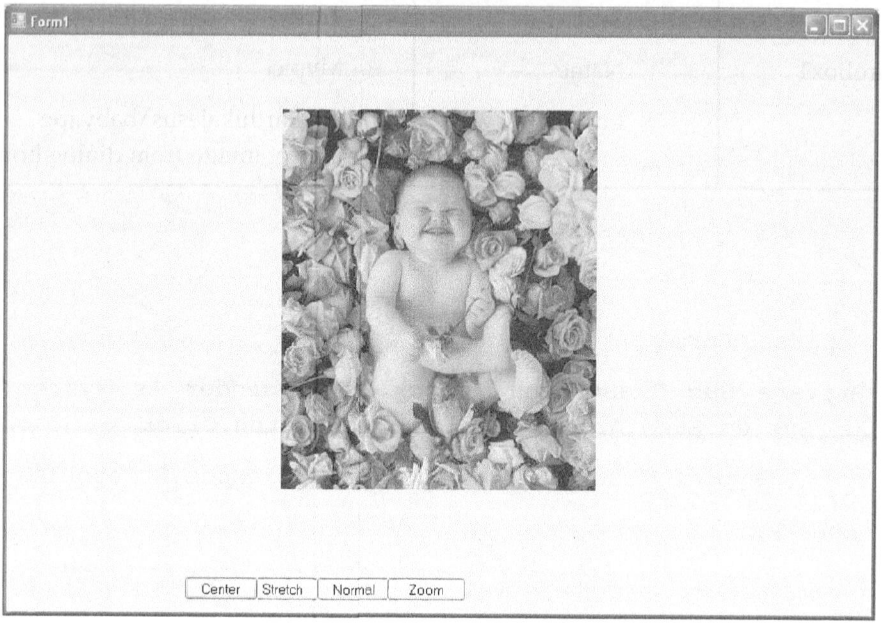

11.2 TIMER CONTROL

This is a component that raises an event at regular intervals. The length of the intervals is defined by the **Interval** property, whose value is in milliseconds. When the component is enabled, the **timer_tick** event is raised at every interval of time specified in the property **Interval**. At the specified interval, the statements in the **timer_tick** procedure are executed repeatedly.

Backcolour Changing

This program changes the back colour of the form automaically at the interval of time specified. **Drawing.Colour.FromArgb()** function takes three arguments and produce System Colour.

Form Designing

Table 11.3 Backcolour Changing

Control	*Property*	*Value*
Timer1	Name	Timer1
	Enabled	True
	Interval	100

Coding

```
Public Class Form1
 Private Sub Timer1_Tick(ByVal sender As System.Object, ByVal e As
System.EventArgs) Handles Timer1.Tick
```

```
            Me.BackColor = Drawing.Color.FromArgb(Rnd() * 255, Rnd()
* 255, Rnd() * 255)
        End Sub
End Class
```

Output

Forecolour Changing

This program changes the fore colour of the TextBox automatically at the interval of time specified.

Form Designing

Table 11.4 Forecolour Changing

Control	*Property*	*Value*
Button1	Name	CmdDemo
	Text	Mouse Button Demo
TextBox1	Name	TxtDisplay
	Text	No fools will mislead that whom following him
Timer1	Enabled	True
	Interval	100

Coding

```
    Public Class Form2
        Private Sub Timer1_Tick(ByVal sender As System.Object, ByVal
e As System.EventArgs) Handles Timer1.Tick
            TxtDisplay.ForeColor = Drawing.Color.FromArgb(Rnd() * 255,
Rnd() * 255, Rnd() * 255)
        End Sub
    End Class
```

Output

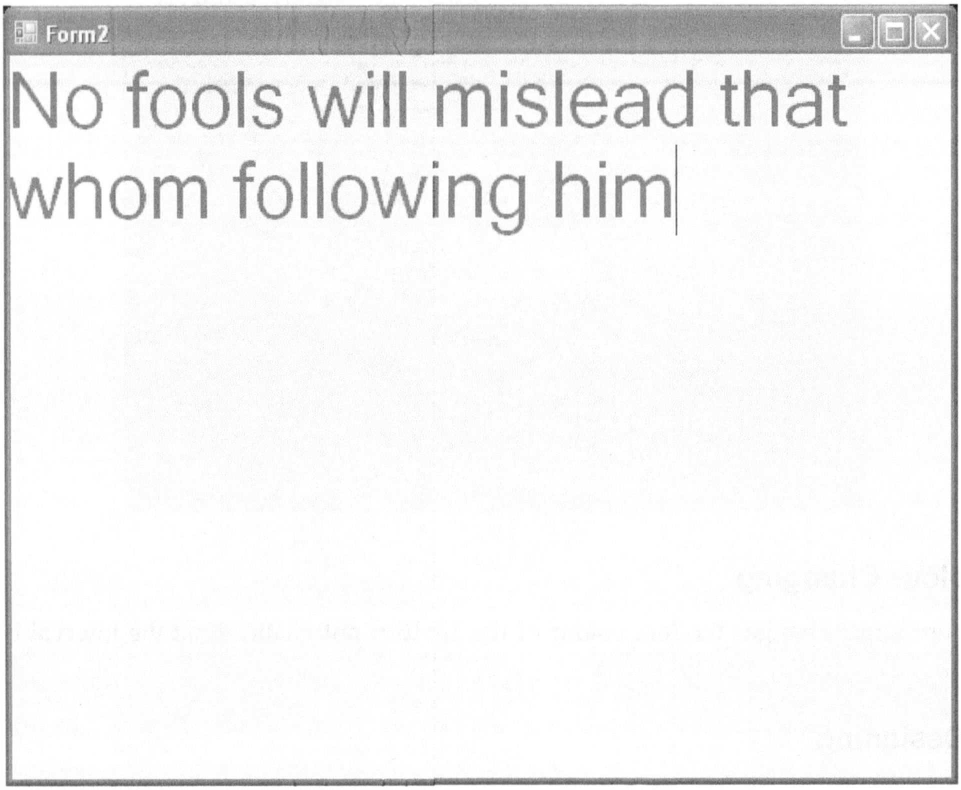

11.3 MENUSTRIP

The **MenuStrip** control represents the container for the menu structure of a form. We can add **ToolStripMenuItem** objects to the **MenuStrip** that represent the individual menu commands in the menu structure. Each **ToolStripMenuItem** can be a command for our application or a parent menu for other submenu items.

MenuStrip is the container for **ToolStripMenuItem, ToolStripComboBox, ToolStripSeparator,** and **ToolStripTextBox** objects. The **MenuStrip** replaces and adds functionality to the MainMenu control of previous versions.

When we add this control to the form, it is added to the component tray, which appears at the bottom of the form. The component tray appears at design time and is used as a container to hold controls, such as **ColorDialog** control, **FontDialog** control, **PrintDialog** control, **MenuStrip** control and **ContextMenuStrip** control.

The following Fig. 11.2 shows that the **MenuStrip** is added to the **Form**.

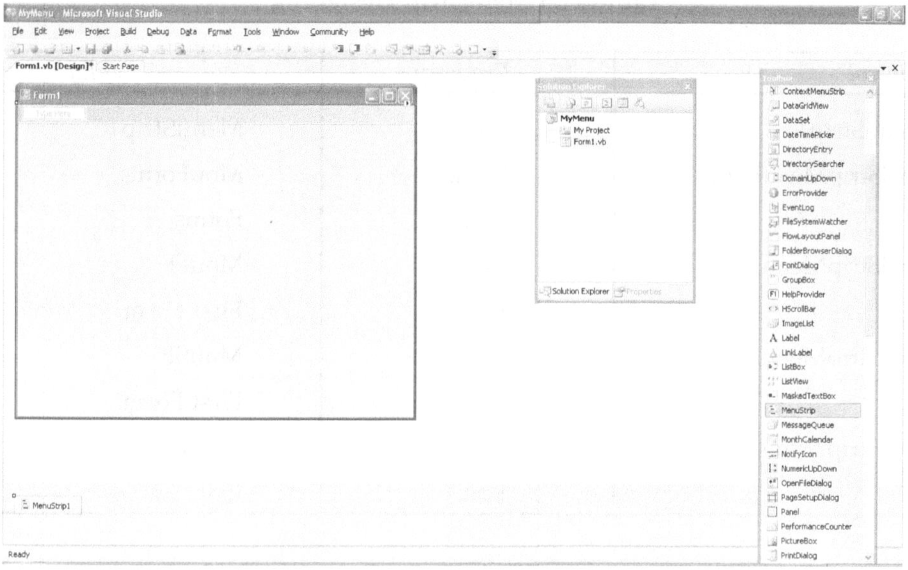

Fig. 11.2 *The MenuStrip is Added to the Form*

In MenuStrip control, Create Menu items as in the following Fig. 11.3 (By typing the menu item text in the Box)

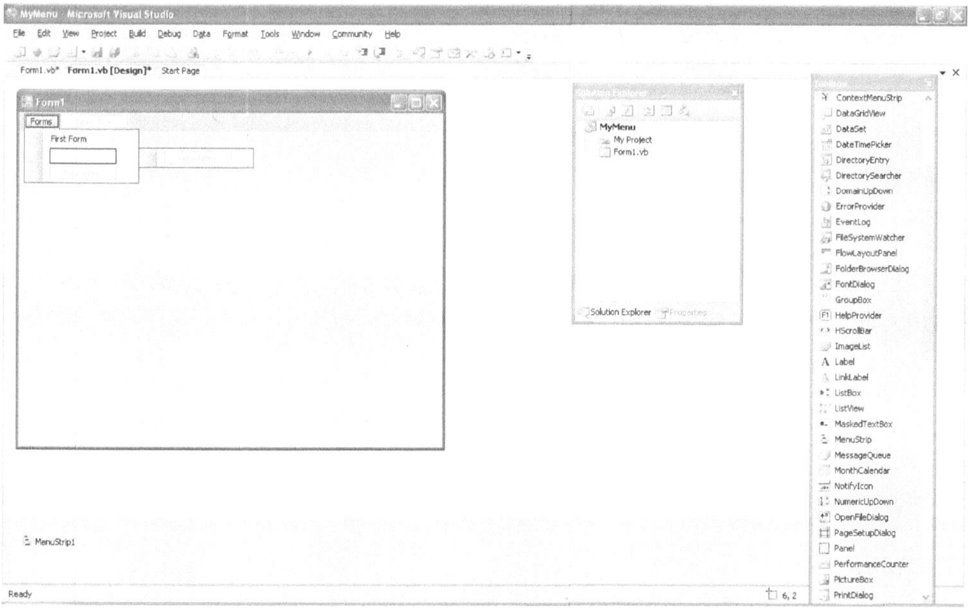

Fig. 11.3 *Creating Menu Items*

If you want to set icons before the menu item, right click the menu item and select the icon from the dialog box. Set the property of each menu item as follows.

Form Designing

Table 11.6 Menustrip Designing

Control	*Property*	*Value*
MenuStrip1	Name	MenuStrip1
ToolStripMenuItem1	Name	MnuForms
	Text	Forms
ToolStripMenuItem2	Name	MnuFF
	Text	First Form
ToolStripMenuItem3	Name	MnuSF
	Text	First Form
ToolStripMenuItem4	Name	MnuExit
	Text	Exit

Coding

```
Public Class Form1
    Private Sub MnuFF _Click(ByVal sender As System.Object, ByVal
e As System.EventArgs) Handles MnuFF.Click
        Dim ff As New Form
        ff.Show()
        ff.Text = "First Form"
     End Sub

    Private Sub MnuSF _Click(ByVal sender As System.Object, ByVal
e As System.EventArgs) Handles MnuSF.Click
        Dim sf As New Form
        sf.Show()
        sf.Text = "Second Form"
     End Sub
End Class
```

Output

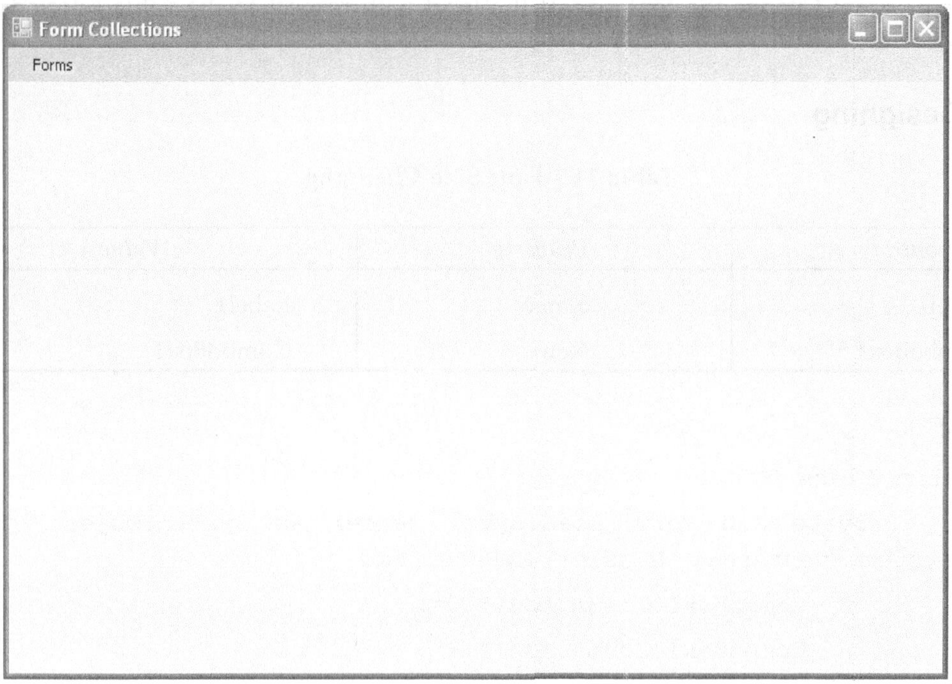

11.4 COMBOBOX

ComboBox control is used to display data in a drop-down combo box. The **ComboBox** initially displays a single item, when we select the combo box, it displays a list of items and we can choose an item from that list. A combo box combines the features of a **TextBox** and a **ListBox**. We can enter information in the **TextBox** portion or select an item from the **ListBox** portion of the control.

Font Size Changing

This program Change the font size of the label with respect to the value selected in the ComboBox

Form Designing

Table 11.7 Font Size Changing

Control	*Property*	*Value*
Label1	Name	Label1
ComboBox1	Name	ComboBox1

Coding

```
Public Class Form1
    Private Sub Form1_Load(ByVal sender As System.Object, ByVal e As System.EventArgs) Handles MyBase.Load
        ComboBox1.Items.Add("10")
        ComboBox1.Items.Add("15")
        ComboBox1.Items.Add("20")
        ComboBox1.Items.Add("22")
        ComboBox1.Items.Add("24")
        ComboBox1.Items.Add("28")
        ComboBox1.Items.Add("30")
        ComboBox1.Items.Add("40")
        ComboBox1.Items.Add("45")
        ComboBox1.Items.Add("50")
        ComboBox1.Items.Add("70")
        Label1.Text = "Before honour is humility"

    End Sub

    Private Sub ComboBox1_SelectedIndexChanged(ByVal sender As System.Object, ByVal e As System.EventArgs) Handles ComboBox1.SelectedIndexChanged
        Label1.Font = New Font("Arial", ComboBox1.SelectedItem, FontStyle.Bold)
    End Sub
End Class
```

Output

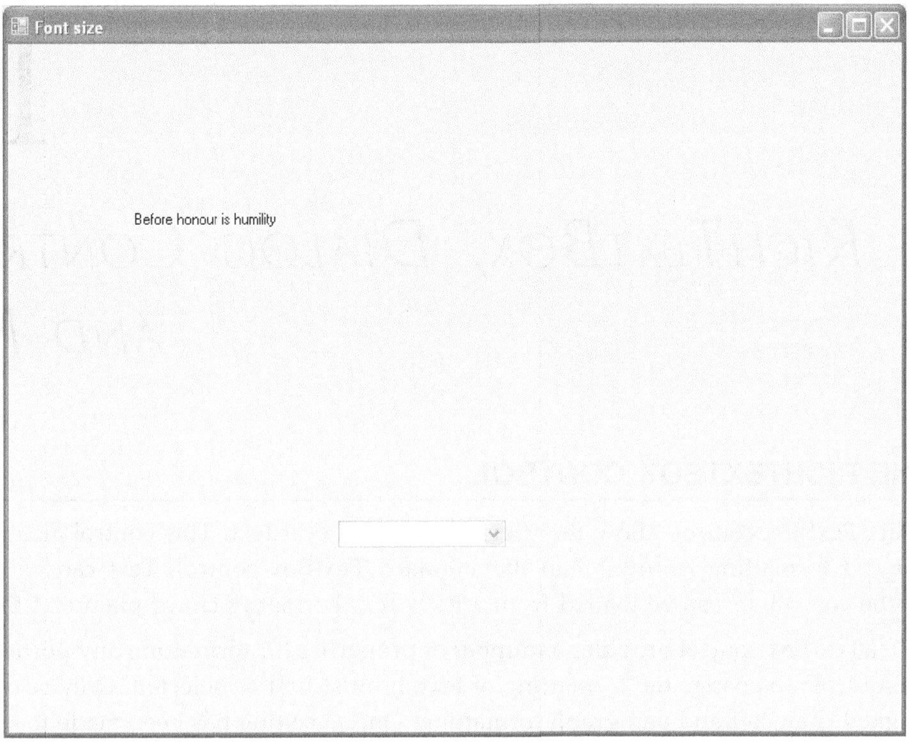
Font size
Before honour is humility

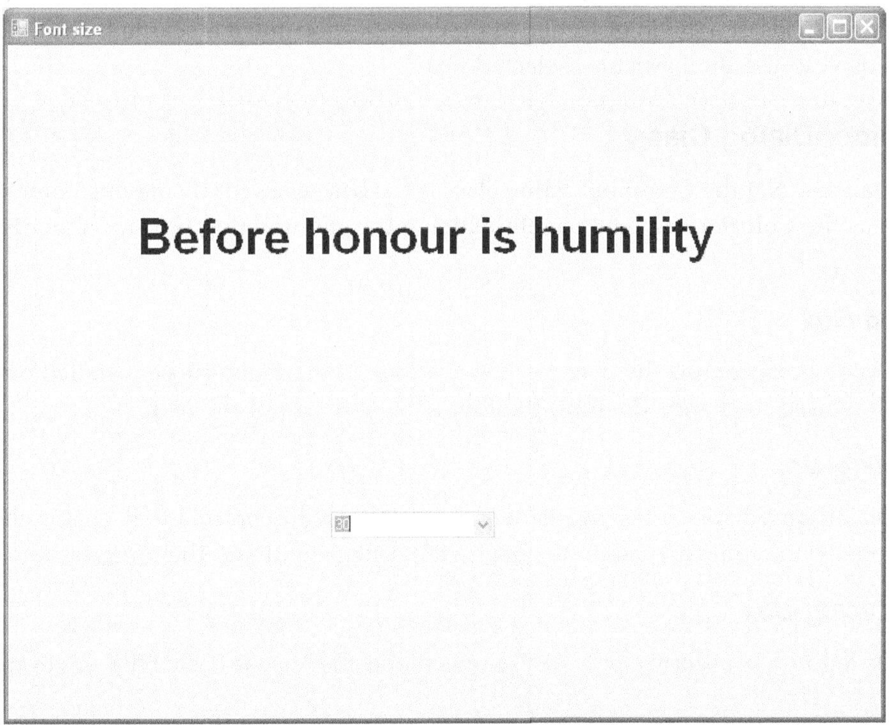
Font size
Before honour is humility
30

CHAPTER

12

RichTextBox, Dialog Controls and Mdi

12.1 THE RICHTEXTBOX CONTROL

The **RichTextBox** control, allow the user to enter and edit text. This control also provides more advanced formatting features than the standard **TextBox** control. Text can be assigned directly to the control, or can be loaded from a Rich Text Format (RTF) or plain text file.

The **RichTextBox** control provides a number of properties for formatting any portion of text within the control. To change the formatting of text, it must first be selected. Only selected text can be assigned character and paragraph formatting. Once a setting has been made to a selected section of text, all text entered after the selection is also formatted with the same settings until a setting change is made or a different section of the control's document is selected. The **SelectedText** property is used to use the particular selected text.

The CommonDialog Class

In VisualBasic.Net the **CommonDialog** class is the base class for displaying common dialog boxes, such as the **ColorDialog** box, **SaveFileDialog** box, **FontDialog** Box and **OpenFileDialog** box.

FontDialog Box

This Dialog box prompts the user to choose a font from among those installed on the local computer. It is used to change the font, the font style and size of the text.

ColourDialog Box

This Dialog box displays the available colors along with controls that enable the user to define custom colors. It is very useful to change the background and the foreground of the text.

OpenFileDialog Box

This Dialog box is used to open an existing file in the Visual Basic.NET environment.

SaveFileDialog Box

This Dialog box is used to overwrite an existing file or create a new file in the Visual Basic.NET environment.

Writing Pad Application

This program uses **RichTextBox** and the dialog controls such as **FontDialog, OpenFileDialog, SaveFileDialog** and **ColorDialog** controls and demonstrates their uses.

Form Designing

Table 12.1 Writing Pad Application

Control	*Property*	*Value*
MenuStrip1	Name	MenuStrip1
ToolStripMenuItem1	Name	MnuFile
	Text	File
ToolStripMenuItem2	Name	MnuNew
	Text	New
ToolStripMenuItem3	Name	MnuOpen
	Text	Open
ToolStripMenuItem4	Name	MnuSave
	Text	Save
ToolStripMenuItem5	Name	MnuClose
	Text	Close
ToolStripMenuItem6	Name	MnuExit
	Text	Exit
ToolStripMenuItem7	Name	MnuEdit
	Text	Edit
ToolStripMenuItem8	Name	MnuCut
	Text	Cut
ToolStripMenuItem9	Name	MnuCopy
	Text	Copy
ToolStripMenuItem10	Name	MnuPaste
	Text	Paste
ToolStripMenuItem11	Name	MnuFormat
	Text	Format
ToolStripMenuItem12	Name	MnuFont

	Text	Font
Color ToolStripMenuItem		
ToolStripMenuItem13	Name	MnuBackcolor
	Text	Backcolor
ToolStripMenuItem14	Name	MnnuForeColor
	Text	ForeColor
RichTextBox1	Name	RT1
FontDialog1	Name	FontDialog1
OpenFileDialog1	Name	OpenFileDialog1
SaveFileDialog1	Name	SaveFileDialog1
ColorDialog1	Name	ColorDialog1

Coding

```
Public Class Form1
      Dim s As String   ' Declare the string for clipboard
operation
      Private Sub MnuNew_Click(ByVal sender As System.Object, ByVal
e As System.EventArgs) Handles  MnuNew.Click
            RT1.Show()          'Enable the RichTextBox
            RT1.Text = ""        'Clear the RichTextBox
      End Sub
      Private Sub MnuOpen_Click(ByVal sender As System.Object, ByVal
e As System.EventArgs) Handles MnuOpen.Click
            OpenFileDialog1.ShowDialog()                 'Opens the
OpenFileDialog control
            RT1.LoadFile(OpenFileDialog1.FileName)'Open the file
mentioned on filename box on the RichTextBox
      End Sub

      Private Sub MnuSave_Click(ByVal sender As System.Object, ByVal
e As System.EventArgs) Handles MnuSave.Click
      SaveFileDialog1.ShowDialog()     'Opens the SaveFileDialog
control
            RT1.SaveFile(SaveFileDialog1.FileName)'Save        the
RichTextBox content with the filename mentioned
      End Sub
```

```
        Private Sub MnuClose_Click(ByVal sender As System.Object,
ByVal e As System.EventArgs) Handles MnuClose.Click
                RT1.Hide()          'Hide the RichTextBox control
        End Sub

        Private Sub MnuExit_Click(ByVal sender As System.Object, ByVal
e As System.EventArgs) Handles MnuExit.Click
                End     'Close the application
        End Sub

        Private Sub MnuCut_Click(ByVal sender As System.Object, ByVal
e As System.EventArgs) Handles MnuCut.Click
                s = RT1.SelectedText        'copy to variable s
                RT1.SelectedText = ""
        End Sub

        Private Sub MnuCopy_Click(ByVal sender As System.Object, ByVal
e As System.EventArgs) Handles MnuCopy.Click
                s = RT1.SelectedText          'copy to variable s


        End Sub

        Private Sub MnuPaste_Click(ByVal sender As System.Object,
ByVal e As System.EventArgs) Handles MnuPaste.Click
                RT1.SelectedText = s        'Display the content in s
        End Sub

        Private Sub MnuFont_Click(ByVal sender As System.Object, ByVal
e As System.EventArgs) Handles MnuFont.Click
                FontDialog1.ShowDialog()       'opens the Fontdialog
                RT1.Font = FontDialog1.Font          'change the font of
the RichTextBox
        End Sub
```

```
        Private Sub MnuForcolor_Click(ByVal sender As System.Object,
ByVal e As System.EventArgs) Handles MnuForcolor.Click
    ' changes the forecolor of the RichTextBox
                ColorDialog1.ShowDialog()      'opens the ColorDialog
                RT1.ForeColor = ColorDialog1.Color
        End Sub

        Private Sub MnuBackcolor_Click(ByVal sender As System.Object,
ByVal e As System.EventArgs) Handles MnuBackcolor.Click
     ' changes the backcolor of the RichTextBox
                ColorDialog1.ShowDialog()
                RT1.BackColor = ColorDialog1.Color
        End Sub
    End Class
```

Output

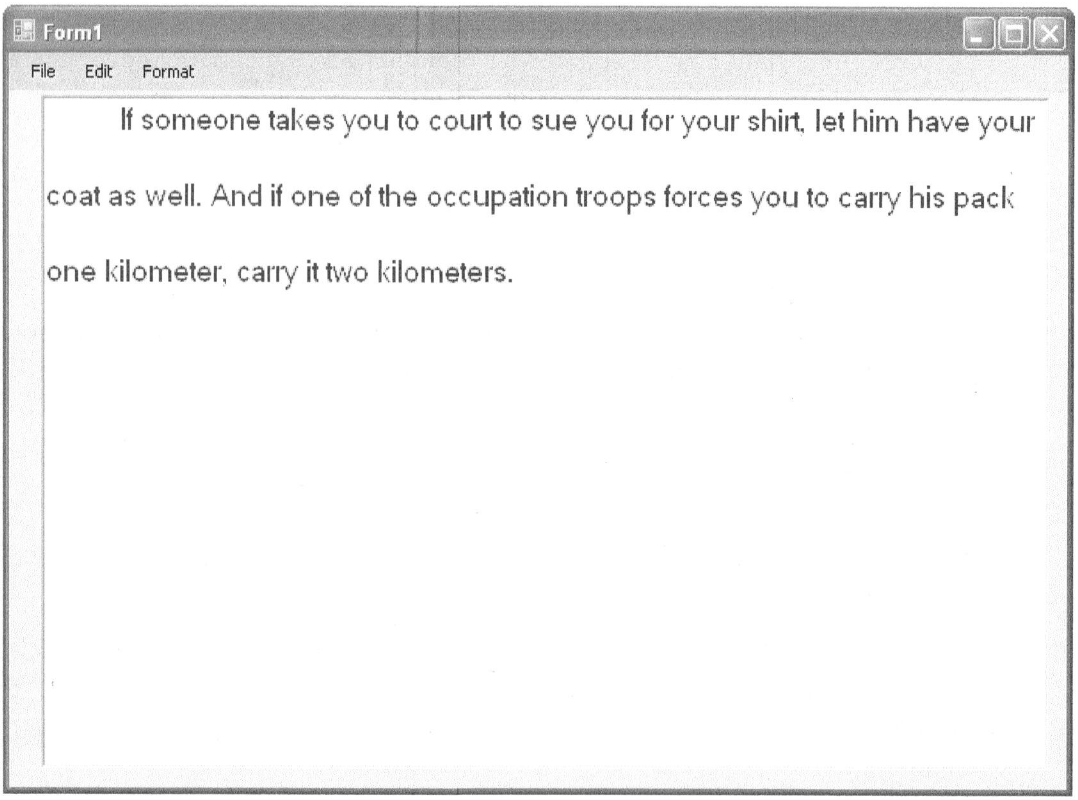

Output Displayed

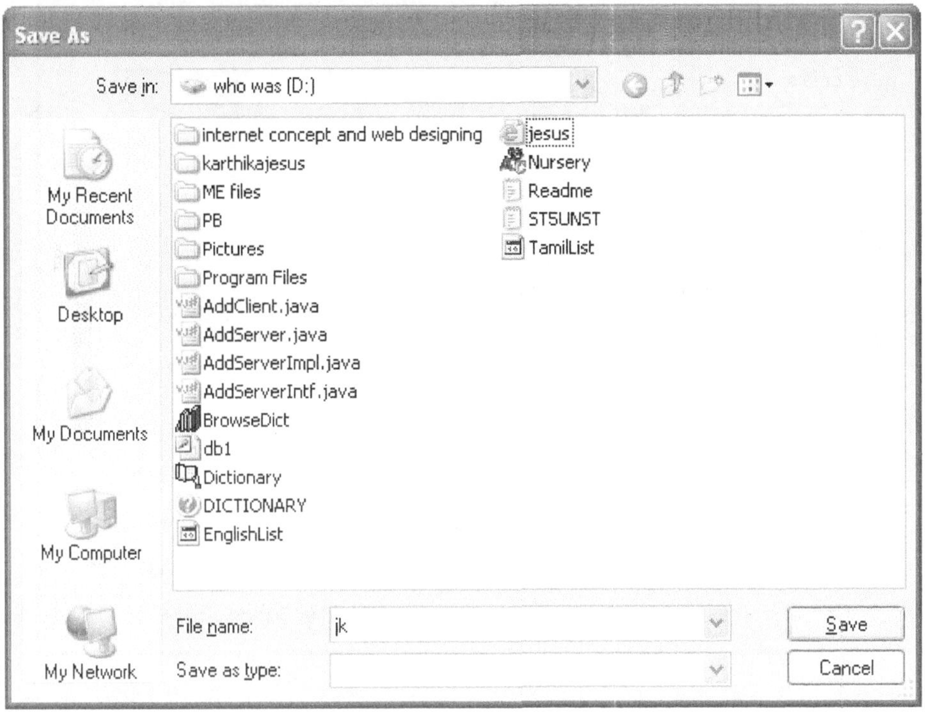

SaveFileDialog Box

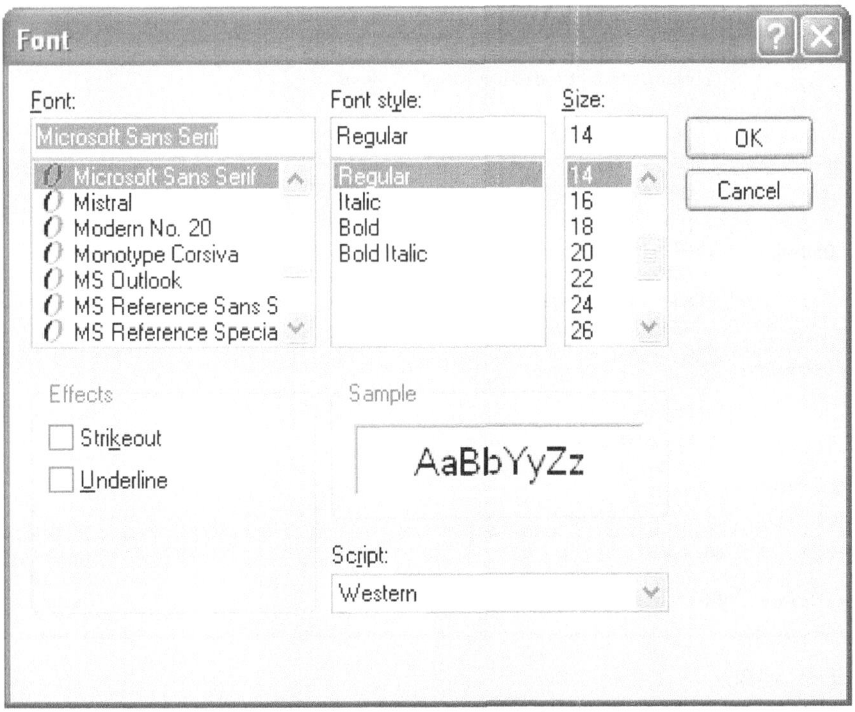

FontDialog Box

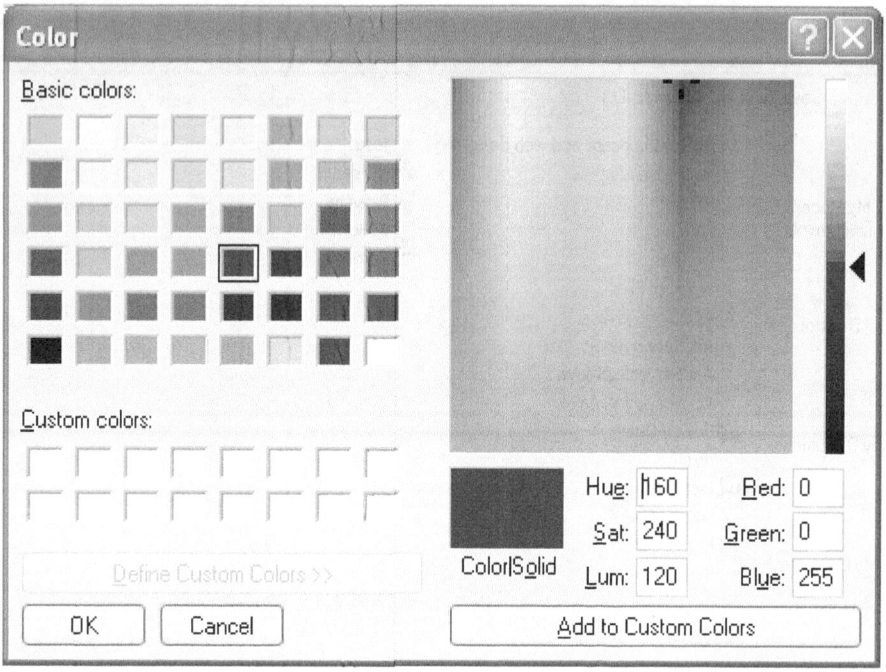

ColourDialog Box

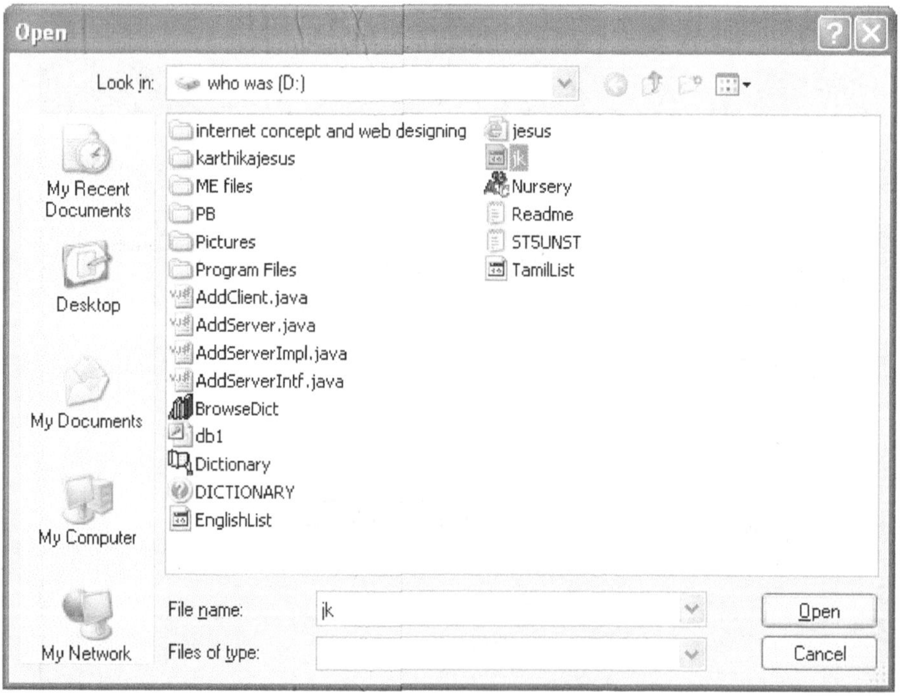

OpenFileDialog Box

12.2 MDI – MULTIPLE DOCUMENT INTERFACE

Visual Basic .NET supports Multiple Document Interface (MDI) applications. MDI applications allow as displaying multiple windows at the same time, with each form sharing a parent- child relationship.

In Single Document Interface (SDI) application we can work with only one window at a time. By default, the Windows Applications in the Visual Basic .NET is a SDI application. To invoke multiple instances of the SDI application, which use more system resources, such as memory. MicroSoft WordPad is an example of an SDI application.

When an application supports multiple windows simultaneously, it is called an MDI application. Microsoft Word is an example of an MDI application.

In Windows application a form is converted to MDI form by setting the **IsMdiContainer** Property to **True**

Form Designing

Table 12.2 Multiple Document Interface

Control	*Property*	*Value*
MenuStrip1	Name	MenuStrip1
ToolStripMenuItem1	Name	MnuData
	Text	Data
ToolStripMenuItem2	Name	MnuExit
	Text	Exit
ToolStripMenuItem3	Name	MnuEntry
	Text	Entry
ToolStripMenuItem4	Name	MnuStyle
	Text	Style
ToolStripMenuItem5	Name	MnuCascade
	Text	Cascade
ToolStripMenuItem6	Name	MnuVertical
	Text	Vertical
ToolStripMenuItem7	Name	MnuHorizontal
	Text	Horizontal
Form1	Name	Form1
	Text	Multiple Document Interface
	IsMdiContainer	True

Coding

```
Public Class Form1

        Private Sub MnuEntry_Click (ByVal sender As System.Object,
ByVal e As System.EventArgs) Handles MnuEntry.Click
                Dim f As New Form
                f.MdiParent = Me
                f.Show()
        End Sub

        Private Sub MnuExit_Click(ByVal sender As System.Object, ByVal
e As System.EventArgs) Handles MnuExit.Click
                End
        End Sub

        Private Sub MnuCascade _Click(ByVal sender As System.Object,
ByVal e As System.EventArgs) Handles MnuCascade.Click
                Me.LayoutMdi(MdiLayout.Cascade)
        End Sub

        Private Sub MnuVertical_Click(ByVal sender As System.Object,
ByVal e As System.EventArgs) Handles MnuVertical.Click
                Me.LayoutMdi(MdiLayout.TileVertical)
        End Sub

        Private Sub MnuHorizontal_Click(ByVal sender As System.Object,
ByVal e As System.EventArgs) Handles MnuHorizontal.Click
                Me.LayoutMdi(MdiLayout.TileHorizontal)
        End Sub

End Class
```

Output

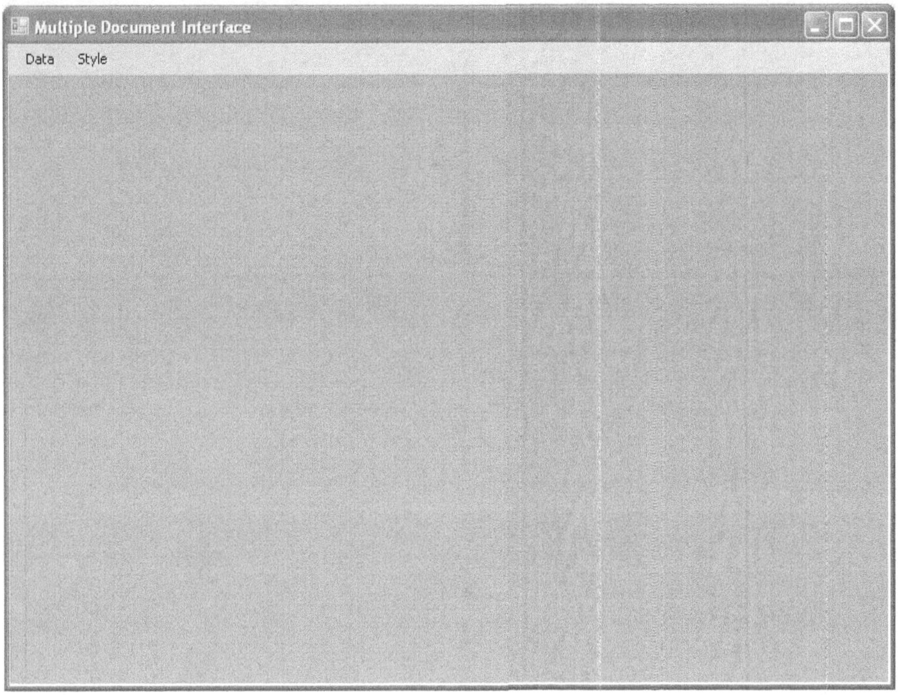

Multiple Document Interface

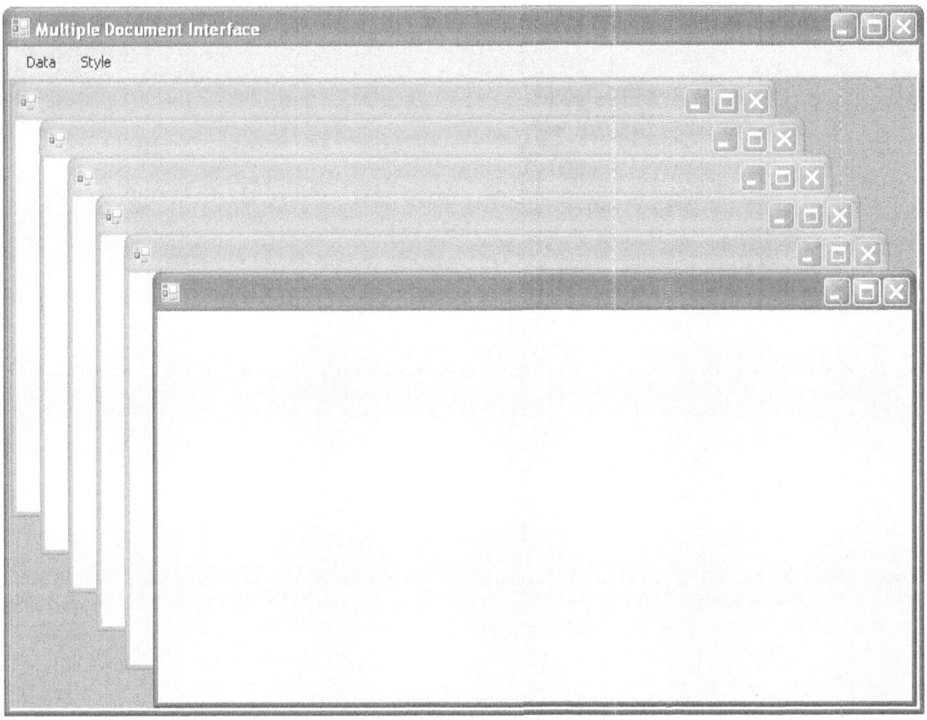

Multiple Document Interface – cascading view

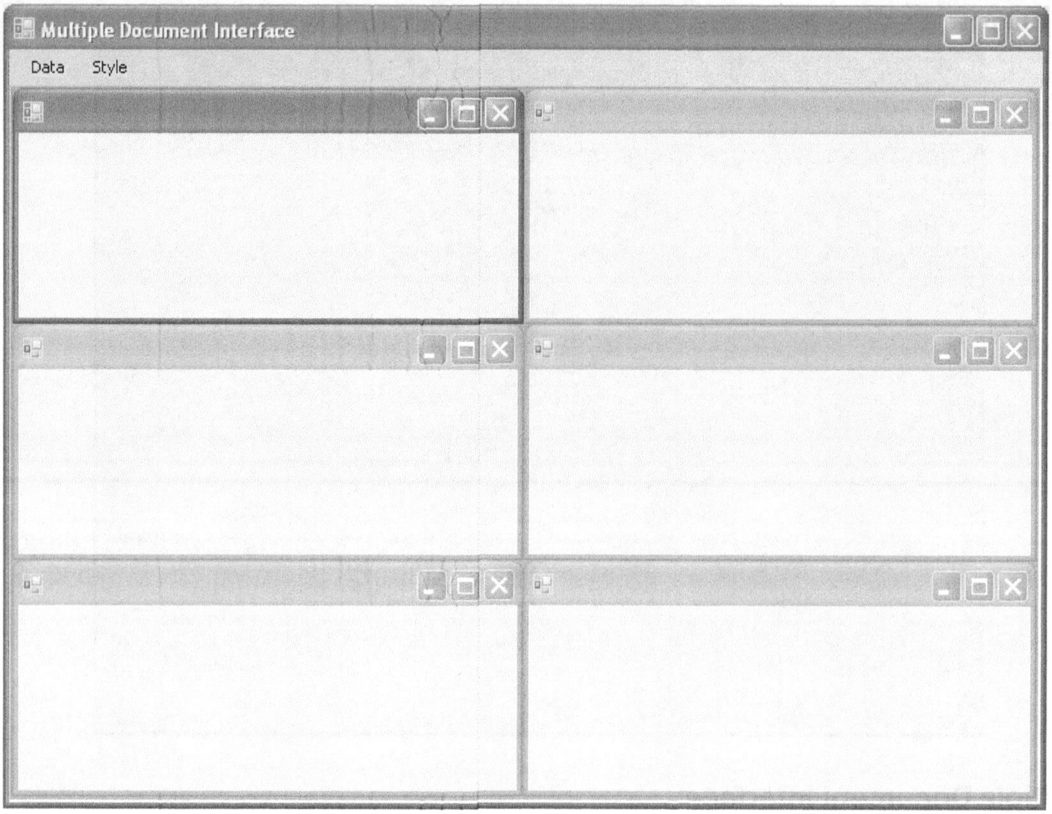

Multiple Document Interface – Horizontal view

CHAPTER

13

MONTH CALENDAR, DATE TIME PICKER, CHECKED LIST BOX

13.1 DATE TIME PICKER

The **DateTimePicker** control is used to allow the user to select a date and time, and to display that date and time in the specified format. We can limit the dates and times that can be selected by setting the **MinDate** and **MaxDate** properties. The **Value** property displays the Date as value whereas the **Text** property displays the Date as Text. The default date Format is DateTimePickerFormat.Long. **DateTimePicker** control is used instead of a **MonthCalendar** (see 13.2) if we need custom date formatting (for example, limiting a selection to just one date). Using the DateTimePicker will limit the need for much data validation of date/time values. Generally this control is used to set the date and time for the applications.

Date Time Picker Demo

This program displays the date selected on the **DateTimePicker** control.

Form Designing

Table 13.1 Date Time Picker Demo

Control	*Property*	*Value*
DateTimePicker1	Name	DTP
TextBox1	Name	TxtDate
Label1	Text	Selected Date is

Coding

```
Public Class Form2
Private Sub DTP_ValueChanged(ByVal sender As System.Object, ByVal
e As System.EventArgs) Handles
```

```
    DTP.ValueChanged
            TxtDate.Text  =  DTP.Text
        End  Sub
End  Class
```

Output

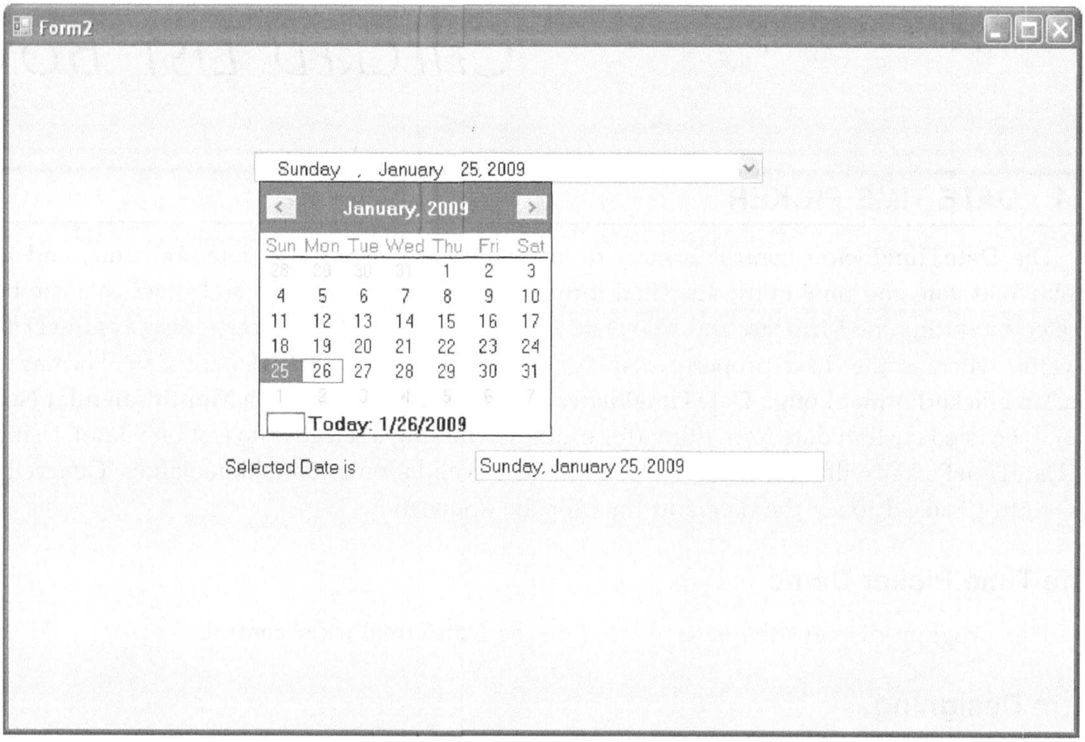

13.2 MONTH CALENDAR

The Windows Forms **MonthCalendar** control presents an intuitive graphical interface for users to view and set date information. The control displays a grid containing the numbered days of the month, arranged in columns underneath the days of the week. You can select a different month by clicking the arrow buttons on either side of the month caption. Using this control, we can select a range of dates from a set of Date information.

Displaying a Range of Date

This program selects the range between two mentioned dates.

Form Designing

Table 13.2 MonthCalendar

Control	*Property*	*Value*
Button1	Name	CmdOk
	Text	OK
Label1	Text	Enter Start date year/month/date
Label2	Text	Enter End date year/month/date
MonthCalendar1	Backcolor	Info
	Name	MC
Textbox1	Name	TxtSDYear
Textbox2	Name	TxtSDMonth
Textbox3	Name	TxtSDDate
Textbox4	Name	TxtEDYear
Textbox5	Name	TxtEDMonth
Textbox6	Name	TxtEDDate

Coding

```
Public Class Form1
    Private Sub Ok_Click(ByVal sender As System.Object, ByVal e
As System.EventArgs) Handles Ok.Click
        Dim SD, ED As Date
        Dim y, m, d As Integer
        y = Integer.Parse(TxtSDYear.Text)
        m = Integer.Parse(TxtSDMonth.Text)
        d = Integer.Parse(TxtSDDate.Text)
        SD = New DateTime(y, m, d)
        y = Integer.Parse(TxtEDYear.Text)
        m = Integer.Parse(TxtEDMonth.Text)
        d = Integer.Parse(TxtEDDate.Text)
        ED = New DateTime(y, m, d)
        MC.SelectionRange = New SelectionRange(SD, ED)
    End Sub
End Class
```

Output

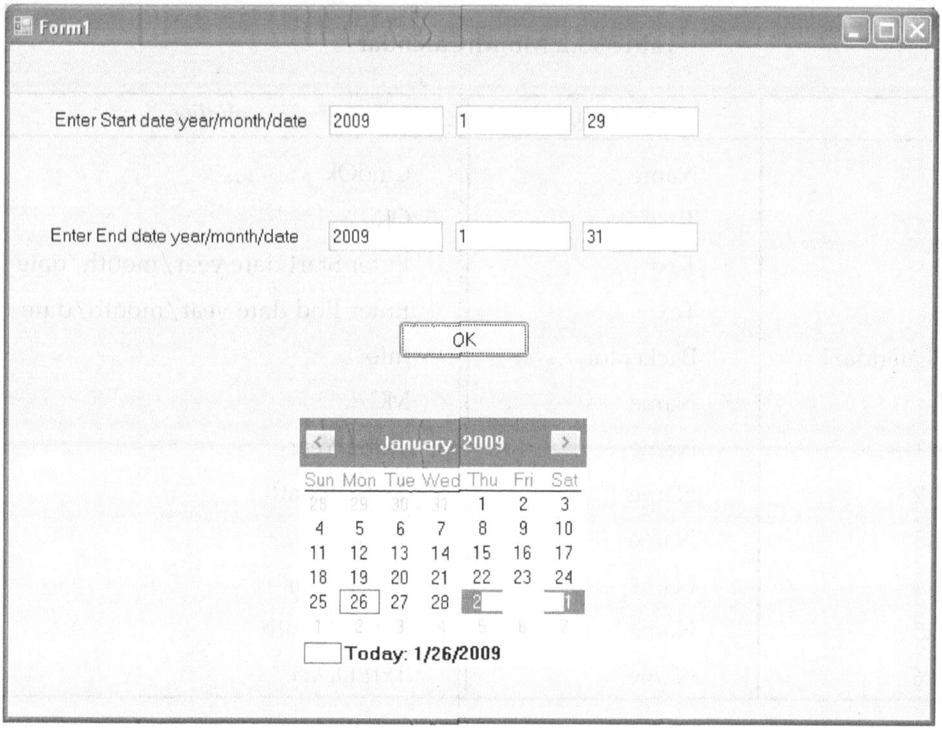

Date Difference

This program displays the difference between two dates in terms of month, year, Date, Hour, Minute and Seconds.

Form Designing

Table 13.3 Date Difference

Control	*Property*	*Value*
DateTimePicker1	Name	DTP1
DateTimePicker2	Name	DTP2
TextBox1	Name	TxtYear
TextBox1	Name	TxtMonth
TextBox1	Name	TxtDay
TextBox1	Name	TxtHour
TextBox1	Name	Txt Minute
TextBox1	Name	TxtSecond
Label1	Text	Select two date, I will show the differences
	Font	Microsoft Sans Serif, 20.25pt

Coding

```
Public Class Form3
    Private Sub DTP2_ValueChanged(ByVal sender As System.Object, ByVal e As System.EventArgs) Handles DTP2.ValueChanged
      Txtyear.Text = DateDiff(DateInterval.Day, DTP1.Value, DTP2.Value)
     TxtMonth.Text = DateDiff(DateInterval.Month, DTP1.Value, DTP2.Value)
      TxtDay.Text = DateDiff(DateInterval.Year, DTP1.Value, DTP2.Value)
     TxtHour.Text = DateDiff(DateInterval.Hour, DTP1.Value, DTP2.Value)
   TextMinute.Text = DateDiff(DateInterval.Minute, DTP1.Value, DTP2.Value e)
    Txtsecond.Text = DateDiff(DateInterval.Second, DTP1.Value, DTP2.Value)
      End Sub
End Class
```

Output

13.3 CHECKED LIST BOX

The **CheckedListBox** Control has the same functionality as the **ListBox** control. In addition, the **CheckedListBox** control also displays a check box next to the items in the list.

To add items in the **CheckedListBox** Control, in the Properties window, select Collection value of the **Items** Property as in Figure 13.3.1, it opens the **String Collection Editor** window in figure 13.3.2 and adds the strings as in Figure 13.3.3

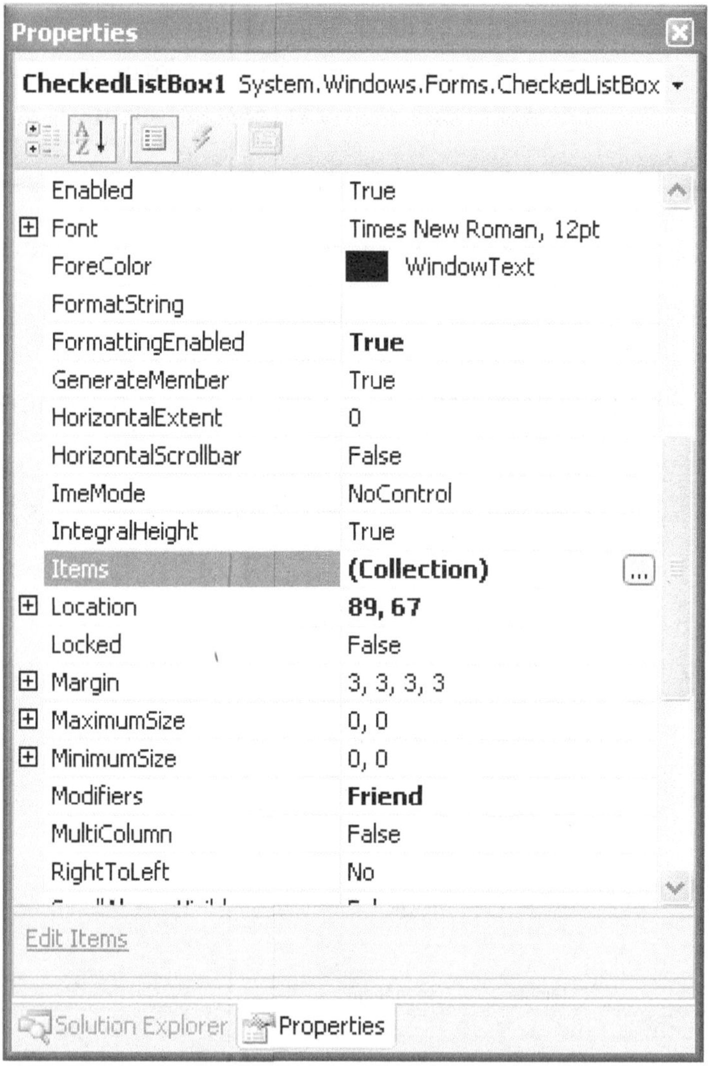

Fig. 13.1 *Properties Window of* ***CheckedListBox*** *Control*

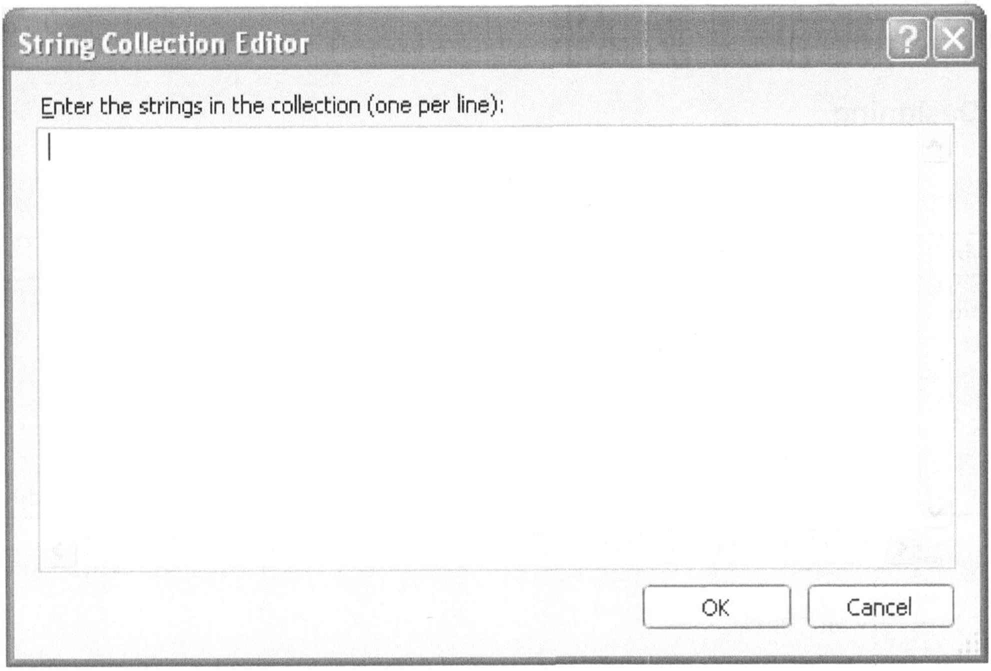

Fig. 13.2 *String Collection Editor Window*

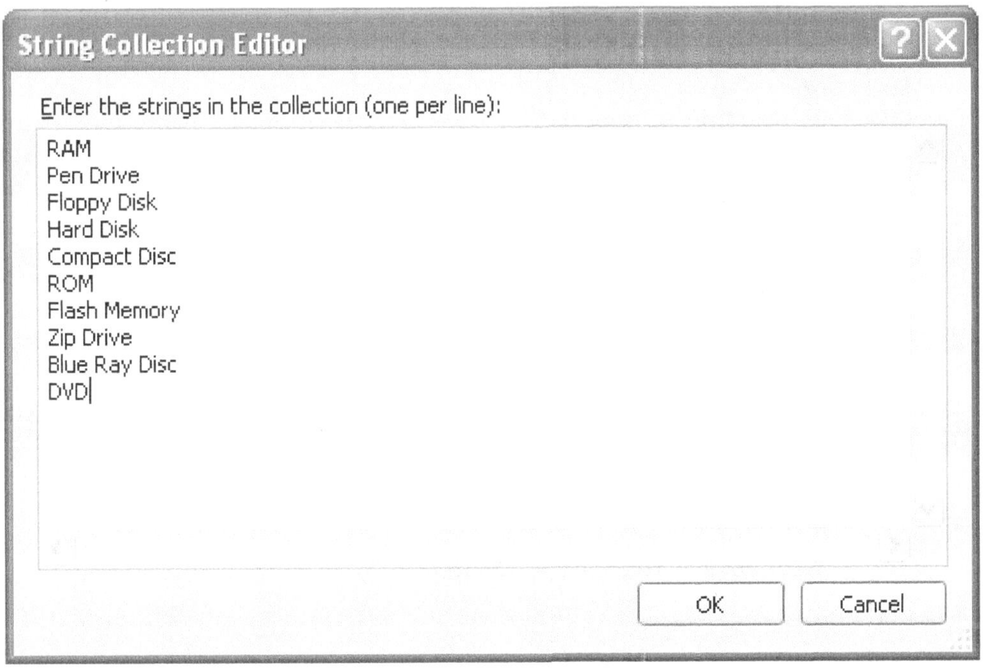

Fig. 13.3 *Items are Added in String Collection Editor Window*

Displaying the Checked Items

This program displays the checked items of the **CheckedListBox** control.

Form Designing

Table 13.4 Checked Items

Control	*Property*	*Value*
Button1	Name	CmdOK
	Text	OK
Label1	Text	Select the Memory you like to work...
CheckedListBox1	Name	CheckedListBox1
	Items	Collection[Select from the String Collection Editor]

Coding

```
Public Class Form1
        Private Sub Form1_Load(ByVal sender As System.Object, ByVal
e As System.EventArgs) Handles MyBase.Load
                ListBox1.Visible = False
                Label2.Visible = False
        End Sub

        Private Sub CmdOK_Click(ByVal sender As System.Object, ByVal
e As System.EventArgs) Handles CmdOK.Click
                Dim mycollection = CheckedListBox1.CheckedIndices()
                Dim item As Integer
                For Each item In mycollection
                ListBox1.Items.Add(CheckedListBox1.Items(item).ToString)
                Next
                Label2.Visible = True
                ListBox1.Visible = True
        End Sub
End Class
```

Output

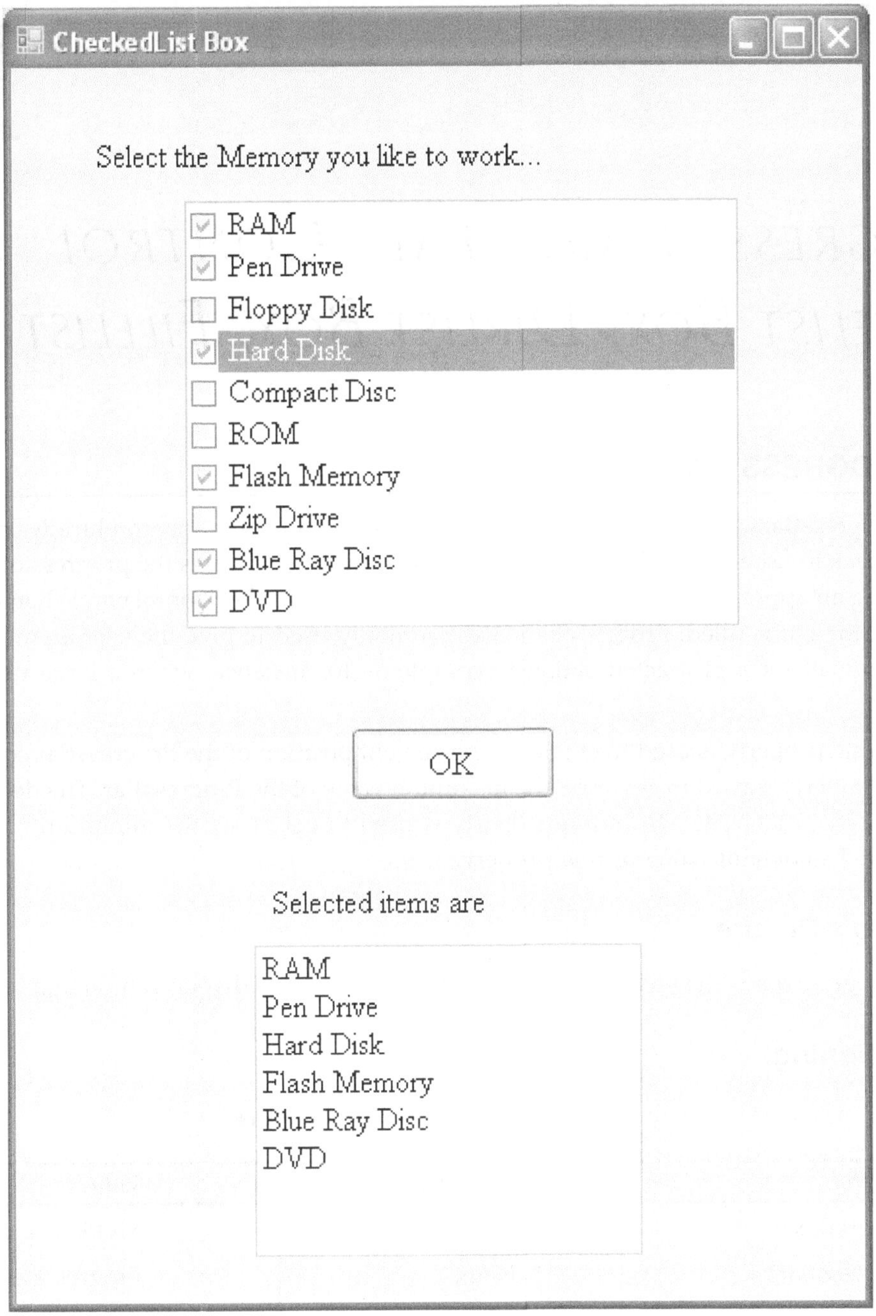
CheckedList Box
Select the Memory you like to work...
RAM
Pen Drive
Floppy Disk
Hard Disk
Compact Disc
ROM
Flash Memory
Zip Drive
Blue Ray Disc
DVD
OK
Selected items are
RAM
Pen Drive
Hard Disk
Flash Memory
Blue Ray Disc
DVD

CHAPTER

14

PROGRESS BAR, TAB CONTROL AND DRIVELIST BOX, DIRLIST BOX, FILELIST BOX

14.1 PROGRESS BAR

The **ProgressBar** control used to display the progress of an operation graphically. It provides visual feedback to users about the status of a particular task. It indicates the progress of an action by displaying an appropriate number of rectangles arranged in a horizontal bar. When the action is complete, the bar is filled. Progress bars are commonly used to give the user an indication of how long to wait for a protracted action to complete—for instance, when a large file is being loaded.

The **Value** property is used to get or set the current position of the **ProgressBar** control. The **Maximum** property is used to get or set the maximum value of the **ProgressBar**. The default value of this property is 100. The **Minimum** property is used to get or set the minimum value of the **ProgressBar**. The default value of this property is 0.

Displaying a Picture

This program loads the picture into PictureBox .Progress bar displays the action to be taken.

Form Designing

Table 14.1 Displaying a Picture

Control	*Property*	*Value*
PictureBox1	Name	MyPicture
ProgressBar1	Name	ProgressBar1
Timer1	Enabled	True
	Interval	100

Coding

```
Public Class Form1
```

```
        Private Sub Timer1_Tick(ByVal sender As System.Object, ByVal
e As System.EventArgs) Handles Timer1.Tick
            If ProgressBar1.Value < ProgressBar1.Maximum Then
                ProgressBar1.Value += 10
            Else
      MyPicture.Image = Image.FromFile("D:\karthikajesus\baby.jpg")
            End If
        End Sub
End Class
```

Output

ProgrssBar

Picture loaded

14.2 TABCONTROL

The **TabControl** displays multiple tabs that contain pictures and other controls. We can use the tab control to produce the kind of multiple-page dialog box that appears many places in the Windows operating system, such as the Control Panel Display Properties. Additionally, the **TabControl** can be used to create property pages, which are used to set a group of related properties.

The most important property of the **TabControl** is **TabPages**, which contains the individual tabs. Each individual tab is a **TabPage** object. When a tab is clicked, it raises the Click event for that **TabPage** object.

To use the **TabControl** in our project, drag the control from the toolbox as pictured in the Fig. 14.1.

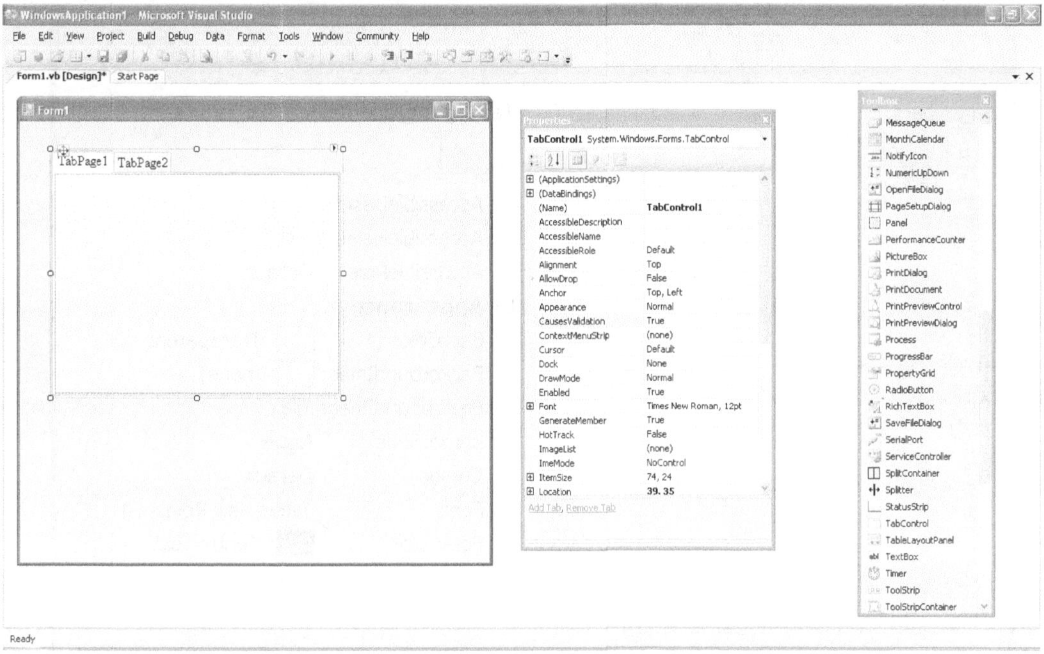

Fig. 14.1 *Tab Control*

In the Properties window (Fig. 14.2), select **Collection** value Button of the **Tabpages** Property, it opens the **TabPage Collection Editor** window (Fig. 14.3)

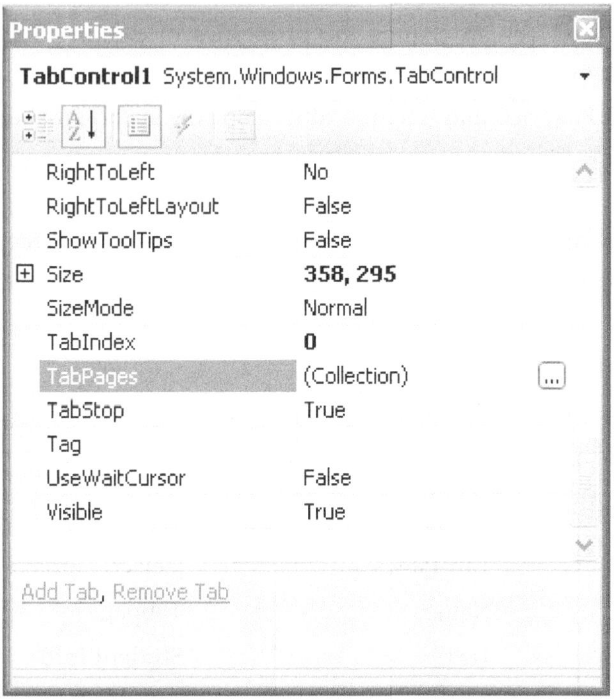

Fig. 14.2 *Properties Window of Tab Control*

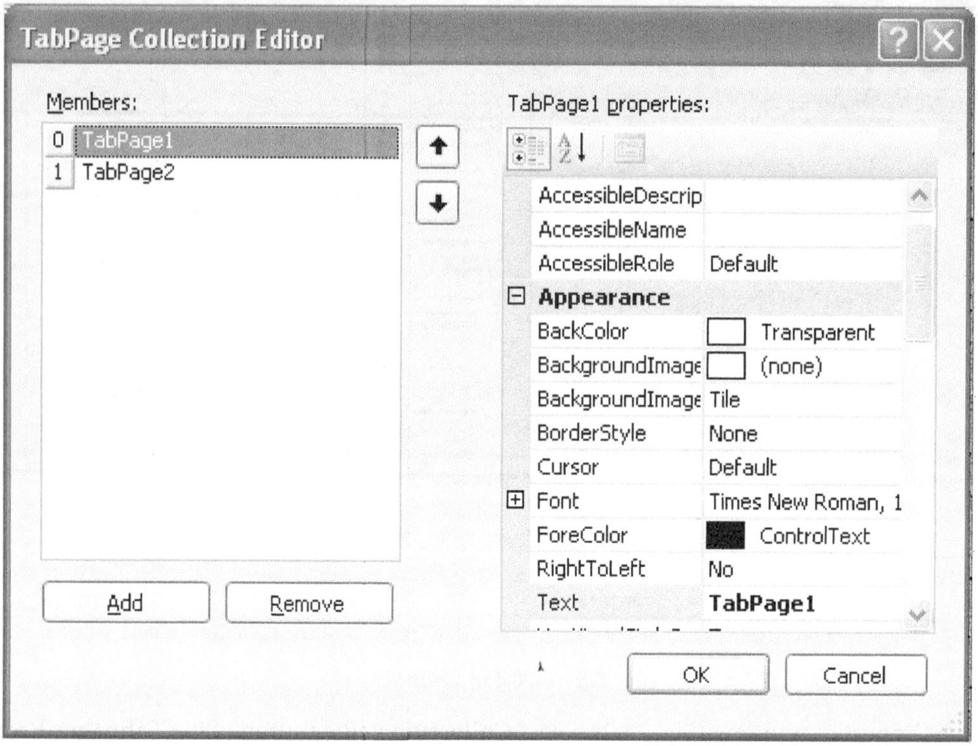

Fig. 14.2 *TabPage Collection Editor Window*

In this editor window we can change the properties of existing TabPage and include or exclude the TabPages by using **Add or Remove** button as required.

In a particular **TabPage** we may include other controls such as Label, Button as required.

Mark Processing

This program does the traditional mark processing such as input three marks and calculates the percentage and Grade.

Form Designing

Table 14.2 Mark Processing

Control	*Property*	*Value*
TabControl1	Name	TabControl1
	Tab Pages	[select Tabpage Collection Editor]
Tabpage1	Name	Tabpage1
	Text	Student Info
TabPage2	Name	Tabpage2
	Text	Mark Details

Tabpage3	Name	Tabpage3
	Text	Result
Label1	Text	Name
Label2	Text	Reg No
Label3	Text	Class
Label4	Text	Institution
Label5	Text	Ad. DataStructure
Label6	Text	High Speed n/w
Label7	Text	Discrete Maths
Label8	Text	Percentage
Label9	Text	Grade
TextBox1	Name	TxtName
TextBox2	Name	TxtRegno
Textbox3	Name	TxtClass
TextBox4	Name	TxtIns
TextBox5	Name	TxtADS
TextBox6	Name	TxtNW
TextBox7	Name	TxtMaths
TextBox8	Name	TxtPercent
TextBox9	Name	TxtGrade
Button1	Name	cmdOk
	Text	Ok

Coding

```
Public Class Form2
    Private Sub CmdOk_Click(ByVal sender As System.Object, ByVal
e As System.EventArgs) Handles CmdOk.Click
        Dim m1, m2, m3 As Integer
        Dim avg As Single
        m1 = Val(TxtADS.Text)
        m2 = Val(TxtNW.Text)
        m3 = Val(TxtMaths.Text)
        avg = (m1 + m2 + m3) / 3.0
        TxtPercent.Text = avg
```

```
                If (avg >= 90) Then
                    TxtGrade.Text = "A"
                ElseIf (avg >= 70) Then
                    TxtGrade.Text = "B"
                ElseIf (avg >= 50) Then
                    TxtGrade.Text = "C"
                Else
                   TxtGrade.Text = "D"
                End If
        End Sub
End Class
```

Output

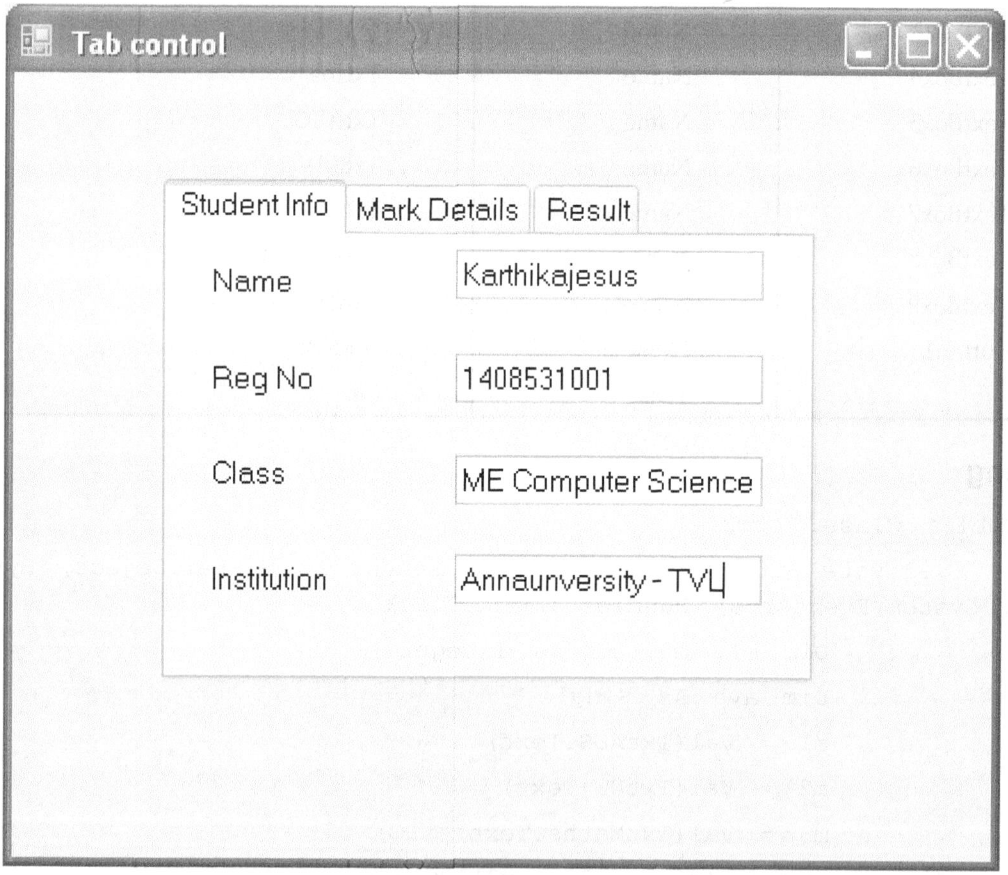

Tab Control student information entered

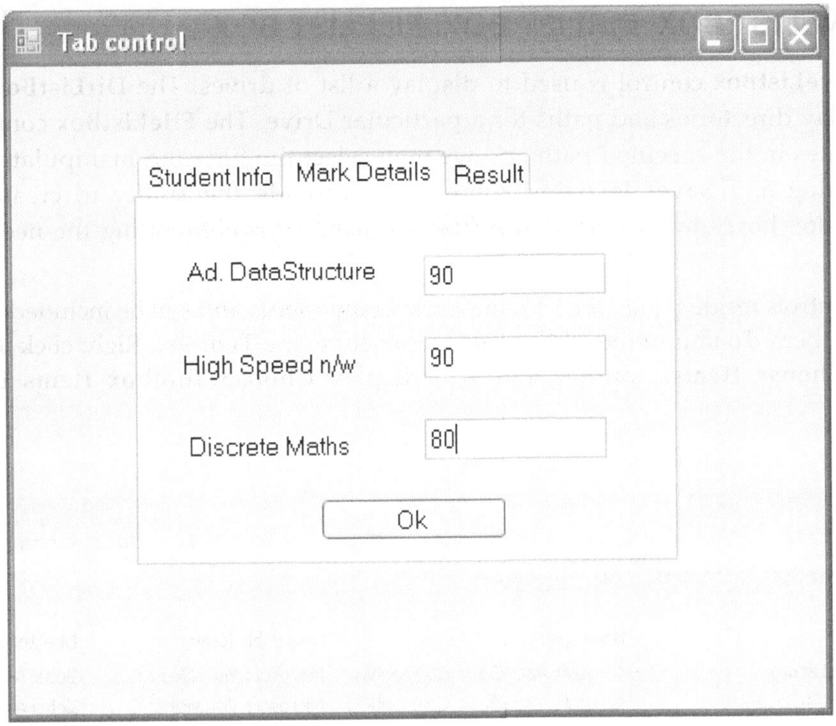

Tab Control mark information entered

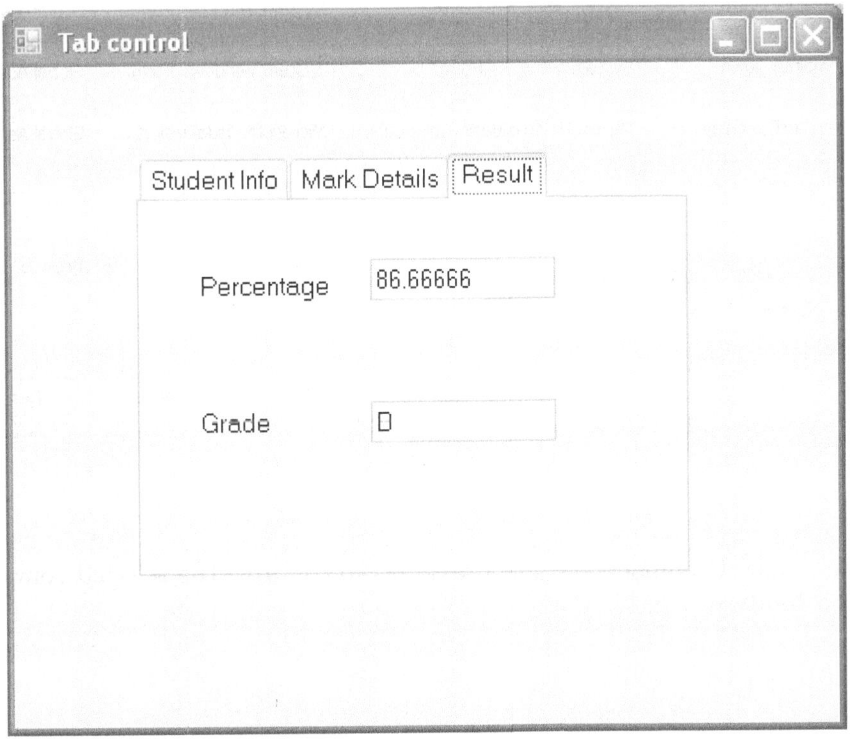

Tab Result Displayed

14.3 DRIVELIST BOX, DIRLIST BOX, FILELIST BOX

The **DriveListBox** control is used to display a list of drives. The **DirListBox** control is used to display directories and paths for a particular Drive. The **FileListBox** control is used display the files in the specified path and we may select the files and manipulate them. The **OpenFileDialog** and **SaveFileDialog** components provide the ability to create standard Windows dialog boxes for working with files, in most cases eliminating the need for these controls.

These controls reside in the **.NET Framework Components** and can be included in our form by importing them. To import the additional component to the **ToolBox**, Right click the **ToolBox** and select **Choose Items...** option that will display **Choose Toolbox Items** Dialog box (Fig. 14.4)

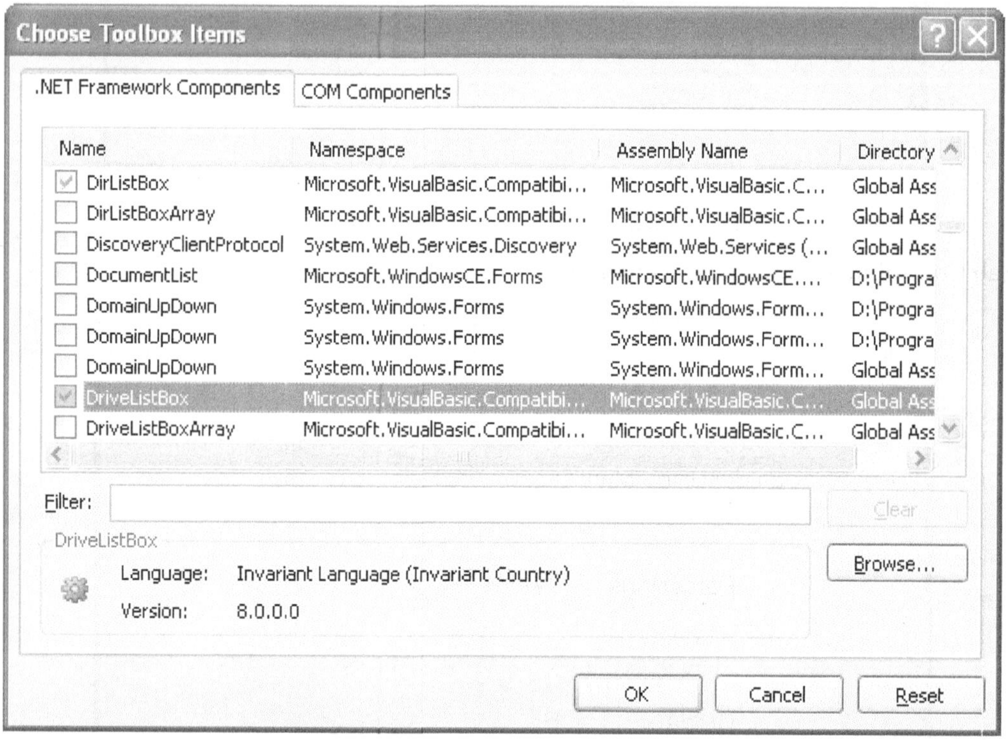

Fig. 14.4 *Choose Toolbox Items Dialog Box*

Select the required componenets and press **OK**, to confirm. The selected components are loaded into the **ToolBox**. (Fig. 14.5)

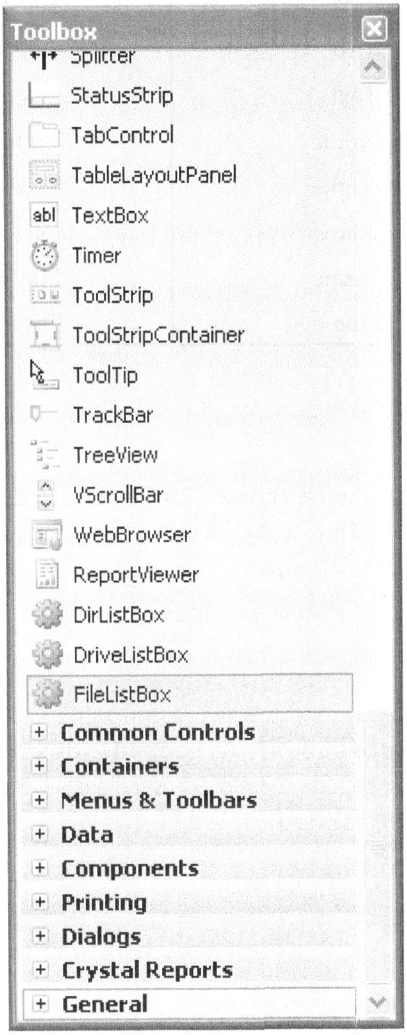

Fig. 14.5 *Components are Loaded into the Tool Box*

Displaying a File Name

This program displays the selected file name from the FileListBox control.

Form Designing

Table 14.3 Displaying a File Name

Control	*Property*	*Value*
Form1	Name	Form1
	Text	Displaying a Filename
Label1	Text	Select the Drive

Label2	Text	Select the Folder
Label3	Text	Select the File
Label4	Text	Selected File Path is
TextBox1	Name	TxtFilter
TextBox2	Name	TxtOut
DirListBox1	Name	DirListBox1
FileListBox1	Name	FileListBox1
DriveListBox1	Name	DriveListBox1

Coding

```
Public Class Form1
    Private Sub DriveListBox1_SelectedIndexChanged(ByVal sender As System.Object, ByVal e As System.EventArgs) Handles DriveListBox1.SelectedIndexChanged
        DirListBox1.Path = DriveListBox1.Drive
    End Sub

    Private Sub DirListBox1_SelectedIndexChanged(ByVal sender As System.Object, ByVal e As System.EventArgs) Handles DirListBox1.SelectedIndexChanged
        FileListBox1.Path = DirListBox1.Path
    End Sub

    Private Sub FileListBox1_SelectedIndexChanged(ByVal sender As System.Object, ByVal e As System.EventArgs) Handles FileListBox1.SelectedIndexChanged
        TxtOut.Text = DriveListBox1.Drive & "\" & DirListBox1.SelectedItem & "\" & FileListBox1.FileName
    End Sub

    Private Sub TextBox1_TextChanged(ByVal sender As System.Object, ByVal e As System.EventArgs) Handles TextBox1.TextChanged
        FileListBox1.Pattern = TextBox1.Text
    End Sub

    Private Sub Form1_Load(ByVal sender As System.Object, ByVal e As System.EventArgs) Handles MyBase.Load
```

```
            TxtFilter.Text  =  "*.*"
        End  Sub
End  Class
```

Output

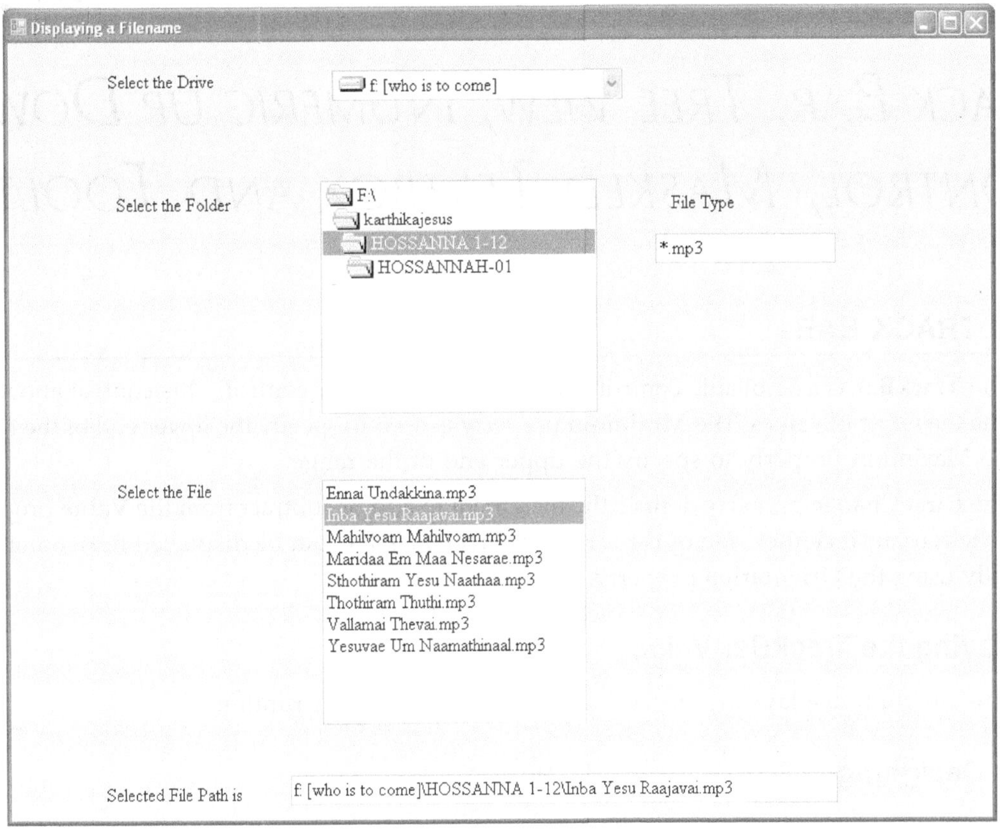

CHAPTER

15

TRACK BAR, TREE VIEW, NUMERIC UP DOWN CONTROL, MASKED TEXTBOX AND TOOLTIP

15.1 TRACK BAR

The **TrackBar** is a scrollable control similar to the **ScrollBar** control. This control allows us to define the range of values. The **Minimum** property is used to specify the lower end of the range and the **Maximum** property to specify the upper end of the range.

The **LargeChange** property defines the increment to add or subtract from the **Value** property when clicks occur on either side of the scroll box. The track bar can be displayed horizontally or vertically using the **Orientation** property.

Displaying the TrackBar Value

This program displays the trackbar value in the **TextBox** at runtime

Form Designing

Table 15.1 Displaying a Trackbar Value

Control	*Property*	*Value*
TrackBar	Name	Trackbar1
	Maximum	100
	Minimum	0
	TickFrequency	10
	TickStyle	BottomRight
	Orientation	Horizontal
Label1	Text	Selected value is
TextBox1	Name	Txtout

Coding

```
Public Class Form3
Private Sub TrackBar1_Scroll(ByVal sender As System.Object, ByVal
e As System.EventArgs) Handles
                                            TrackBar1.Scroll
            TxtOut.Text = TrackBar1.Value
        End Sub
End Class
```

Output

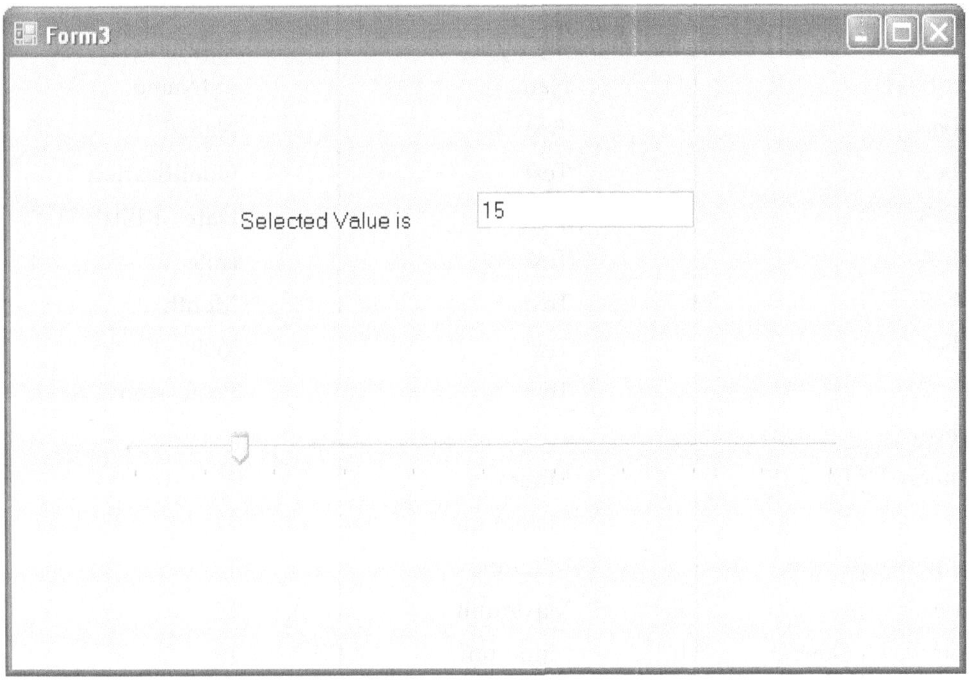

15.2 NUMERICUPDOWN CONTROL

A **NumericUpDown** control contains a single numeric value that can be incremented or decremented by clicking the up or down buttons of the control. The user can also enter a value, unless the **ReadOnly** property is set to **True**.

The numeric display can be formatted by setting the **DecimalPlaces, Hexadecimal**, or **ThousandsSeparator** properties. To display hexadecimal values in the control, set the **Hexadecimal property** to **True**. To display a thousands separator in decimal numbers when appropriate, set the **ThousandsSeparator** property to **True**. To specify the number of digits displayed after the decimal symbol, set the **DecimalPlaces** property to the number of decimal places to display.

The **Minimum** and **Maximum** properties are used to specify the range of values. Set the **Increment** property value to specify the value to be incremented or decremented to the **Value** property when the user clicks the up or down arrow buttons.

Registration Form

This program input the Date of birth using Numeric up down control

Form Designing

Table 15.2 Numeric Up Down Control

Control	*Property*	*Value*
Button1	Name	CmdSubmit
	Text	Submit
TextBox1	Name	TxtName
Label	Text	Name
Labe2	Text	Qualification
Labe3	Text	Date of Birth
Labe4	Text	Date
Labe5	Text	Month
Labe6	Text	Year
Labe7	Text	Profession
Labe8	-	-
NumericUpDown1	Minimum	1
	Maximum	31
NumericUpDown2	Minimum	1
	Maximum	12
NumericUpDown3	Minimum	1947
	Maximum	2000

Coding

```
Public Class Form1
        Private Sub CmdSubmit_Click(ByVal sender As System.Object,
ByVal e As System.EventArgs) Handles CmdSubmit.Click
            Dim na As String
            na = TxtName.Text
            MsgBox("Miss/Mr/Mrs/ " & na & " Thank you for Your
Registration", MsgBoxStyle.Information, "Registration")
```

```
                Label8.Text = "Registered!" & " Your DOB is " & NumericUpDown1.Value & "/" & NumericUpDown2.Value & "/" & NumericUpDown3.Value
                Label8.Visible = True
        End Sub

        Private Sub Form1_Load(ByVal sender As System.Object, ByVal e As System.EventArgs) Handles MyBase.Load
                Label8.Visible = False
        End Sub
    End Class
```

Output

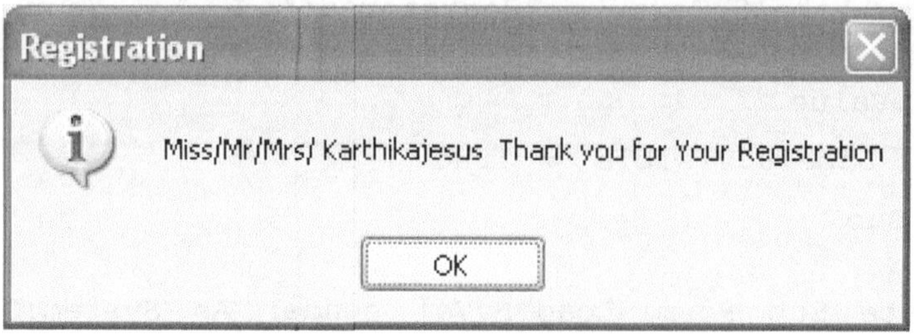

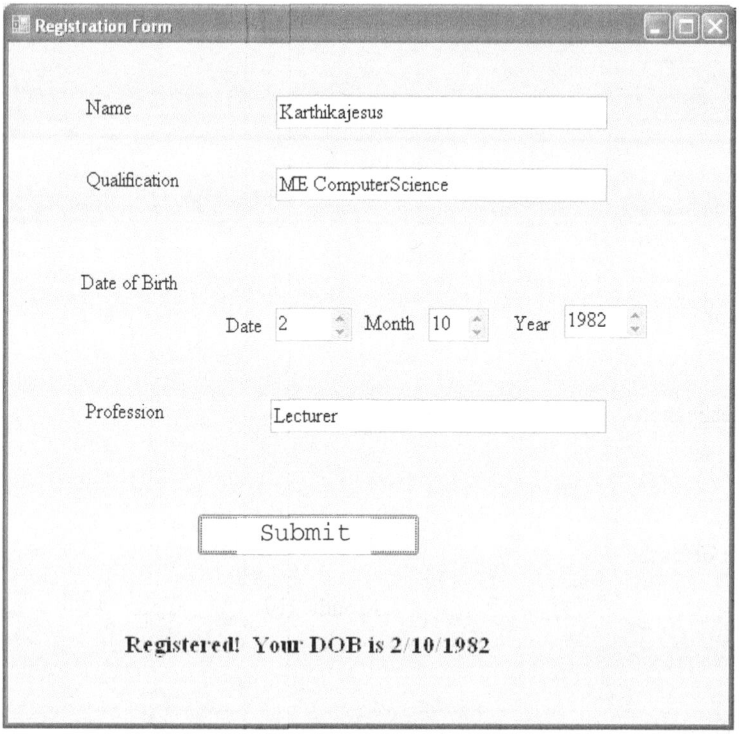

15.3 TREEVIEW

The **TreeView** control is used to display hierarchical data, such as a table of contents or file directory, in a tree structure and supports the following features:

- Data binding that allows the nodes of the control to be bound to XML, tabular, or relational data.
- Site navigation through integration with the **SiteMapDataSource** control.
- Node text can be displayed as either plain text or hyperlinks.
- Programmatic access to the TreeView object model to create trees, populate nodes, set properties, and so on dynamically.
- Client-side node population (on supported browsers).

- The ability to display a check box next to each node.
- Customizable appearance through themes, user-defined images, and styles.

The TreeView control is made up of nodes. Each entry in the tree is called a node and is represented by a **TreeNode** object. Node types are defined as follows:

- A node that contains other nodes is called a parent node.
- The node that is contained by another node is called a child node.
- A node that has no children is called a leaf node.
- The node that is not contained by any other node but is the ancestor to all the other nodes is the root node.

A node can be both a parent and a child, but root, parent, and leaf nodes are mutually exclusive. Several visual and behavioral properties of nodes are determined by whether a node is a root, parent, or leaf node.

Although a typical tree structure has only one root node, the TreeView control allows us to add multiple root nodes to our tree structure. This is useful to display item listings without displaying a single root node, as in a list of product categories.

Each node has a **Text** property and a **Value** property. The value of the **Text** property is displayed in the **TreeView**, while the **Value** property is used to store any additional data about the node, such as data that is passed to the **postback** event that is associated with the node.

A node can be in one of two modes namely selection mode and navigation mode. By default, a node is in selection mode.

To add nodes in the **TreeView** Control, in the Properties window (Fig. 15.1), select **Collection** value Button of the **Nodes** Property. It opens the **TreeNode Editor** window (Fig. 15.2)

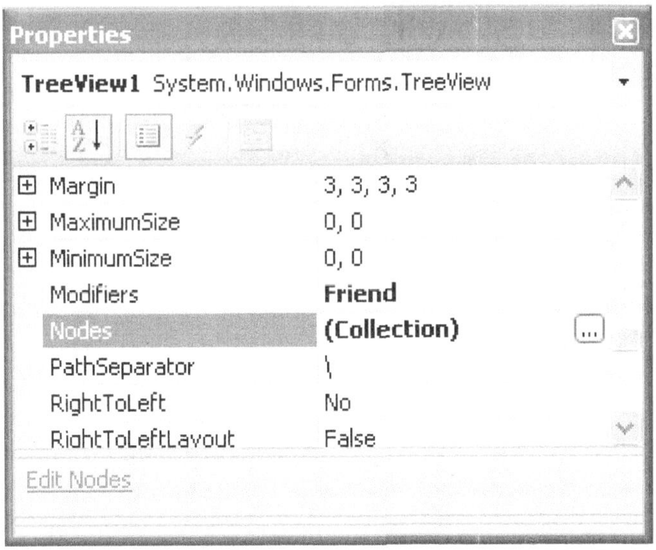

Fig. 15.1 *The Properties Window of* ***TreeView*** *Control*

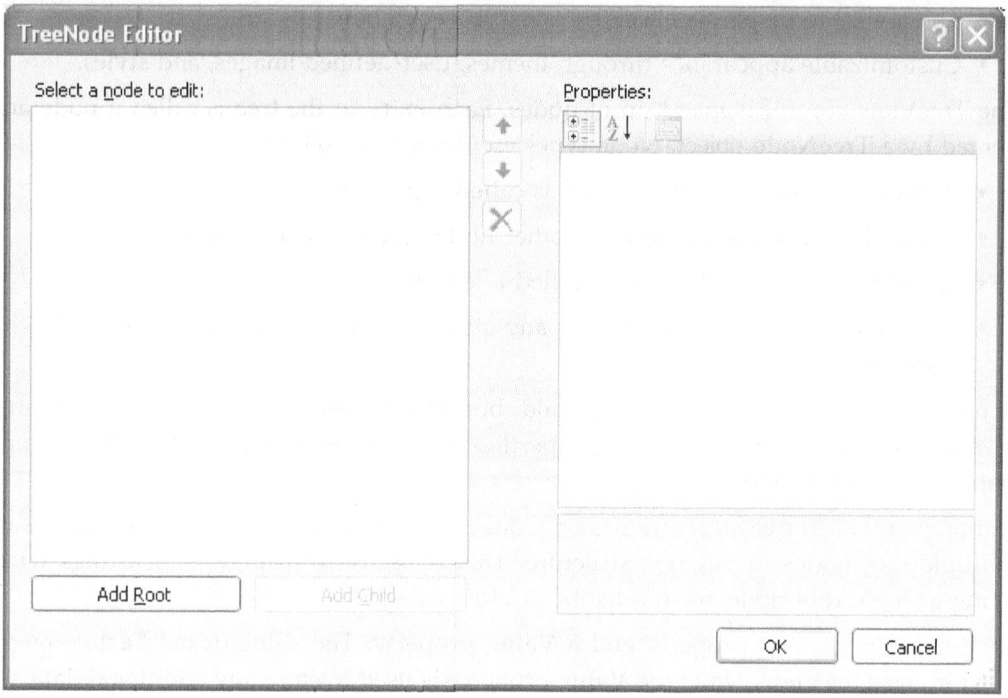

Fig. 15.2 *The* ***TreeNode Editor*** *Window*

In this window, using **Add Root** and **Add Child** Button we can add the nodes in hierarchical manner as below. (Fig. 15.3)

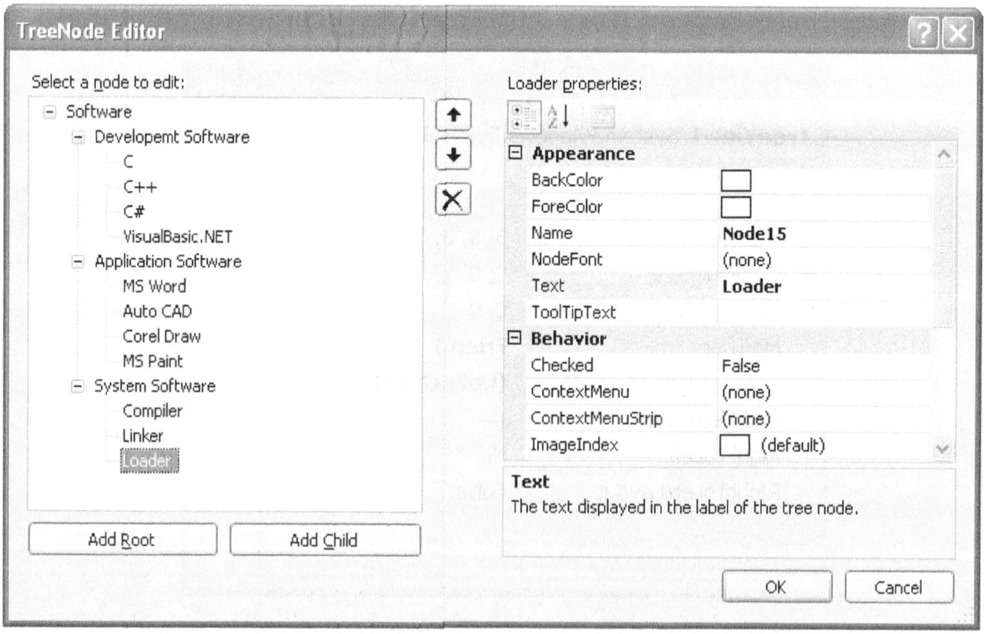

Fig. 15.3 *Item Included in the TreeView Control*

Displaying the Selected Node

This program dispalys the selected node in text

Form Designing

Table 15.3 Tree View

Control	*Property*	*Value*
TreeView1	Name	TreeView1
	Nodes	TreeNode Editor
Node0	Text	Software
Node1	Text	Development Software
Node2	Text	C
Node3	Text	C++
Node4	Text	C#
Node5	Text	VisualBasic.NET
Node6	Text	Application Software
Node7	Text	MS Word
Node8	Text	Auto CAD
Node9	Text	Corel Draw
Node10	Text	MS Paint
Node11	Text	System Software
Node12	Text	Compiler
Node13	Text	Linker
Node14	Text	Loader

Coding

```
Public Class Form1
    Private Sub TreeView1_AfterSelect(ByVal sender As System.Object,
ByVal e As System.Windows.Forms.TreeViewEventArgs) Handles
TreeView1.AfterSelect

        Label1.Text = "Path:" & " " & e.Node.FullPath
        Label1.Visible = True
        'displaying the path of the selected node
```

```
        Label2.Text ="Current node selected  :  " & " " & e.Node.Text
        Label2.Visible = True
        'displaying the selected node
        End Sub

        Private Sub Form1_Load(ByVal sender As System.Object, ByVal
e As System.EventArgs) Handles MyBase.Load
                Label1.Visible = False
                Label2.Visible = False

        End Sub
    End Class
```

Output

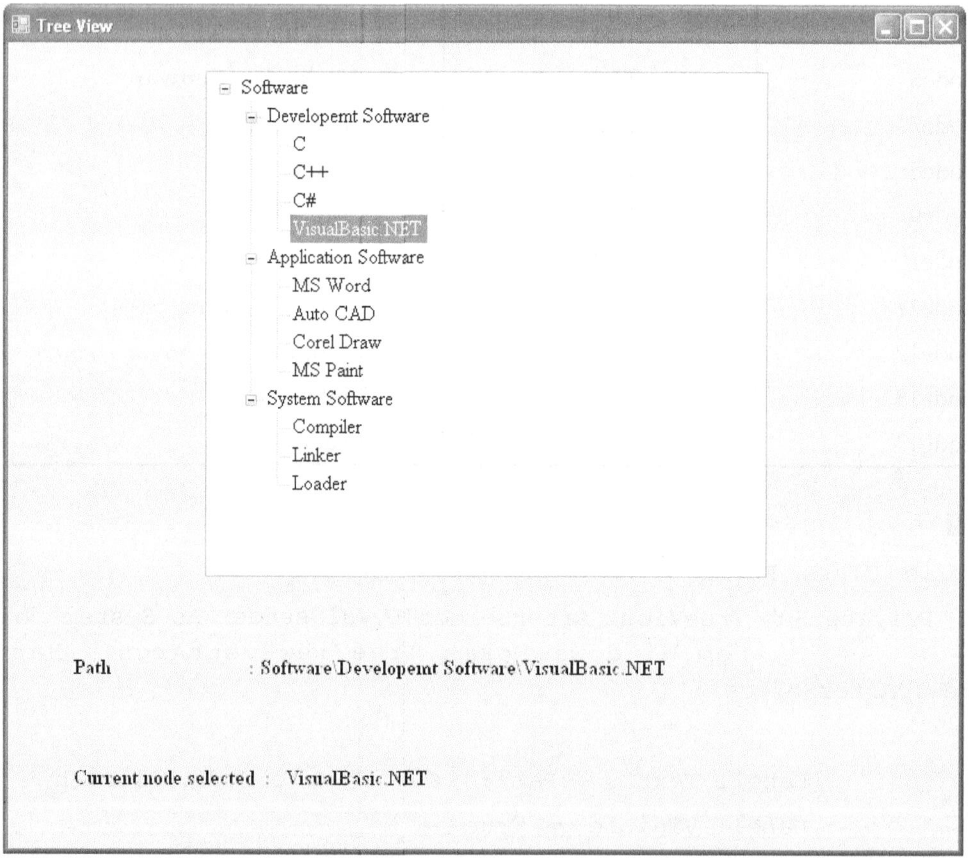

15.4 TOOL TIP

The **ToolTip** Control displays a small rectangular pop-up window that displays a brief description about the control, when the user rests the pointer on the control. The **ToolTip** control can be used in any container.

Picture Info

This program displays the picture information when mouse over the control.

Form Designing

Table 15.4 Tool Tip Text

Control	*Property*	*Value*
ToolTip1	Name	ToolTip1
	IsBalloon	True
Button1	Name	CmdInfo
	Text	Picture Info
	ToolTip on ToolTip1	Click to see the Picture Information
PictureBox1	Name	MyPicture
	ToolTip on ToolTip1	Picture Box
TextBox1	Name	TxtHeight
	ToolTip on ToolTip1	Picture Height
TextBox1	Name	TxtWidth
	ToolTip on ToolTip1	Picture Width

Coding

```
Public Class Form1
        Private Sub CmdInfo _Click(ByVal sender As System.Object,
ByVal e As System.EventArgs) Handles CmdInfo.Click
              TxtHeight.Text = MyPicture.Height
              TxtWidth.Text = MyPicture.Width
        End Sub
End Class
```

Output

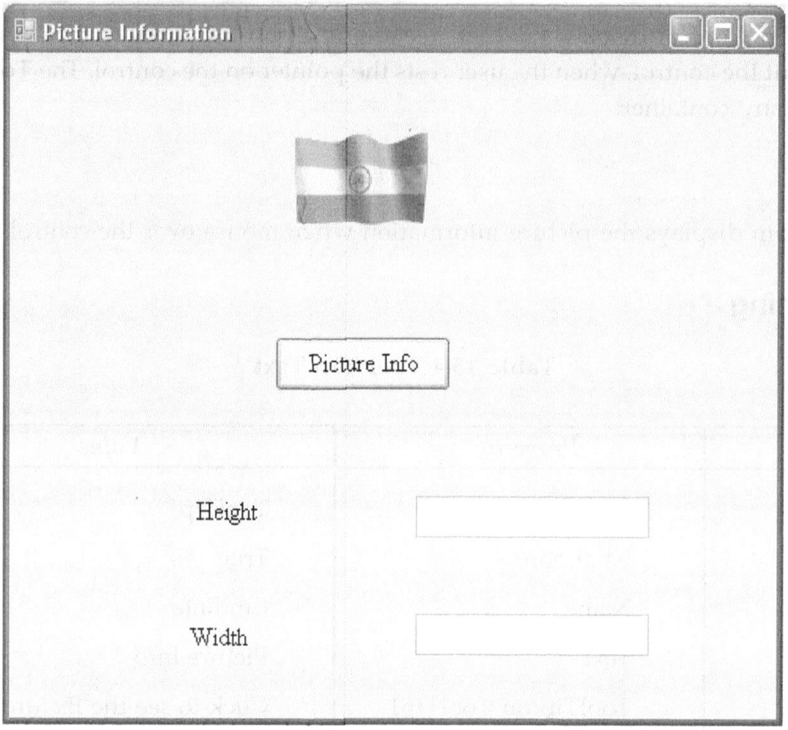
Picture Information
Picture Info
Height
Width

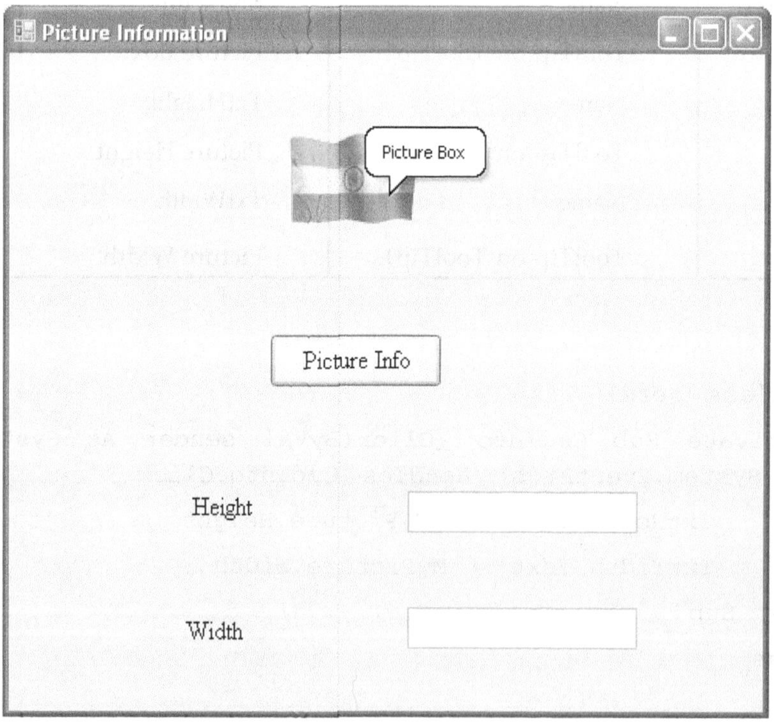
Picture Information
Picture Box
Picture Info
Height
Width

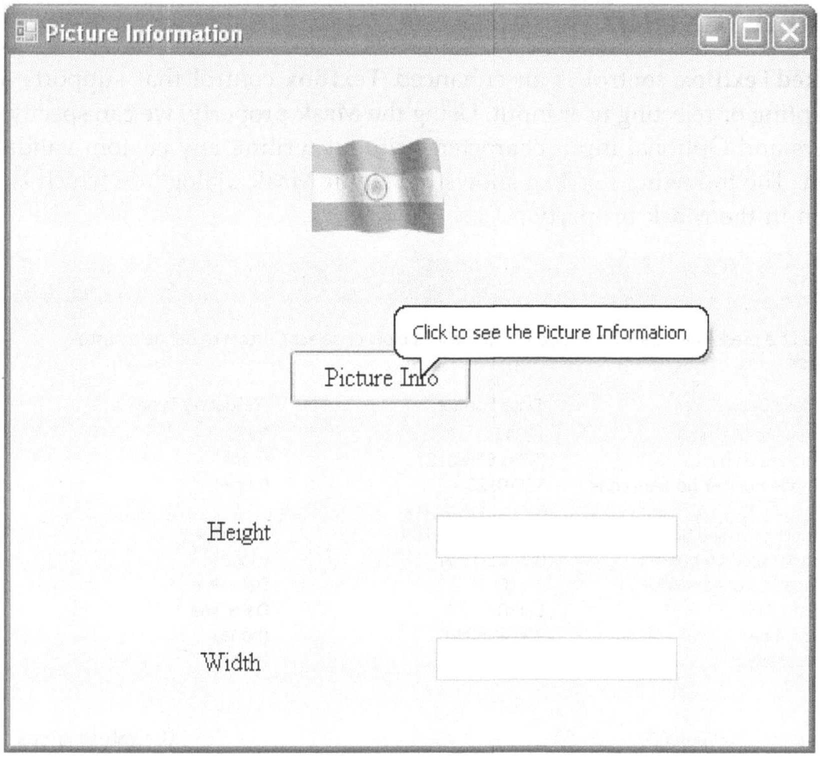
Picture Information
Click to see the Picture Information
Picture Info
Height
Width

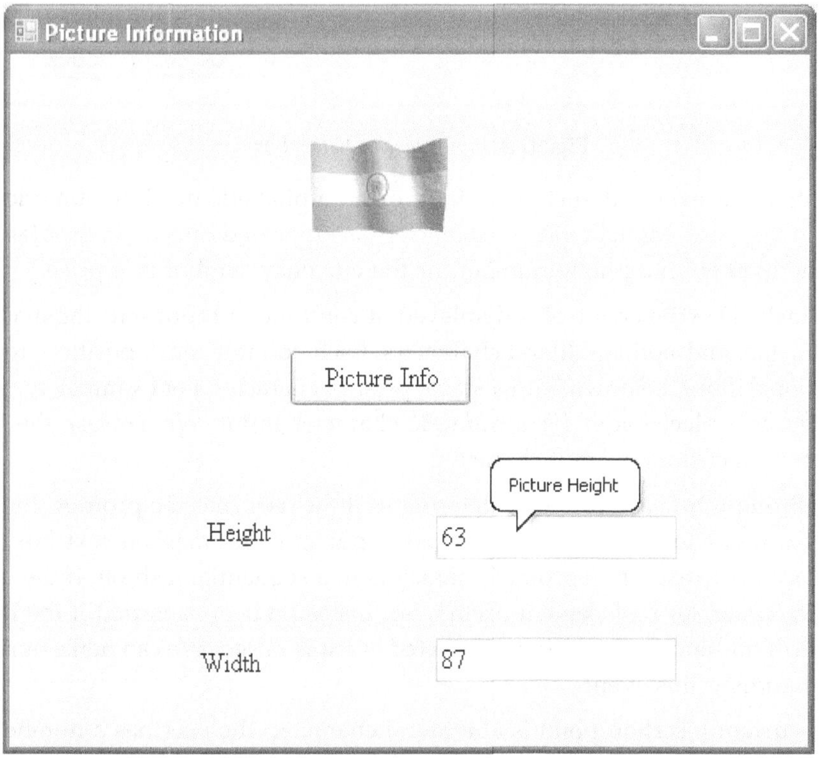
Picture Information
Picture Info
Picture Height
Height
63
Width
87

15.5 MASKED TEXTBOX

The **MaskedTextBox** control is an enhanced **TextBox** control that supports a declarative syntax for accepting or rejecting user input. Using the **Mask** property, we can specify the required input characters and Optional input characters without writing any custom validation logic in our application. The following fig. 15.4 shows the **Input Mask** dialog box which is activated by click the button in the **Mask** property.

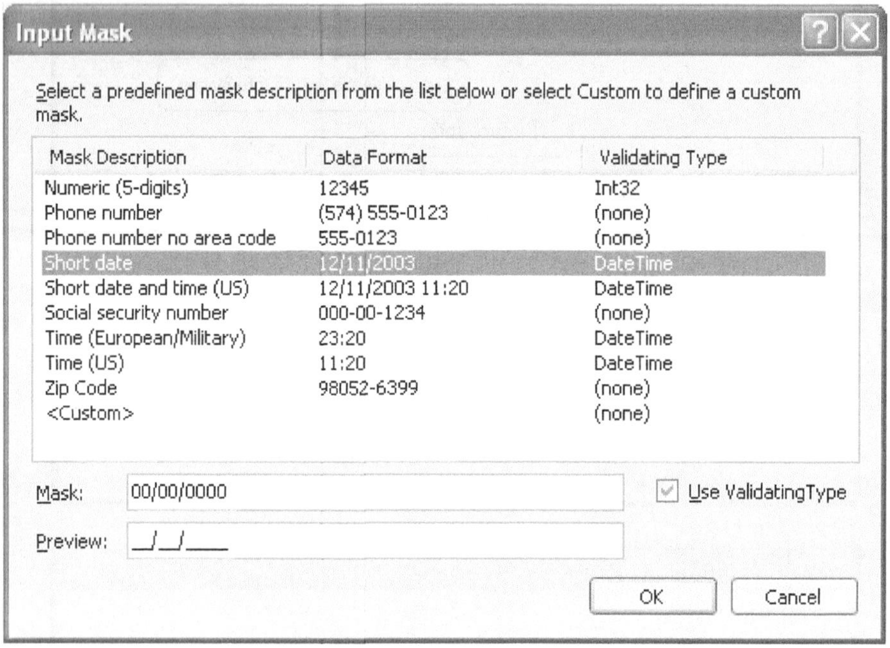

Fig. 15.4 *Input Mask Dialog Box*

The type of input expected such as a digit, or an alphabetic or alphanumeric character is given position in the mask. Mask literals, or characters are appeared directly in the **MaskedTextBox**. For example the hyphen in a phone number, or the currency symbol in a price.

When a **MaskedTextBox** control is displayed at run time, it represents the mask as a series of prompt characters and optional literal characters. Each editable mask position, representing a required or optional input, is shown with a single prompt character. For example, the number sign (#) is often used as a placeholder for a numeric character input. We can use the **PromptChar** property to specify a custom prompt character.

The **HidePromptOnLeave** property determines if the user sees the prompt characters when the control loses input focus. As the user types input into the masked text box, valid input characters replace their respective prompt characters in a sequential fashion. If the user types an invalid input character, no replacement occurs, but instead a beep is issued if the **BeepOnError** property is set to **True,** and the **MaskInputRejected** event is raised. We can make our own custom error logic by handling this event.

When the current insertion point is at a literal character, the user has a number of options:

If a character other than the prompt character is typed, the literal will automatically be skipped and the input character will be applied to the next editable position, represented by the next prompt character.

If the prompt character is typed and the **AllowPromptAsInput** property is **True**, the input will overtype the prompt character and insertion point will be moved to the next position in the mask. As is always the case, the arrow keys can be used to navigate to a previous or subsequent position.

We can use the **MaskFull** property to verify whether or not the user has entered all of the required input. The **Text** property will always retrieve the user's input format according to the **Mask** and the **TextMaskFormat** property.

As with the TextBox control, several common keyboard shortcuts do not work with MaskedTextBox. In particular, CTRL-R (right justify text), CTRL-L (left justify text), and CTRL-L (center text) have no effect

Validation Form

This program demonstrates the **Masked Textbox** control.

Form Designing

Table 15.5 MaskedTextBox

Control	*Property*	*Value*
Button1	Name	CmdSubmit
	Text	Submit
Label1	Text	Name
Label2	Text	Qualification
Label3	Text	Date of Birth
Label4	Text	Fix salary for You...
Label5	Text	Five digits only
TextBox1	Name	TxtName
TextBox2	Name	TxtQuali
MaskedTextBox1	Name	MaskedTxtDOB
	BeepOnError	True
	Mask	00/00/0000[selected from the Input Mask dialog box]
MaskedTextBox2	Name	MaskedTxtSalary
	BeepOnError	True
	MASK	00000 [Selected from the input mask dialog box]

Coding

```
Public Class Form1

        Private Sub MaskedTxtDOB _MaskInputRejected(ByVal sender As
System.Object, ByVal e As System.Windows.Forms.MaskInputRejectedEventArgs)
Handles MaskedTxtDOB.MaskInputRejected
            MsgBox("Your input must be in 5 digits")
            MaskedTxtDOB.Focus()
        End Sub

        Private Sub CmdSubmit_Click(ByVal sender As System.Object,
ByVal e As System.EventArgs) Handles CmdSubmit.Click
            MsgBox("Thank You!!! Mr/Mrs/Miss  " & TextBox1.Text)
        End Sub

        Private Sub MaskedTxtSalary _MaskInputRejected(ByVal sender
As Object, ByVal e As System.Windows.Forms.MaskInputRejectedEventArgs)
Handles MaskedTxtSalary.MaskInputRejected
            MsgBox("Enter Valid Date")
            MaskedTxtSalary.Focus()
        End Sub
End Class
```

Output

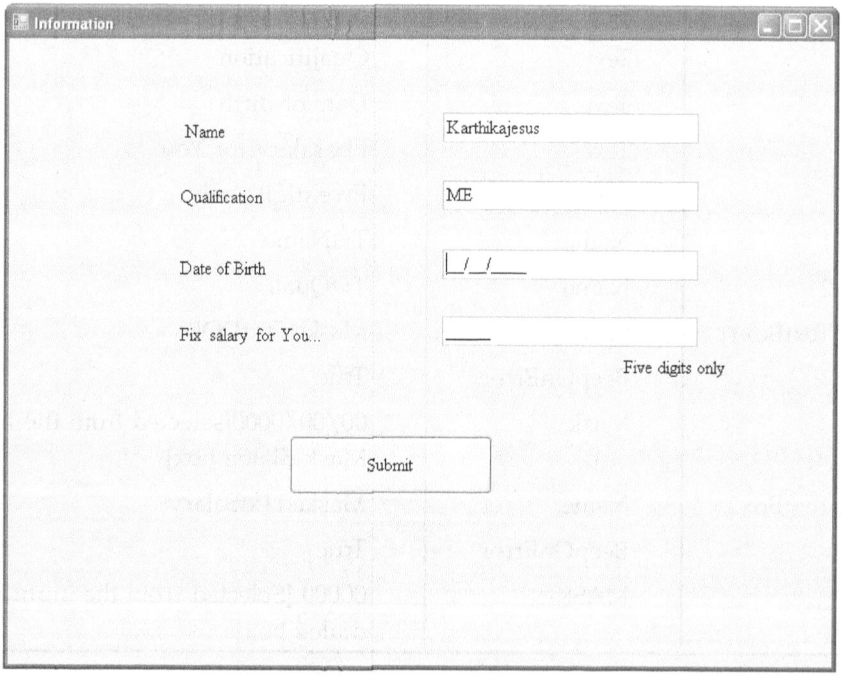

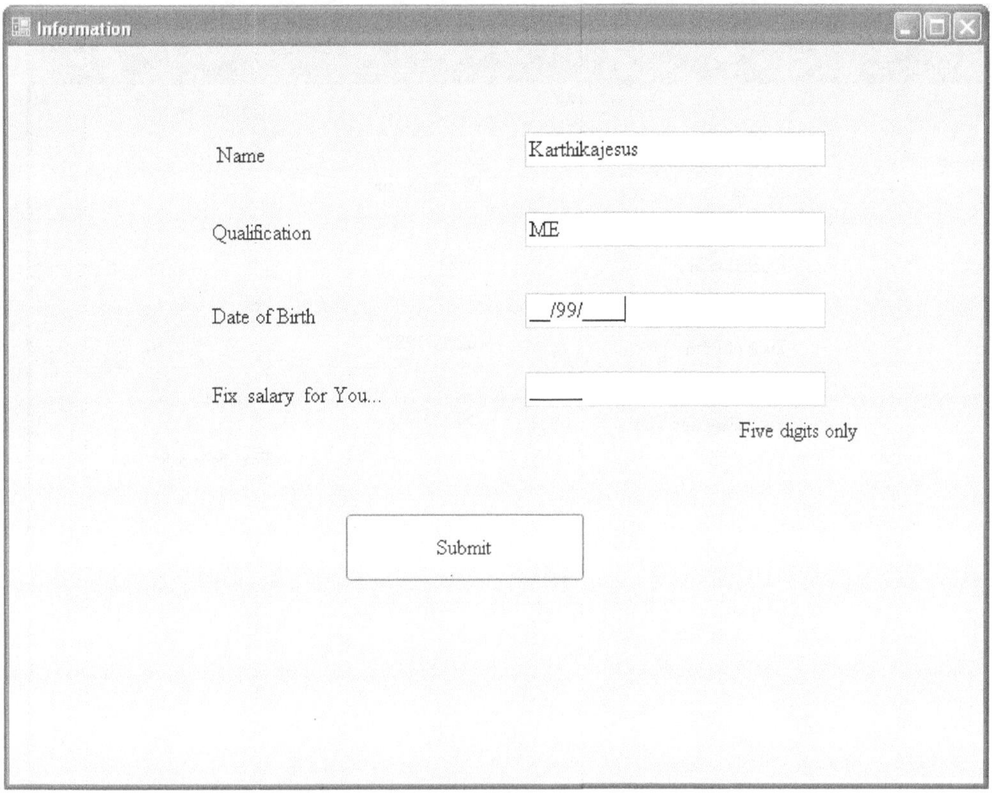
Information
Name
Karthikajesus
Qualification
ME
Date of Birth
__/99/____
Fix salary for You...
Five digits only
Submit

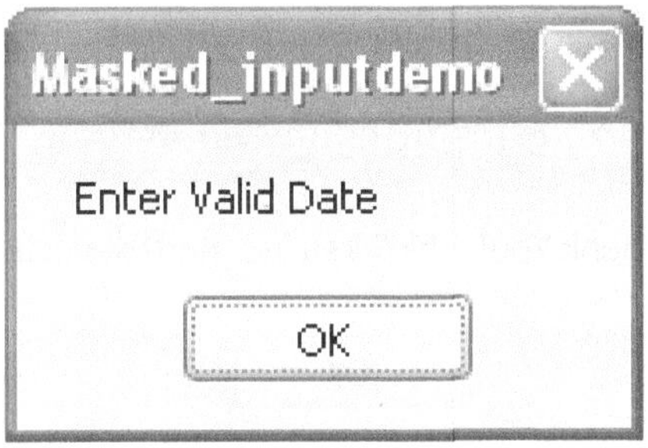
Masked_inputdemo
Enter Valid Date
OK

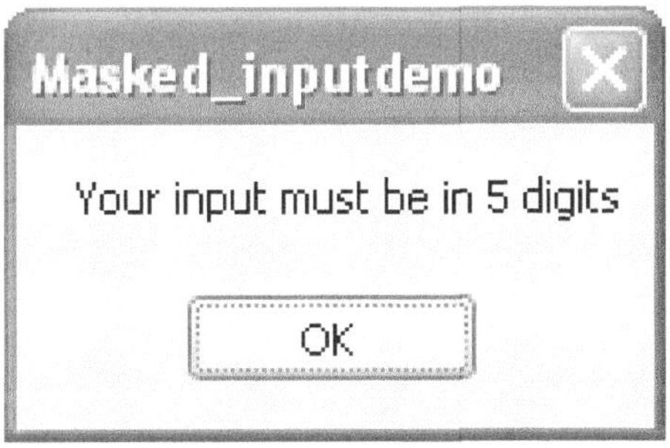
Masked_inputdemo
Your input must be in 5 digits
OK

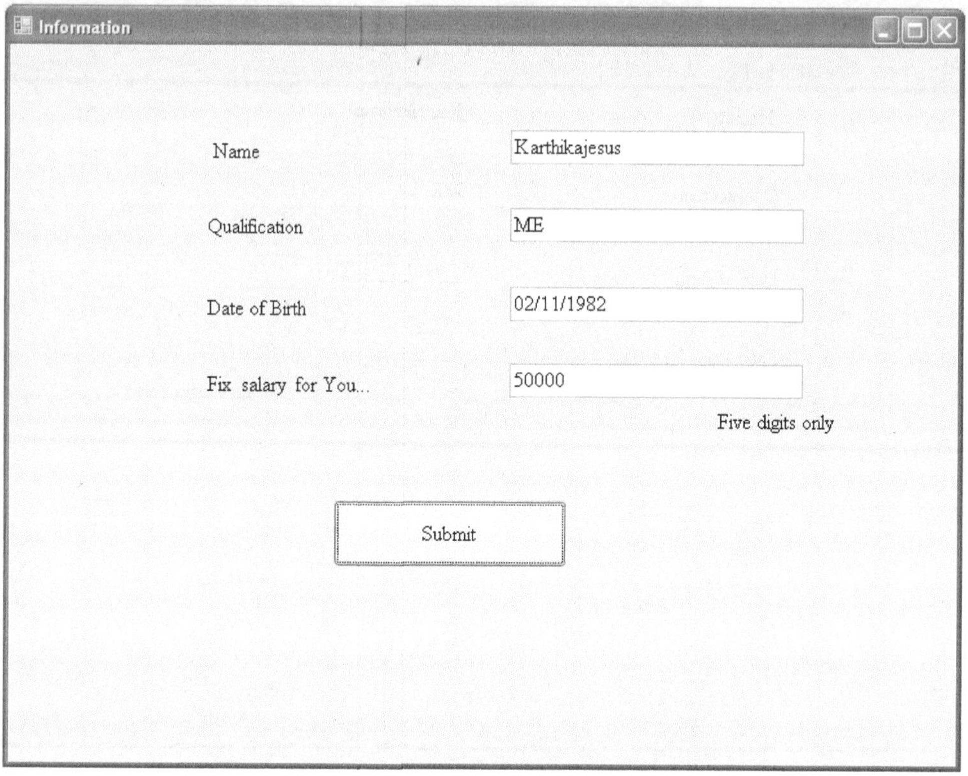
Information
Name
Karthikajesus
Qualification
ME
Date of Birth
02/11/1982
Fix salary for You...
50000
Five digits only
Submit

Masked_inputdemo
Thank You!!! Mr/Mrs/Miss Karthikajesus
OK

CHAPTER

16

IMAGE LIST, LIST VIEW, PROPERTY GRID AND TOOLSTRIP

16.1 IMAGE LIST

The **ImageList** control is used to store images, which can then be displayed by controls. In **ImageList** we can write code for a single, consistent catalog of images.

The **ImageList** is typically used by other controls, such as the **ListView, TreeView**, or **ToolBar.** We can add bitmaps or icons to the **ImageList**, and the other controls are able to use the images as required. The **Images** property of the **ImageList** contains the pictures to be used by the associated control. Each individual image can be accessed by its index value or by its key. When this control is invoked from the Toolbox, it goes to the component tray as in Fig. 16.1

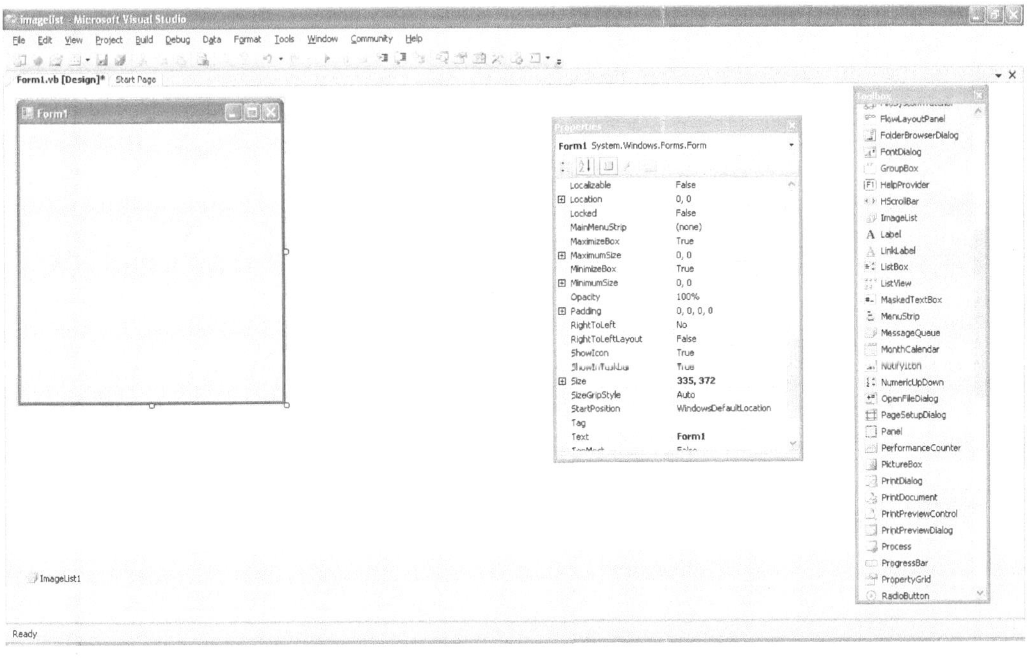

Fig. 16.1 *ImageList on the Component Tray*

To add images in the **ImageList** Control, in the Properties window, select **Collection** value of the **Images** Property as in Fig. 16.2, it opens the **Images Collection Editor** window in Fig. 16.3.

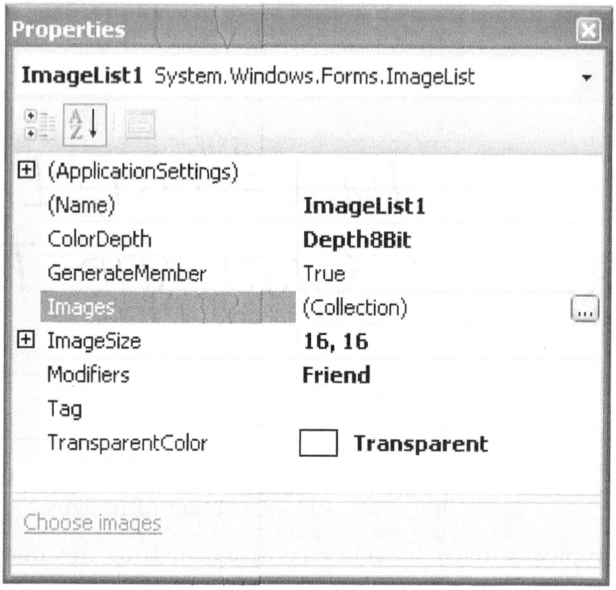

Fig. 16.2 *The Properties Window of ImageList*

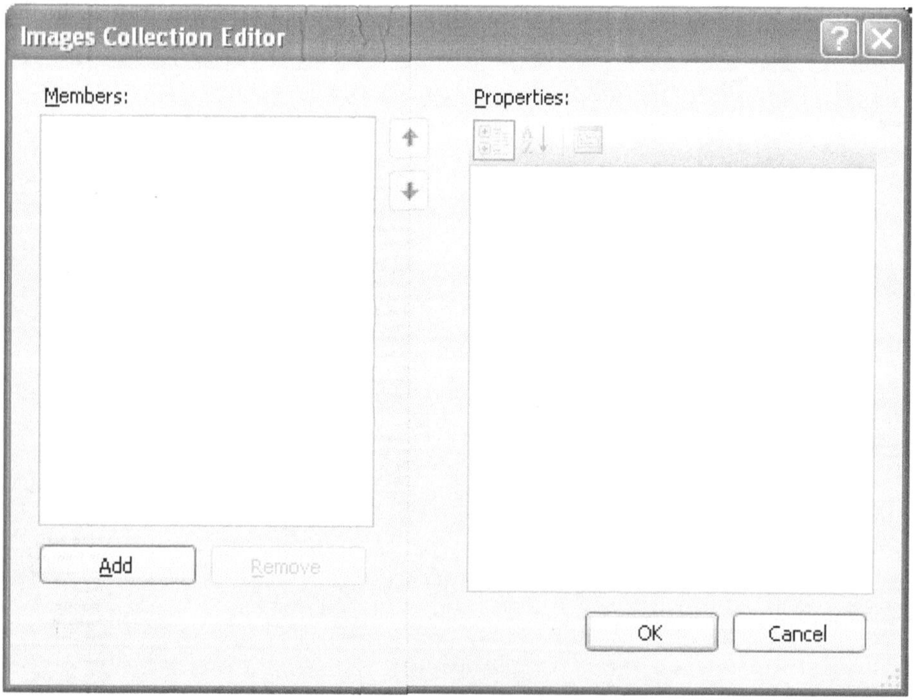

Fig. 16.3 *Images Collection Editor Window*

In this window, using **Add** and **Remove** Button we can add the pictures as in the Fig. 16.4 below.

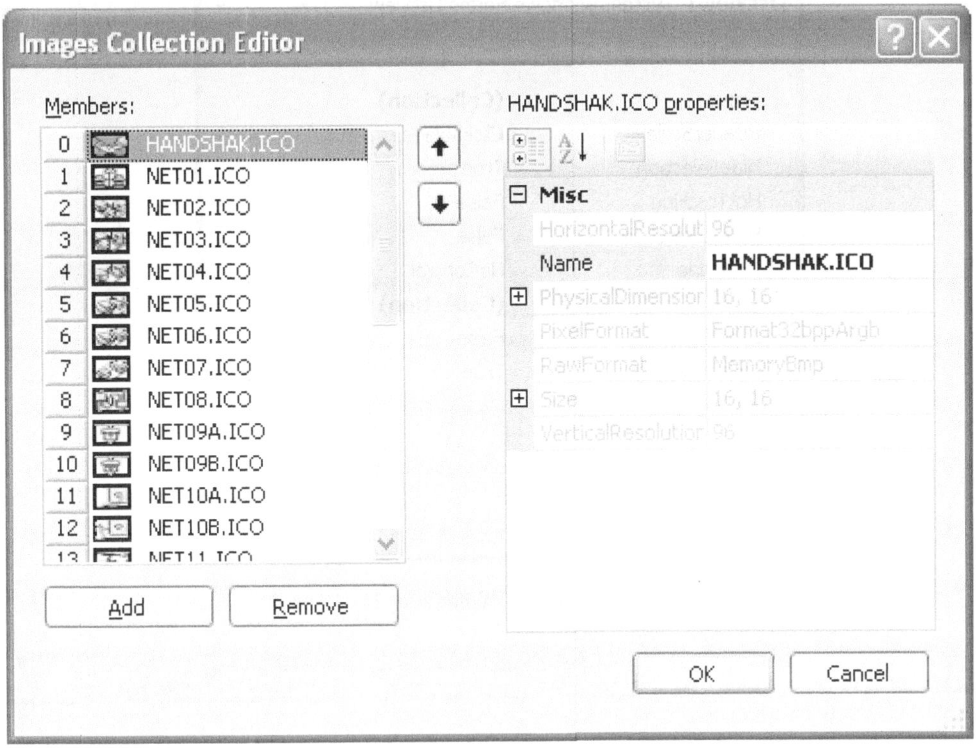

Fig. 16.4 *Picture Files Added to the Images Collection Editor Window*

This **ImageList** can be used in the subsequent examples.

16.2 LISTVIEW

The **ListView** control is used to display a list of items with item text and, optionally, an icon to identify the type of item. For example, the Windows Explorer list of files is similar in appearance to a **ListView** control. It displays a list of the files and folders currently selected in the tree. Each file and folder displays an icon associated with it which helps to identify the type of file or folder. The **ListViewItem** class represents an item within a **ListView** control. The items that are displayed in the list can be shown in one of five different views. **ListView** supports single or multiple selections. The multiple selection feature lets the user select from a list of items in a way similar to a **ListBox** control. Additionally, the user can activate selected items to perform a task. We can use the **ListView** control in a variety of ways. The control can be used to display information from an application, a database, or a text file. The **ListView** can also be used to obtain information from the user, such as selecting a set of files to process.

To add items in the **ListView** Control, in the Properties window, select Collection value of the **Items** Property as in Fig. 16.5, it opens the **ListViewItem Collection Editor** window in Fig. 16.6.

Fig. 16.1 *Properties Window of ListView*

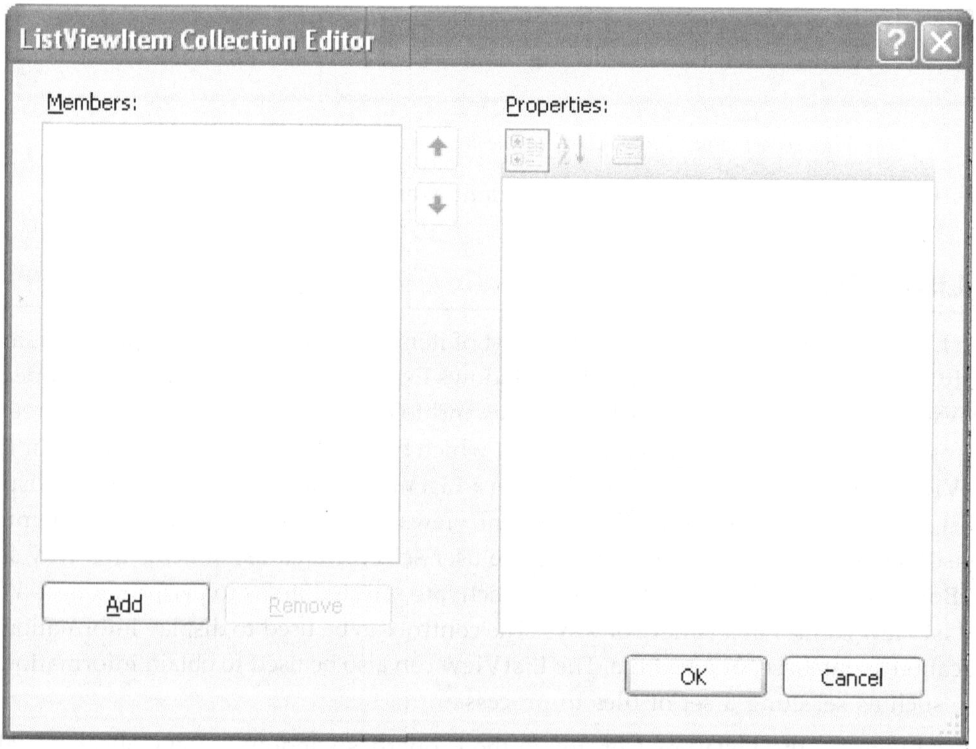

Fig. 16.6 *ListViewItem Collection Editor Window*

In this window, using **Add** and **Remove** Button we can add the items as in the Fig. 16.7 below.

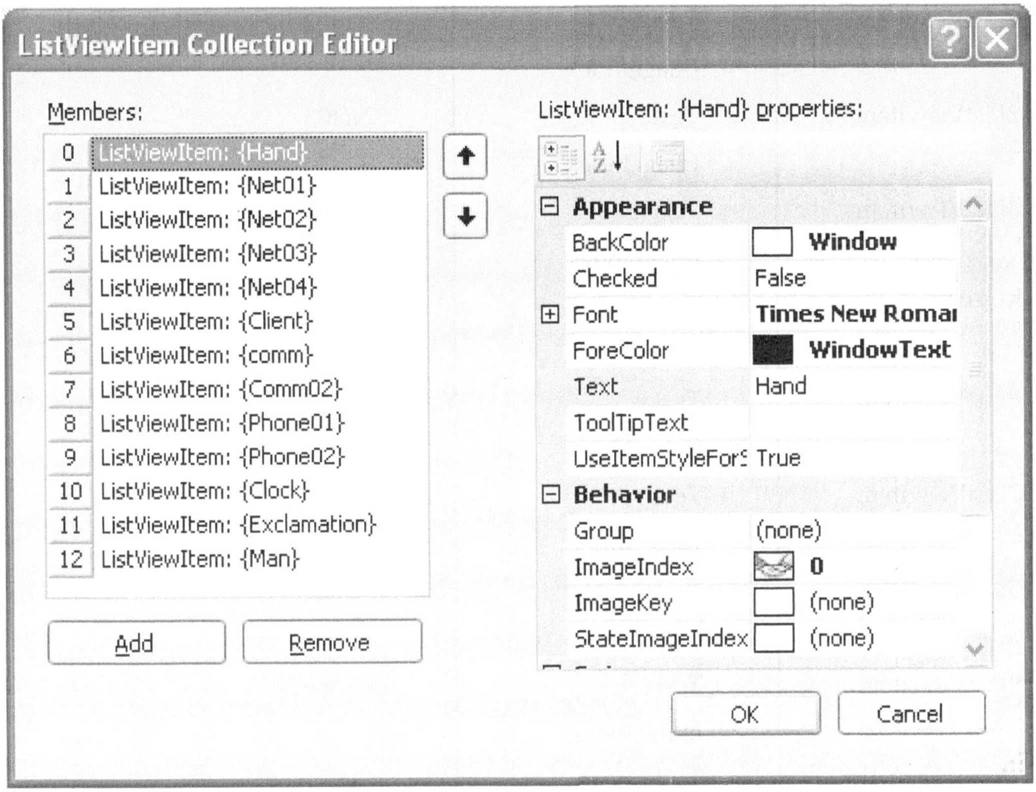

Fig. 16.7 *Items Added to the ListViewItem Collection Editor Window*

Displaying ListView in Various Styles

This program displays the **ListView** in various styles.

Form Designing

Table 16.1 Displaying ListView in Various Styles

Control	*Property*	*Value*
ImageList1	Name	ImageList1
	Image	(Collection)
ListView1	Name	ListView1
	LargeImageList	ImageList1
0ListViewItem	Text	Head
	ImageIndex	0

1ListViewItem	Text	Net01
	ImageIndex	1
2ListViewItem	Text	Net02
	ImageIndex	2
3ListViewItem	Text	Net03
	ImageIndex	3
4ListViewItem	Text	Net04
	ImageIndex	4
5ListViewItem	Text	Client
	ImageIndex	5
6ListViewItem	Text	Comm
	ImageIndex	6
7ListViewItem	Text	Comm2
	ImageIndex	7
8ListViewItem	Text	Phone01
	ImageIndex	8
9ListViewItem	Text	Phone2
	ImageIndex	9
10ListViewItem	Text	Clock
	ImageIndex	10
11ListViewItem	Text	Exclamation
	ImageIndex	11
12ListViewItem	Text	Man
	ImageIndex	12
RadioButton1	Name	RadioDetails
	Text	Details View
RadioButton2	Name	RadioLargeIcon
	Text	LargeIcon View
RadioButton3	Name	RadioList
	Text	List View
RadioButton4	Name	RadioTile
	Text	Tile View

Coding

```
Public Class Form1

 Private Sub RadioDetails _CheckedChanged(ByVal sender As System. Object,
ByVal e As System.EventArgs) Handles RadioDetails.CheckedChanged

        If RadioDetails.Checked = True Then

            ListView1.View = View.Details

        End If

    End Sub


    Private Sub RadioLargeIcon _CheckedChanged(ByVal sender As
System.Object, ByVal e As System.EventArgs) Handles RadioLargeIcon.
CheckedChanged

        If RadioLargeIcon.Checked = True Then

            ListView1.View = View.LargeIcon

        End If

    End Sub


    Private Sub RadioLargeIcon _CheckedChanged(ByVal sender As
System.Object, ByVal e As System.EventArgs)Handles RadioLargeIcon.
CheckedChanged

        If RadioLargeIcon.Checked = True Then

            ListView1.View = View.List

        End If

    End Sub


    Private Sub RadioList _CheckedChanged(ByVal sender As
System.Object, ByVal e As System.EventArgs)Handles RadioList.
CheckedChanged

        If RadioList.Checked = True Then

            ListView1.View = View.Tile

        End If

    End Sub

End Class
```

Output

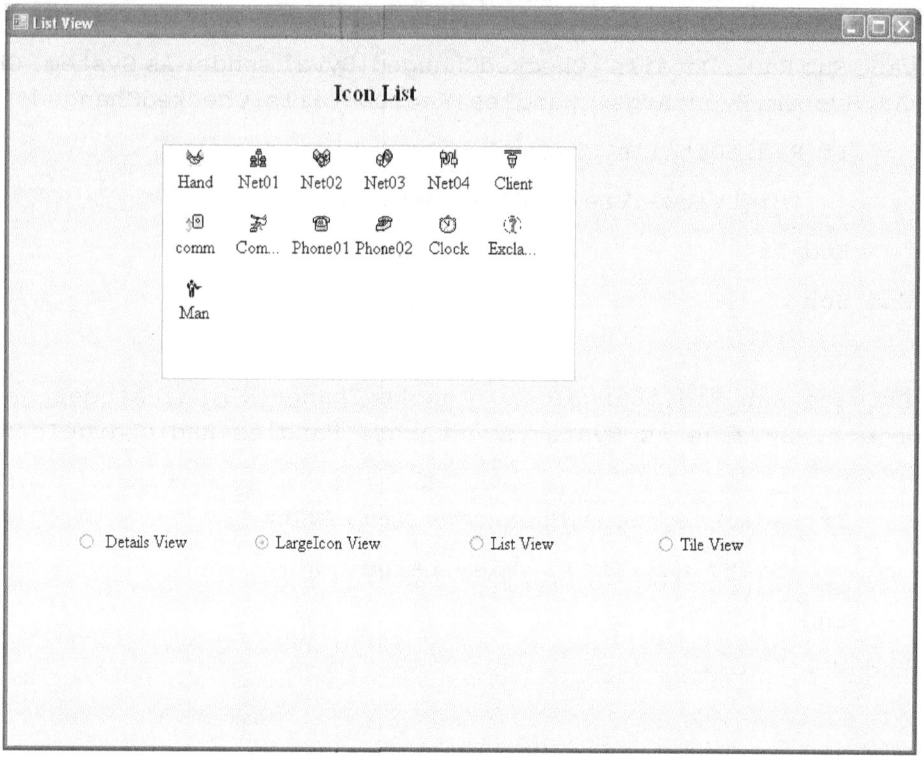
List View
Icon List
Hand
Net01
Net02
Net03
Net04
Client
comm
Com...
Phone01
Phone02
Clock
Excla...
Man
Details View
LargeIcon View
List View
Tile View

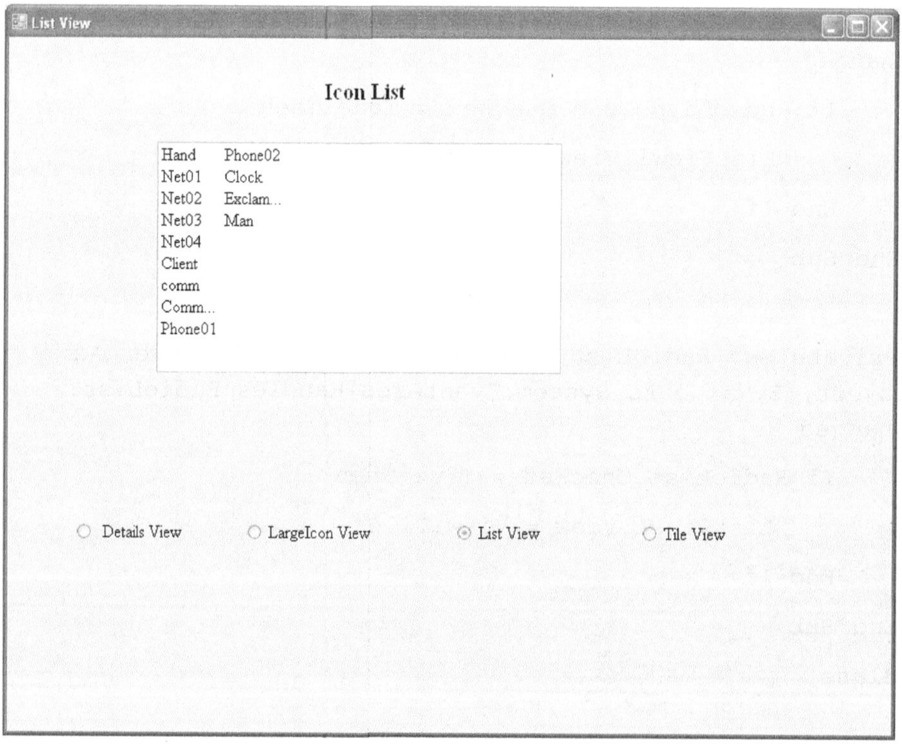
List View
Icon List
Hand
Net01
Net02
Net03
Net04
Client
comm
Comm...
Phone01
Phone02
Clock
Exclam...
Man
Details View
LargeIcon View
List View
Tile View

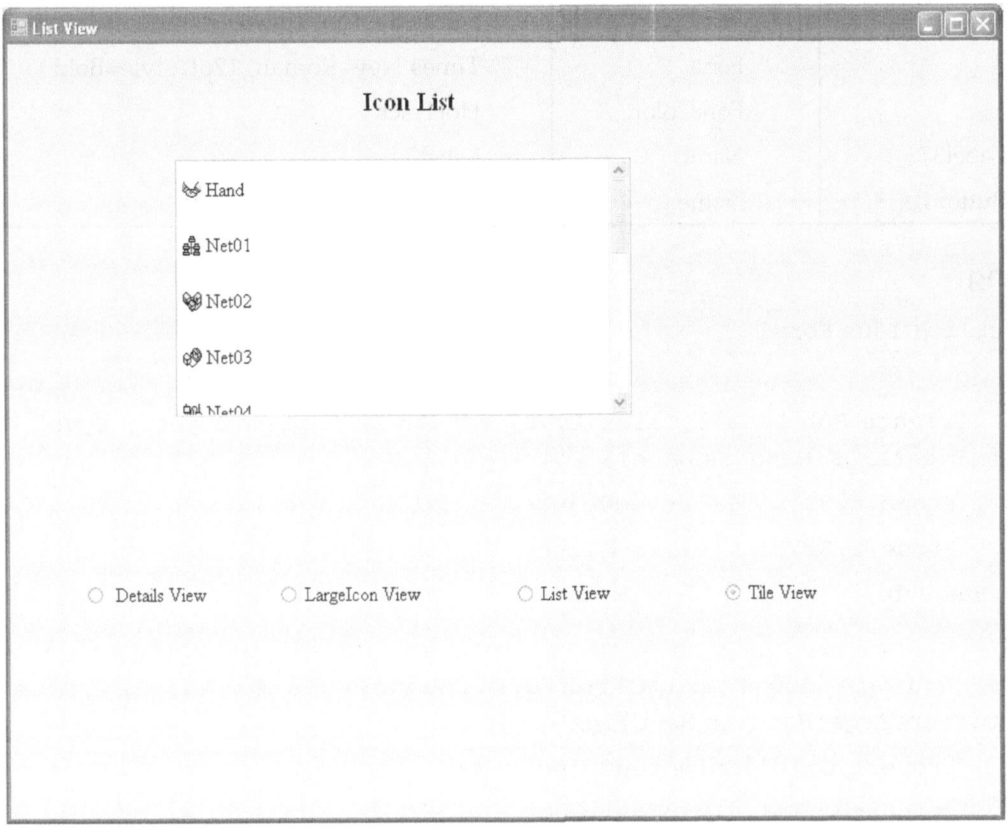

16.3 PROPERTY GRID

The **PropertyGrid** control is used to display the properties of the object assigned at that time. The information displayed in the grid is a snapshot of the properties at the time the object is assigned.

The property **SelectedObject** is used to assign the control to the **PropertyGrid.**

Designing the Form at Run Time

This program changes the properties of the form controls at runtime.

Form Designing

Table 16.2 Designing the Form at Run Time

Control	*Property*	*Value*
PropertyGrid1	Name	PropertyGrid1
Label1	Text	Form Designing at Runtime

	Font	Times New Roman, 24pt, style=Bold, Italic
Label2	Text	Select the Controls to change its properties
	Font	Times New Roman, 12pt, style=Bold
	ForeColor	HotTrack
Label3	Name	Label3
Button1	Name	Button1

Coding

```
Public Class Form1

    Private Sub Label3_Click(ByVal sender As System.Object, ByVal e As System.EventArgs)Handles Label3.Click
        PropertyGrid1.SelectedObject = Label3
        PropertyGrid1.Visible = True
    End Sub

    Private Sub Form1_Click(ByVal sender As Object, ByVal e As System.EventArgs)Handles Me.Click
        PropertyGrid1.SelectedObject = Me
        PropertyGrid1.Visible = True
    End Sub

    Private Sub Form1_Load(ByVal sender As System.Object, ByVal e As System.EventArgs) Handles MyBase.Load
        PropertyGrid1.Visible = False
    End Sub

    Private Sub Button1_Click(ByVal sender As System.Object, ByVal e As System.EventArgs) Handles Button1.Click
        PropertyGrid1.SelectedObject = Button1
        PropertyGrid1.Visible = True
    End Sub
End Class
```

Output

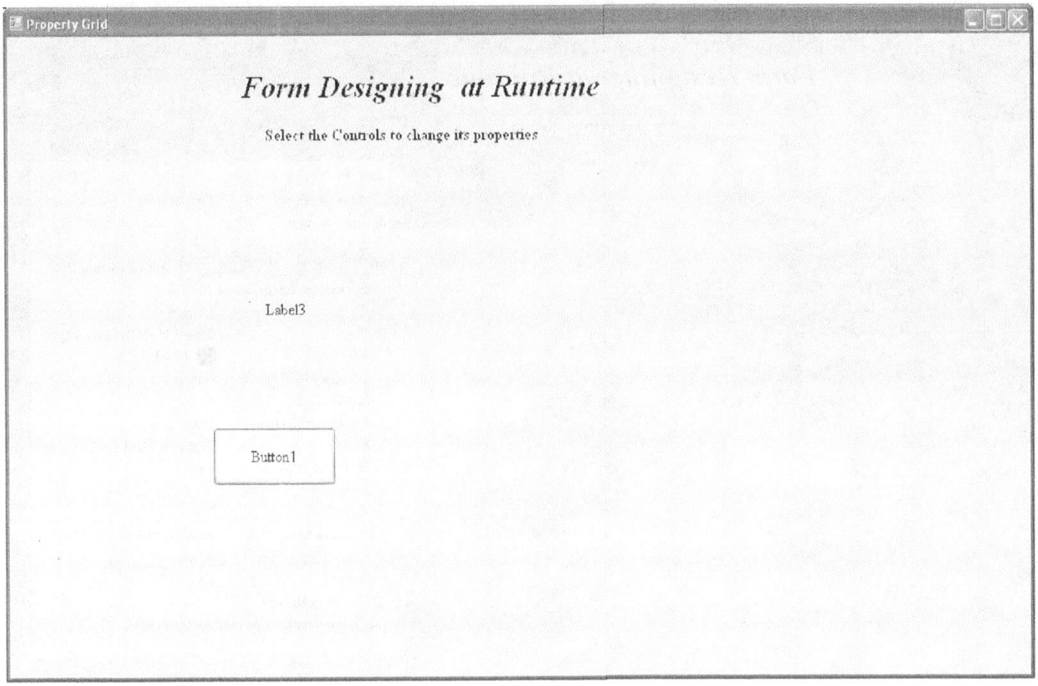
Property Grid
Form Designing at Runtime
Select the Controls to change its properties
Label3
Button1

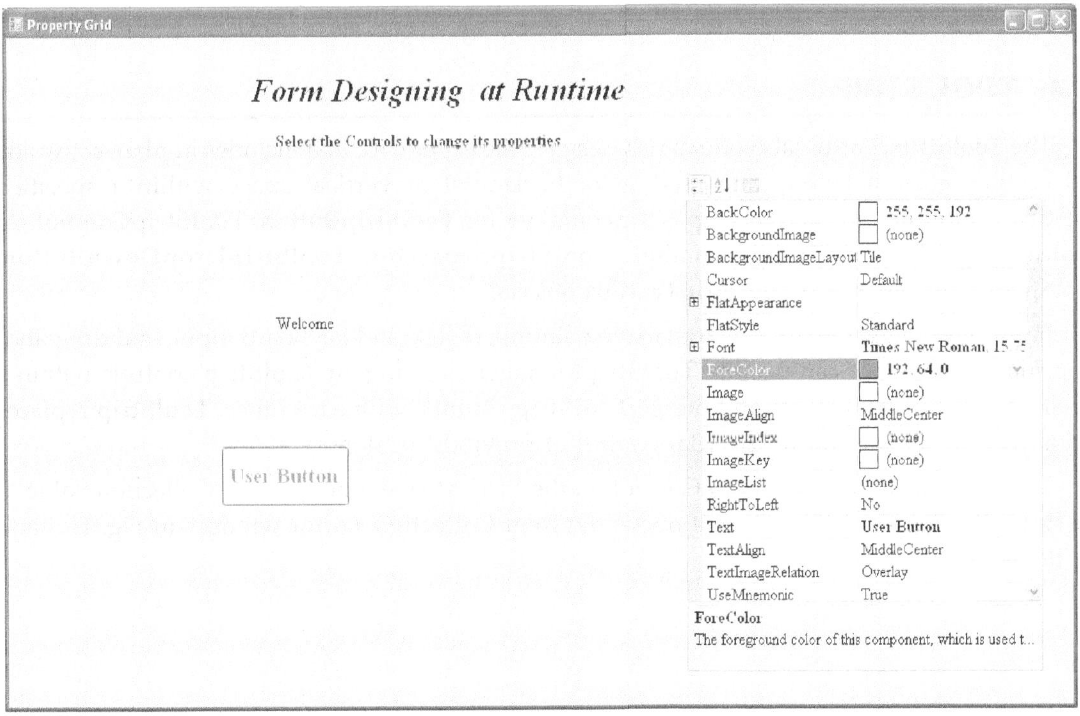
Property Grid
Form Designing at Runtime
Select the Controls to change its properties
Welcome
User Button
BackColor 255, 255, 192
BackgroundImage (none)
BackgroundImageLayout Tile
Cursor Default
FlatAppearance
FlatStyle Standard
Font Times New Roman, 15.75
ForeColor 192, 64, 0
Image (none)
ImageAlign MiddleCenter
ImageIndex (none)
ImageKey (none)
ImageList (none)
RightToLeft No
Text User Button
TextAlign MiddleCenter
TextImageRelation Overlay
UseMnemonic True
ForeColor
The foreground color of this component, which is used t...

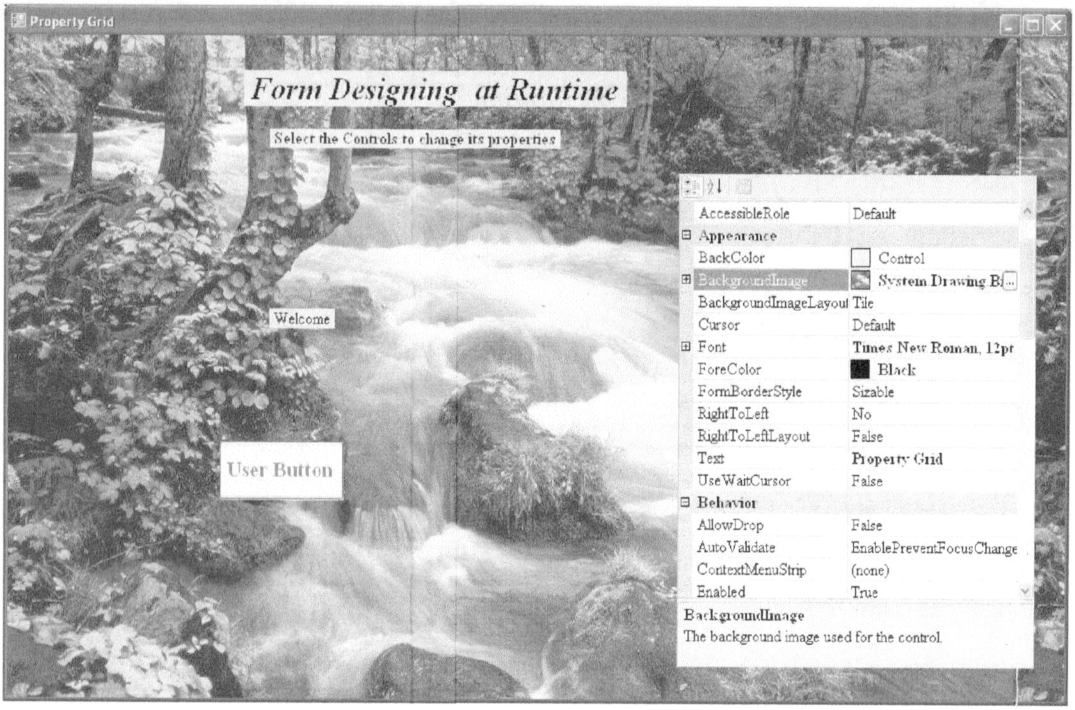

16.4 TOOL STRIP

The **ToolStrip** controls also offer a rich design-time experience that includes in-place activation and editing, custom layout, and sharing of horizontal or vertical space within a specified **ToolStripContainer**. This **ToolStrip** is the container for **ToolStripButton**, **ToolStripComboBox**, **ToolStripSplitButton**, **ToolStripLabel**, **ToolStripSeparator**, **ToolStripDropDownButton**, **ToolStripProgressBar**, and **ToolStripTextBox** objects.

It provides many members that manage painting, mouse and keyboard input, and drag-and-drop functionality, we can use the **ToolStripManager** class to join **ToolStrip** controls within a specified **ToolStripContainer** and merge **ToolStrip** controls with each other. **ToolStrip** replaces and adds functionality to the **ToolBar** control of previous versions.

To add items in the **ToolStrip** Control, in the Properties window, select Collection value of the **Items** Property as in Fig. 16.8, it opens the **Item Collection Editor** window in Fig. 16.9 and the Items as in Fig. 16.10.

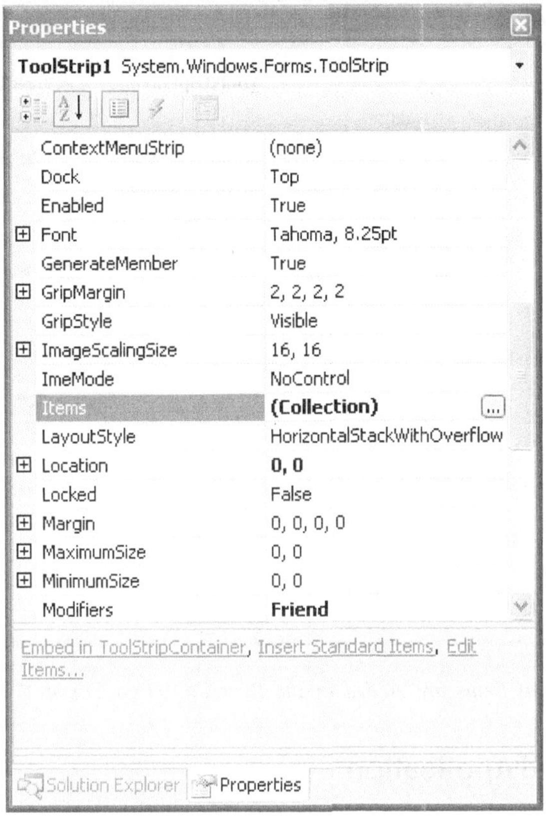

Fig. 16.8 *Properties Window of ToolStrip*

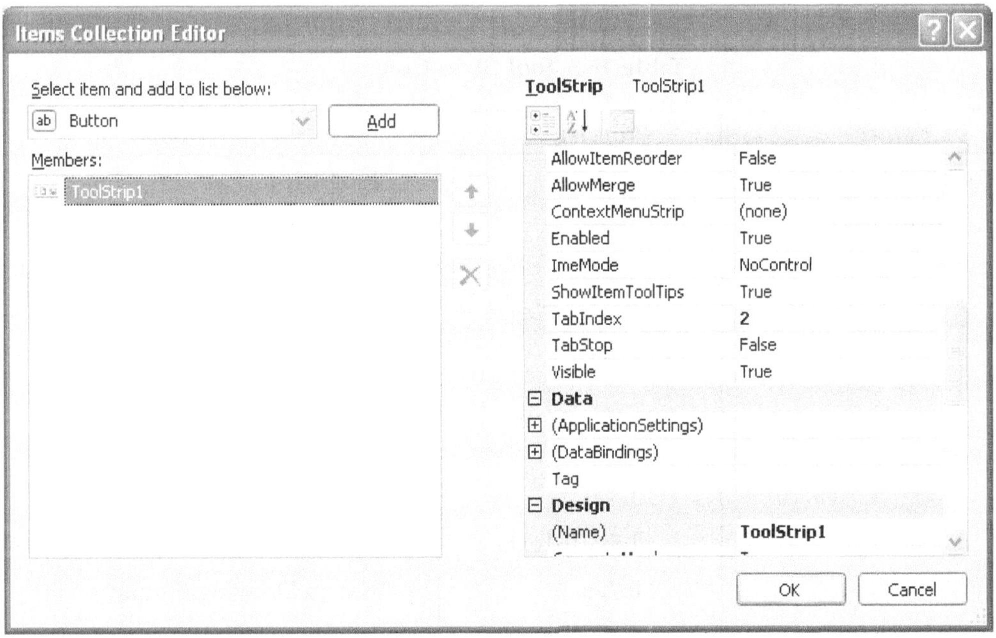

Fig. 16.9 *Item Collection Editor Window*

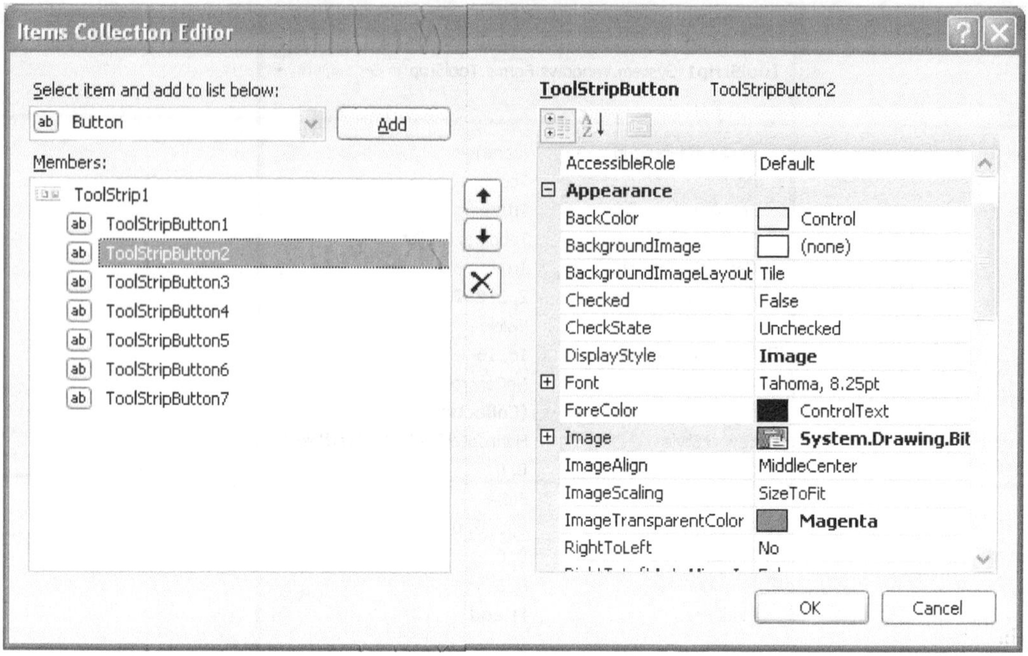

Fig. 16.10 *Items are Added in the Item Collection Editor Window*

Optimized Writing Pad Application

This program optimizes the writing pad application with the help of **ToolStrip** control.

Form Designing

Table 16.3 Tool Strip Control

Control	*Property*	*Value*
ToolStrip1	Name	ToolStrip1
ToolStripButton1	Name	ToolStripNew
	Text	New
	ToolTipText	New
	Image	System.Drawing.Bitmap [select icon file]
ToolStripButton2	Name	ToolStripOpen
	Text	Open
	ToolTipText	Open
	Image	System.Drawing.Bitmap [select icon file]

ToolStripButton3	Name	ToolStripSave
	Text	Save
	ToolTipText	Save
	Image	System.Drawing.Bitmap
		[select icon file]
ToolStripButton4	Name	ToolStripCut
	Text	Cut
	ToolTipText	Cut
	Image	System.Drawing.Bitmap
		[select icon file]
ToolStripButton5	Name	ToolStripCopy
	Text	Copy
	ToolTipText	Copy
	Image	System.Drawing.Bitmap
		[select icon file]
ToolStripButton6	Name	ToolStripPaste
	Text	Paste
	ToolTipText	Paste
	Image	System.Drawing.Bitmap
		[select icon file]
ToolStripButton7	Name	ToolStripPrint
	Text	Print
	ToolTipText	Print
	Image	System.Drawing.Bitmap
		[select icon file]
ToolStripButton8	Name	ToolStripPrintPreview
	Text	Print Preview
	ToolTipText	Print Preview
	Image	System.Drawing.Bitmap
		[select icon file]
MenuStrip1	Name	MenuStrip1
ToolStripMenuItem	Name	MnuFile
	Text	File
ToolStripMenuItem	Name	MnuNew

	Text	New
ToolStripMenuItem	Name	MnuOpen
	Text	Open
ToolStripMenuItem	Name	MnuSave
	Text	Save
ToolStripMenuItem	Name	MnuClose
	Text	Close
ToolStripMenuItem	Name	MnuExit
	Text	Exit
ToolStripMenuItem	Name	MnuEdit
	Text	Edit
ToolStripMenuItem	Name	MnuCut
	Text	Cut
ToolStripMenuItem	Name	MnuCopy
	Text	Copy
ToolStripMenuItem	Name	MnuPaste
	Text	Paste
ToolStripMenuItem	Name	MnuFormat
	Text	Format
ToolStripMenuItem	Name	MnuFont
	Text	Font
Color ToolStripMenuItem		
ToolStripMenuItem	Name	MnuBackcolor
	Text	Backcolor
ToolStripMenuItem	Name	MnuForeColor
	Text	ForeColor
ToolStripMenuItem	Name	MnuPrint
	Text	Print
ToolStripMenuItem	Name	MnuPrintPreview
	Text	Print Preview
ToolStripMenuItem	Name	MnuPagesetup
	Text	Page setup
PrintDocument1	Name	PrintDocument1
PageSetupDialog1	Name	PageSetupDialog1

	Document	PrintDocument1
PrintDialog1	Name	PrintDialog1
	Document	PrintDocument1
	AllowSelection	True
	AllowSomePages	True
PrintPreviewDialog1	Name	PrintPreviewDialog1
	Document	PrintDocument1
RichTextBox1	Name	RT1
FontDialog1	Name	FontDialog1
OpenFileDialog1	Name	OpenFileDialog1
SaveFileDialog1	Name	SaveFileDialog1
ColorDialog1	Name	ColorDialog1

Coding

```
Public Class Form1
  Dim s As String
  Private Sub NewToolStripMenuItem_Click(ByVal sender As System.Object, ByVal e As System.EventArgs) Handles Newmenu.Click
    RT1.Show()
    RT1.Text = ""
  End Sub
  Private Sub Openmnu_Click(ByVal sender As System.Object, ByVal e As System.EventArgs) Handles Openmnu.Click
    OpenFileDialog1.ShowDialog()
    RT1.LoadFile(OpenFileDialog1.FileName)
  End Sub

  Private Sub Savemnu_Click(ByVal sender As System.Object, ByVal e As System.EventArgs) Handles Savemnu.Click
    SaveFileDialog1.ShowDialog()
    RT1.SaveFile(SaveFileDialog1.FileName)
  End Sub

  Private Sub Closemnu_Click(ByVal sender As System.Object, ByVal e As System.EventArgs) Handles Closemnu.Click
    RT1.Hide()
```

```
    End Sub

    Private Sub Exitmnu_Click(ByVal sender As System.Object, ByVal e As
System.EventArgs) Handles Exitmnu.Click
        End
    End Sub

    Private Sub Cutmnu_Click(ByVal sender As System.Object, ByVal e As
System.EventArgs) Handles Cutmnu.Click
        s = RT1.SelectedText
        RT1.SelectedText = ""
    End Sub

    Private Sub Copymnu_Click(ByVal sender As System.Object, ByVal e As
System.EventArgs) Handles Copymnu.Click
        s = RT1.SelectedText
    End Sub

    Private Sub Pastemnu_Click(ByVal sender As System.Object, ByVal e As
System.EventArgs) Handles Pastemnu.Click
        RT1.SelectedText = s
    End Sub

    Private Sub Fontmnu_Click(ByVal sender As System.Object, ByVal e As
System.EventArgs) Handles Fontmnu.Click
        FontDialog1.ShowDialog()
        RT1.Font = FontDialog1.Font
    End Sub

    Private Sub Forcolor_Click(ByVal sender As System.Object, ByVal e As
System.EventArgs) Handles Forcolor.Click
        ColorDialog1.ShowDialog()
        RT1.ForeColor = ColorDialog1.Color
    End Sub

    Private Sub Backcolor_Click(ByVal sender As System.Object, ByVal e As
System.EventArgs) Handles Backcolor.Click
        ColorDialog1.ShowDialog()
        RT1.BackColor = ColorDialog1.Color
```

```
    End Sub

    Private Sub MnuPrint_Click(ByVal sender As System.Object, ByVal e As System.EventArgs) Handles MnuPrint.Click
        If PrintDialog1.ShowDialog = Windows.Forms.DialogResult.OK Then
            'showDialog method makes the dialog box visible at run time
            PrintDocument1.Print()
        End If

    End Sub

    Private Sub MnuPrintPreview_Click(ByVal sender As System.Object, ByVal e As System.EventArgs) Handles MnuPrintPreview.Click

        'Print preview

        Try
            PrintPreviewDialog1.ShowDialog()
            PrintPreviewDialog1.Update()

        Catch es As Exception
            MessageBox.Show(es.Message)
        End Try

    End Sub

    Private Sub MnuPageSetup_Click(ByVal sender As System.Object, ByVal e As System.EventArgs) Handles MnuPageSetup.Click

        'page setup
        With PageSetupDialog1
            .PageSettings = PrintDocument1.DefaultPageSettings
        End With
        Try
            If PageSetupDialog1.ShowDialog = Windows.Forms.DialogResult.OK Then
                PrintDocument1.DefaultPageSettings =
```

```
    PageSetupDialog1. PageSettings
          End If
        Catch es As Exception
          MessageBox.Show(es.Message)
        End Try
      End Sub

      Private Sub PrintDocument1_PrintPage(ByVal sender As Object, ByVal e
As System.Drawing.Printing.PrintPageEventArgs) Handles PrintDocument1.
PrintPage

        Static intCurrentChar As Int32    'to store the position of the last
printed char
        Dim font As New Font("Times New Roman", 16)    ' initializing the font
to be used for printing
        Dim PrintAreaHeight, PrintAreaWidth, marginLeft, marginTop As Int32

        'Default Page Settings
        With PrintDocument1.DefaultPageSettings
          ' initializing the bounds of the printing area
          PrintAreaHeight = .PaperSize.Height - .Margins.Top - .Margins.Bottom
          PrintAreaWidth = .PaperSize.Width - .Margins.Left - .Margins.Right
          ' initializing margin values
          marginLeft = .Margins.Left
          marginTop = .Margins.Top
        End With

        ' if the selection is landscape mode, swap the printing area height
and width
        If PrintDocument1.DefaultPageSettings.Landscape Then
          Dim intTemp As Int32
          intTemp = PrintAreaHeight
          PrintAreaHeight = PrintAreaWidth
          PrintAreaWidth = intTemp
        End If
```

```
        ' calculating the total number of lines
        Dim intLineCount As Int32 = CInt(PrintAreaHeight / font.Height)

        ' initializing the printing area
            Dim rectPrintingArea As New RectangleF(marginLeft, marginTop,
PrintAreaWidth, PrintAreaHeight)

        'instantiating the StringFormat class for text layout information
        Dim fmt As New StringFormat(StringFormatFlags.LineLimit)

        'determine the number of characters in the printing area rectangle
        Dim intLinesFilled, intCharsFitted As Int32
         e.Graphics.MeasureString(Mid(RT1.Text, intCurrentChar + 1), font,
New SizeF(PrintAreaWidth, PrintAreaHeight), fmt, intCharsFitted,
intLinesFilled)

        ' print the text to the page
           e.Graphics.DrawString(Mid(RT1.Text, intCurrentChar + 1), font,
Brushes.Black, rectPrintingArea, fmt)

      End Sub

    Private Sub ToolStripNew_Click(ByVal sender As System.Object, ByVal e
As System.EventArgs) Handles ToolStripNew.Click
        RT1.Show()
        RT1.Text = ""
      End Sub

      Private Sub ToolStripOpen_Click(ByVal sender As System.Object, ByVal
e As System.EventArgs) Handles ToolStripOpen.Click
        OpenFileDialog1.ShowDialog()
        RT1.LoadFile(OpenFileDialog1.FileName)
      End Sub

      Private Sub ToolStripSave_Click(ByVal sender As System.Object, ByVal
e As System.EventArgs) Handles ToolStripSave.Click
```

```
        SaveFileDialog1.ShowDialog()
        RT1.SaveFile(SaveFileDialog1.FileName)
    End Sub

    Private Sub ToolStripCut_Click(ByVal sender As System.Object, ByVal e
As System.EventArgs) Handles ToolStripCut.Click
        s = RT1.SelectedText
        RT1.SelectedText = ""
    End Sub

    Private Sub ToolStripCopy_Click(ByVal sender As System.Object, ByVal
e As System.EventArgs) Handles ToolStripCopy.Click
        s = RT1.SelectedText
    End Sub

    Private Sub ToolStripPrint_Click(ByVal sender As System.Object, ByVal
e As System.EventArgs) Handles ToolStripPrint.Click
        If PrintDialog1.ShowDialog = Windows.Forms.DialogResult.OK Then
            'showDialog method makes the dialog box visible at run time
            PrintDocument1.Print()
        End If
    End Sub

    Private Sub ToolStripPrintPreview_Click(ByVal sender As System.Object,
ByVal e As System.EventArgs) Handles ToolStripPrintPreview.Click
        'Print preview

        Try
            PrintPreviewDialog1.ShowDialog()
            PrintPreviewDialog1.Update()

        Catch es As Exception
            MessageBox.Show(es.Message)
        End Try
    End Sub
```

```
    Private Sub ToolStripPaste_Click(ByVal sender As System.Object, ByVal
e As System.EventArgs) Handles ToolStripPaste.Click
      RT1.SelectedText = s
    End Sub
End Class
```

output

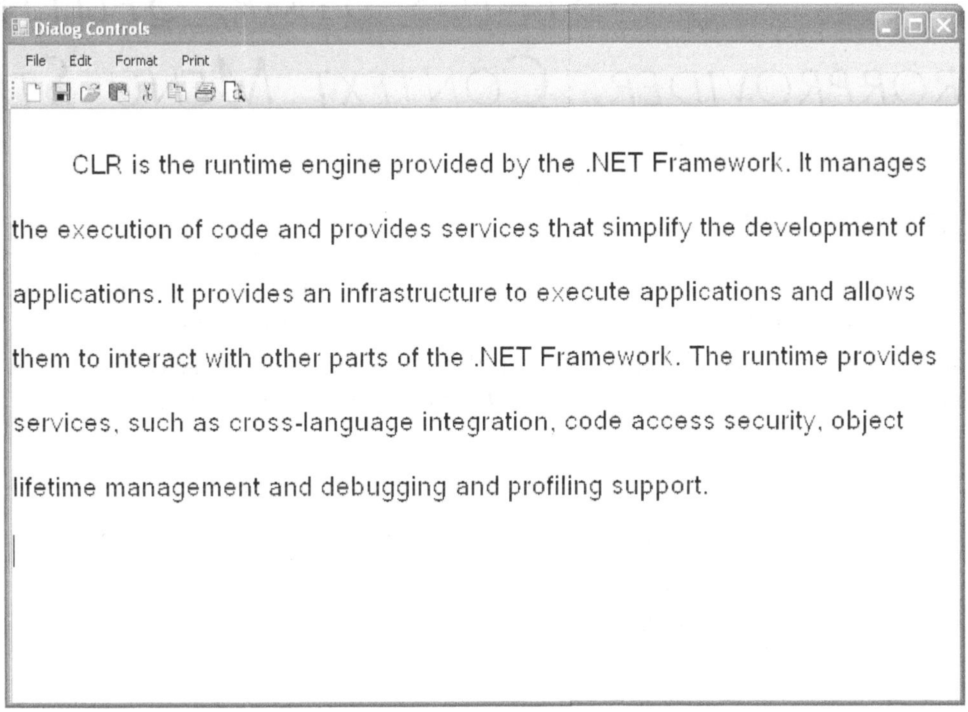

CHAPTER

17

STATUS STRIP, SPLITTER, ERRORPROVIDER, CONTEXT MENU STRIP

17.1 STATUS STRIP

StatusStrip is used to display status messages at the bottom of the form. They are generally used to provide additional information such as page numbers, display a message, etc

To add items in the **StatusStrip** Control, in the Properties window, select Collection value of the **Items** Property as in Fig. 17.1, it opens the **Items Collection Editor** window in Fig. 17.2 and adds the items as in Fig. 17.3

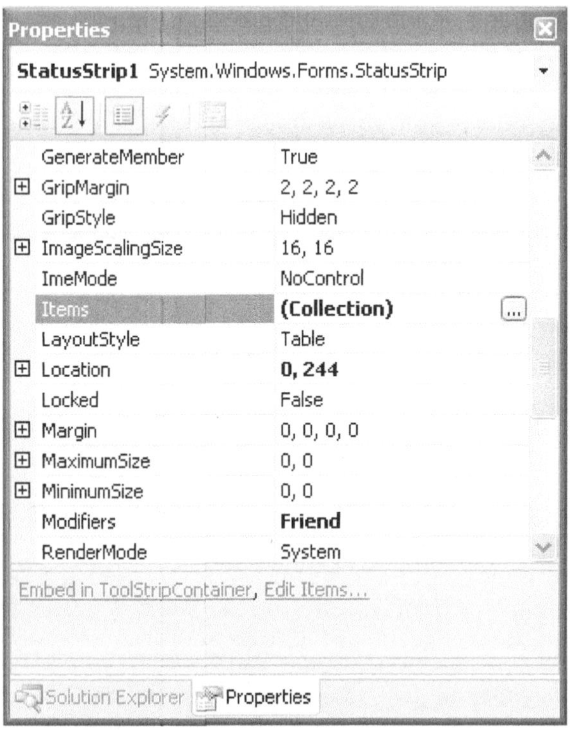

Fig. 17.1 *Properties Window of Status Strip*

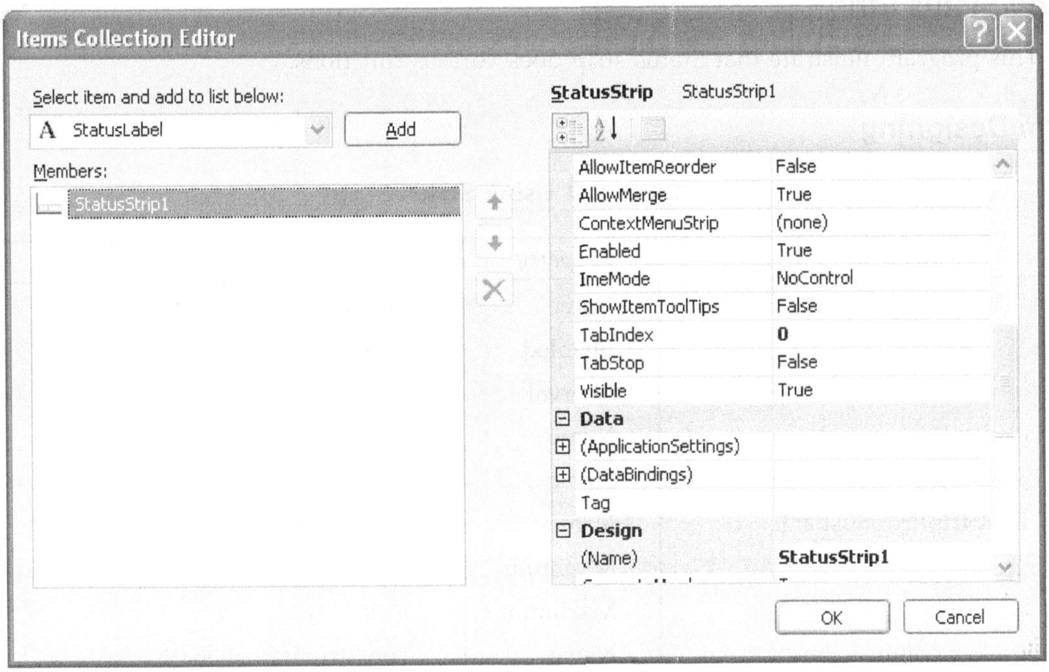

Fig. 17.2 *Items Collection Editor*

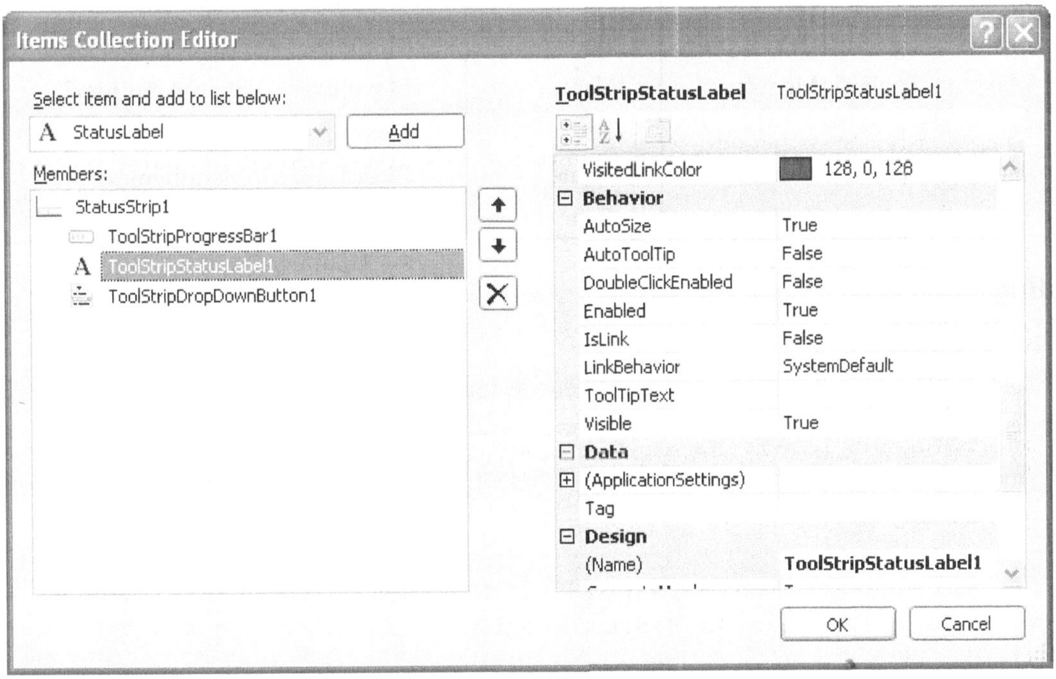

Fig. 17.3 *Items Added in the Items Collection Editor*

Using Status Strip

This program illustrate that Status strip does various functions.

Form Designing

Table 17.1 Using Status Strip

Control	*Property*	*Value*
Timer1	Name	Timer1
	Enabled	True
	Interval	100
Picture1	Name	MyPicture
StatusStrip1	Name	StatusStrip1
ToolStripProgressBar1	Name	ToolStripProgressBar1
	Minimum	0
	Maximum	100
ToolStripStatusLabel1	Name	ToolStripStatusLabel1
ToolStripDropDownButton1	Name	ToolStripDropDownButton1
MinimizeToolStripMenuItem1	Name	MinimizeToolStripMenuItem1
	Text	Minimize
MaximizeToolStripMenuItem	Name	MaximizeToolStripMenuItem2
	Text	Maximize
CloseToolStripMenuItem	Name	CloseToolStripMenuItem
	Text	Close

Coding

```
Public Class Form1
    Private Sub Form1_MouseMove(ByVal sender As Object, ByVal e As
System.Windows.Forms.MouseEventArgs) Handles Me.MouseMove
    ToolStripStatusLabel1.Text = e.X & " , " & e.Y
  End Sub

    Private Sub MinimizeToolStripMenuItem1_Click(ByVal sender As
System.Object, ByVal e As System.EventArgs) Handles MinimizeToolStrip
MenuItem1.Click
    Me.WindowState = FormWindowState.Minimized
  End Sub
```

```
    Private Sub MaximizeToolStripMenuItem_Click(ByVal sender As
System.Object, ByVal e As System.EventArgs) Handles MToolStripMenuItem.Click
        Me.WindowState = FormWindowState.Maximized
    End Sub

    Private Sub CloseToolStripMenuItem_Click(ByVal sender As System.Object,
ByVal e As System.EventArgs) Handles CloseToolStripMenuItem.Click
        End
    End Sub

    Private Sub Timer1_Tick(ByVal sender As System.Object, ByVal e As
System.EventArgs) Handles Timer1.Tick
        If ToolStripProgressBar1.Value < ToolStripProgressBar1.Maximum Then
            ToolStripProgressBar1.Value += 10
        Else
    MyPicture.Image = Image.FromFile("D:\karthikajesus\Scenary.jpg")
        End If
    End Sub
End Class
```

Output

17.2 SPLITTER

The **Splitter** control is used to resize other controls. The main purpose of **Splitter** control is to save space on the form. When we finish the work with a particular control we can move it away from their position or resize them with **Splitter** control. The **Splitter** control is invisible at runtime. If so, when the mouse is moved over it, the cursor of mouse is changed to indicating that it's a **Splitter** control and it can be resized. The **Splitter** control is based on the **Control** class.

Resize the TextBox at Run Time

This program resizes the textbox at run time.

Form Designing

The Fig. 17.4 shows the design view of form

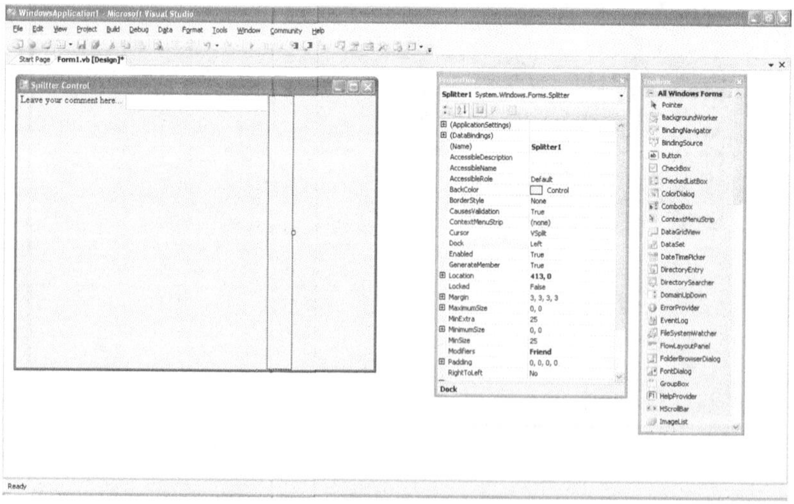

Fig. 17.4 *The Design View of Form*

Form Designing

Table 17.2 Resize the Textbox at Run Time

Control	*Property*	*Value*
Label1	Text	Leave your comment here...
Splitter1	Name	Splitter1
	Dock	Left [select the value]
TextBox1	Dock	Left [select the value]

Running of the above program will give the following output.

Output

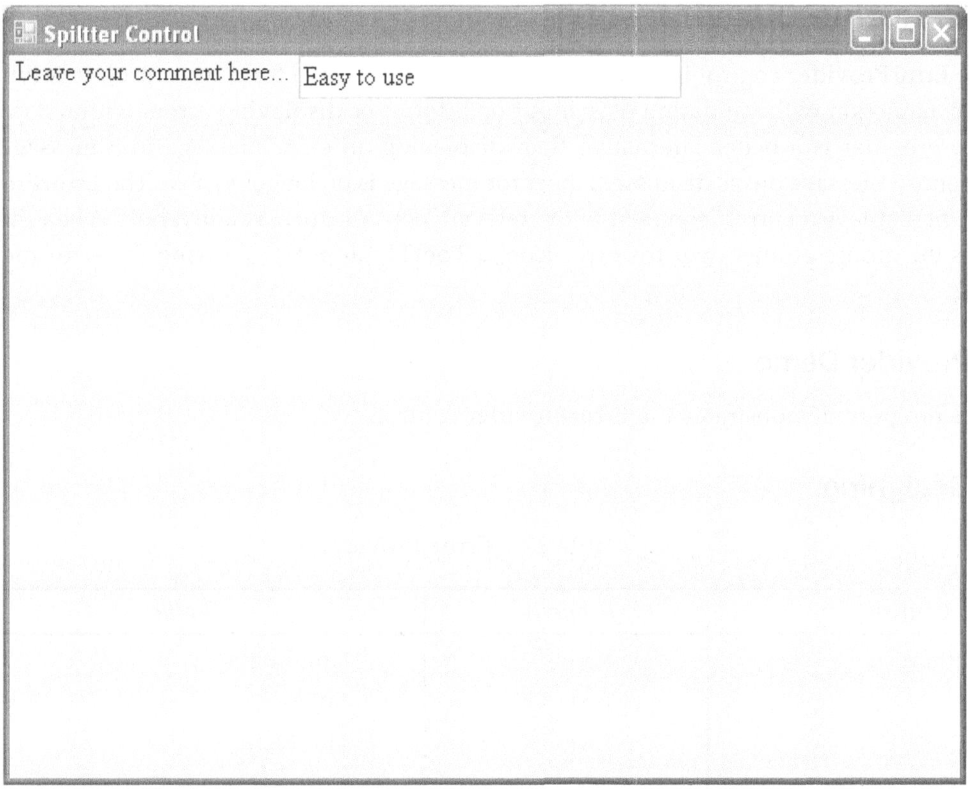

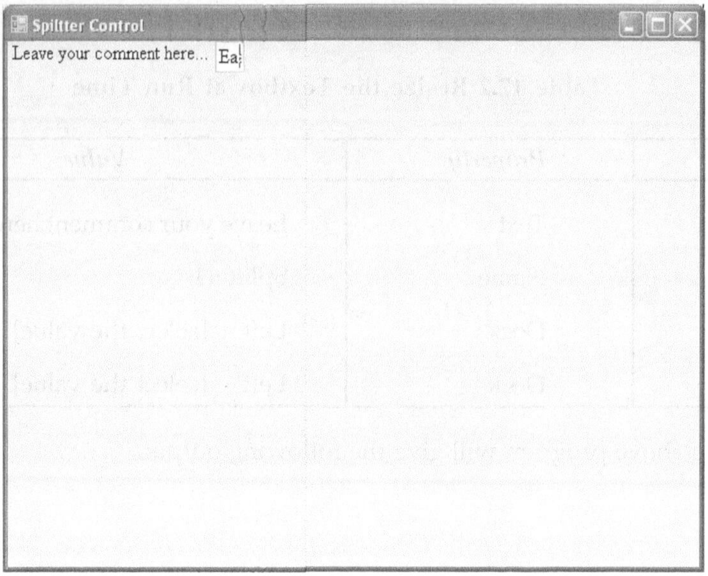

17.3 ERROR PROVIDER

The **ErrorProvider** control is used to validate user input on a form or control. It is typically used in conjunction with validating user input on a form, or displaying errors within a dataset. An error provider is a better alternative than displaying an error message in a message box, because once a message box is dismissed, the error message is no longer visible. The **ErrorProvider** component displays an error icon next to the relevant control, such as a text box. When the user positions the mouse pointer over the error icon, a **ToolTip** appears, showing the error message as string.

Error Provider Demo

This program demonstrates the **ErrorProvider** control.

Form Designing

Table 17.3 Error Provider

Control	*Property*	*Value*
Button1	Name	CmdLogin
	Text	Login
Label1	Text	UserName
Label2	Text	Password
TextBox1	Name	TxtUser
TextBox2	Name	TxtPwd
ErrorProvider1	Name	ErrorProvider1

Coding

```
Public Class Form1
    Private Sub CmdLogin_Click(ByVal sender As System.Object, ByVal e As System.EventArgs) Handles CmdLogin.Click
        MessageBox.Show("Welcome to Doamin", "Info")
    End Sub

    PrivateSubTxtUser_Leave(ByValsenderAsObject,ByValeAsSystem.EventArgs) Handles TextBox1.Leave
        If TxtUser.Text = "" Then
        ErrorProvider1.SetError(TxtUser, "You Must Enter Username")
        End If
    End Sub

    PrivateSubTxtPwd_Leave(ByValsenderAsObject,ByValeAsSystem.EventArgs) Handles TextBox2.Leave
        If TxtPwd.Text = "" Then
      ErrorProvider1.SetError(TxtPwd, "You Must Enter Password")
        End If
    End Sub
End Class
```

Output

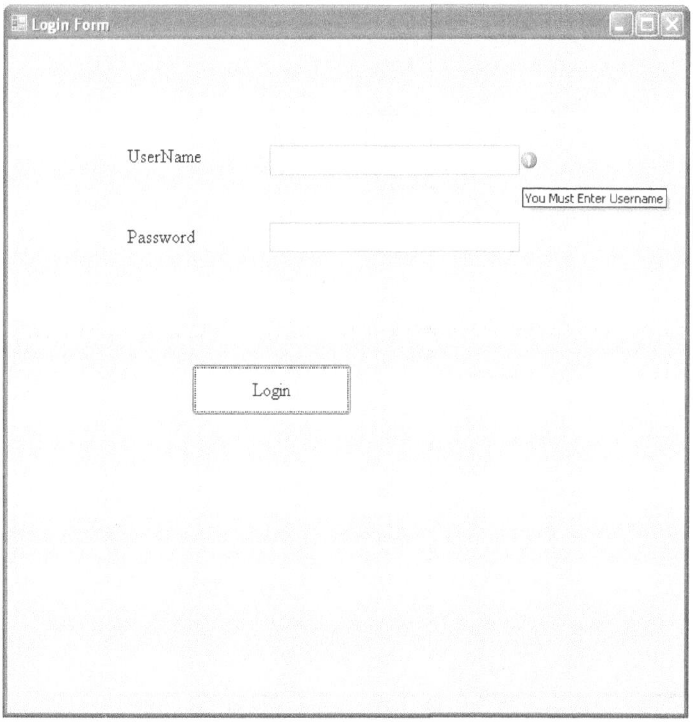

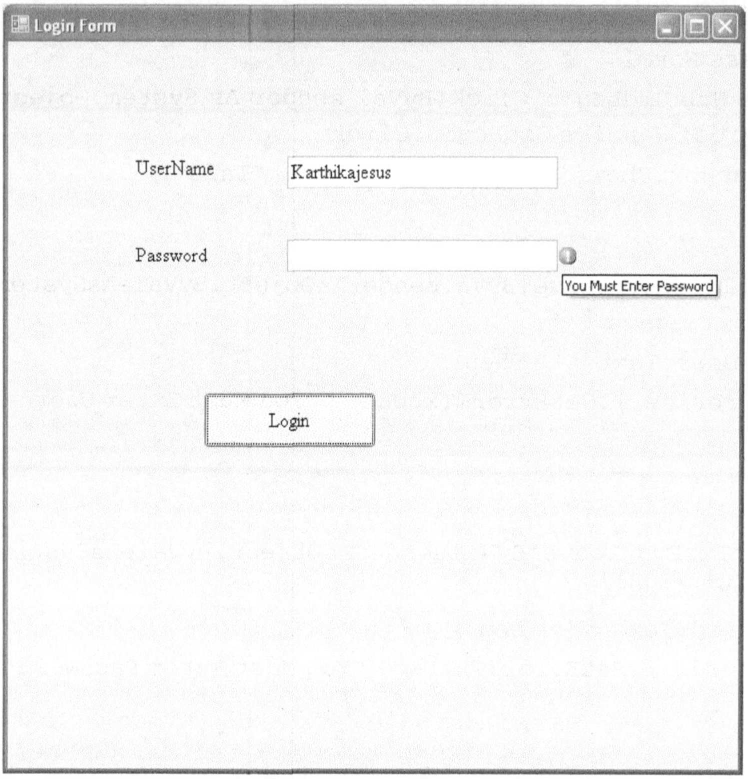
Login Form
UserName
Karthikajesus
Password
You Must Enter Password
Login

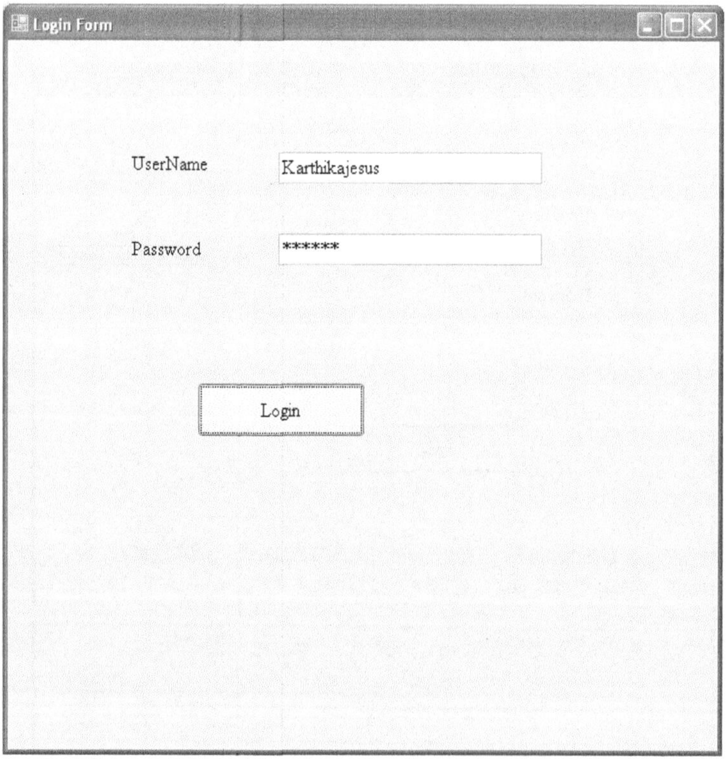
Login Form
UserName
Karthikajesus
Password
******
Login

17.4 CONTEXT MENU STRIP

ContextMenuStrip are shortcut menus that are displayed when right click the mouse button on the control such us **TextBox.** When we add this control to the form, it is added to the component tray, which appears at the bottom of the form. The component tray appears at design time and is used as a container to hold controls, such as **ColorDialog** control, **FontDialog** control, **PrintDialog** control, **MenuStrip** control and **ContextMenuStrip** control.

Context Menu Strip Demo

This program demonstrates the use of **ContextMenuStrip** control.

Form Designing

Table 17.4 Context Menu Strip

Control	*Property*	*Value*
ContextMenuStrip1	Name	ContextMenuStrip1
ToolStripMenuItem	Name	RedToolStripMenuItem
	Text	Red
ToolStripMenuItem	Name	BlueToolStripMenuItem
	Text	Blue
ToolStripMenuItem	Name	GreenToolStripMenuItem
	Text	Green
Label1	Text	Type Your Text Here
TextBox1	Name	TxtDisplay
	ContextMenuStrip	ContextMenuStrip1

Coding

```
Public Class Form1
  Private Sub BlueToolStripMenuItem_Click(ByVal sender As Object, ByVal
e As System.EventArgs) Handles BlueToolStripMenuItem.Click
    TextBox1.ForeColor = Color.Blue
  End Sub
```

```
    Private Sub RedToolStripMenuItem_Click(ByVal sender As System.Object,
ByVal e As System.EventArgs) Handles RedToolStripMenuItem.Click
        TextBox1.ForeColor = Color.Red
    End Sub

    Private Sub GreenToolStripMenuItem_Click(ByVal sender As System.Object,
ByVal e As System.EventArgs) Handles GreenToolStripMenuItem.Click
        TextBox1.ForeColor = Color.Green
    End Sub
End Class
```

Output

While running the program right clicks the text box, the context menu strip appears.

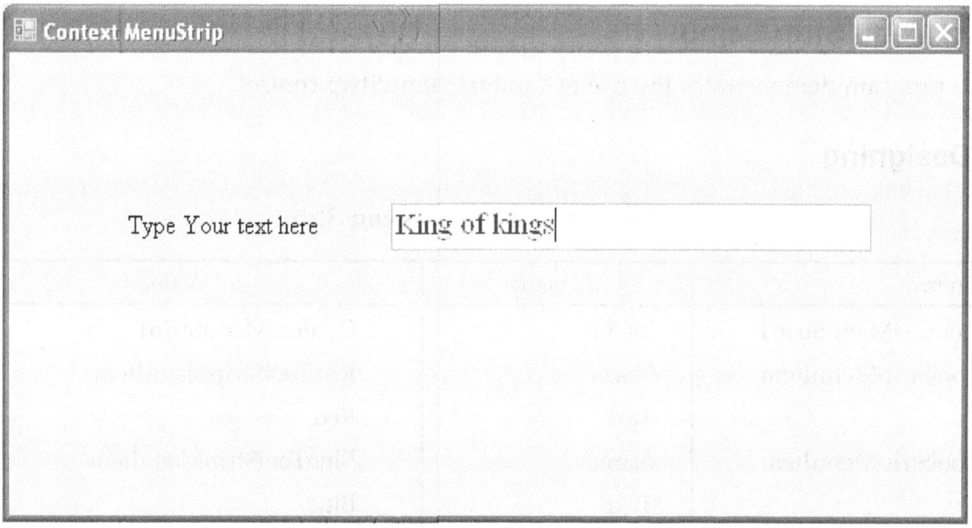

CHAPTER

18

DIALOG CONTROLS IN PRINT OPERATION

18.1 PRINT DIALOGS

Providing support for Printing is one of the common tasks during application development. The .NET Framework provides excellent support for printing documents.

PrintDocument Component

In the .NET Framework, a printed document is represented by the **PrintDocument** component. The **PrintDocument** object encapsulates all the information needed to print a page. They handle the events and operations of printing. **PrintPage** is the foundational printing event. This event gets fired for every page that will be printed

PageSetupDialog

Page Setup dialogs are used to specify page details for printing. This dialog allows us to set borders and adjustments, portraits, orientation, etc. You use the **PrinterSettings** property of this dialog to get a Printer Settings object that holds settings the user specified. The **PageSetupDialog** exposes a Document property that specifies the **PrintDocument** to use. Setting the Document property binds the specified **PrintDocument** to the **PageSetupDialog** and any changes made in this dialog are updated in the **PrinterSettings** property.

PrintPreviewDialog

Print Preview dialogs are supported by the **PrintPreviewDialog** class and they allow us to preview the document before printing. You can preview a document by setting the **Document** property of the **PrintPreviewDialog** object to the **PrintDocument** object. Once set, the **PrintPreviewDialog** provides functionality to zoom, print, to view multiple pages of the preview, etc.

Printing the Document

This program prints the document.

Form Designing

Table 18.1 Printing the Document

Control	*Property*	*Value*
MenuStrip1	Name	MenuStrip1
ToolStripMenuItem	Name	MnuFile
	Text	File
ToolStripMenuItem	Name	MnuNew
	Text	New
ToolStripMenuItem	Name	MnuOpen
	Text	Open
ToolStripMenuItem	Name	MnuSave
	Text	Save
ToolStripMenuItem	Name	MnuClose
	Text	Close
ToolStripMenuItem	Name	MnuExit
	Text	Exit
ToolStripMenuItem	Name	MnuEdit
	Text	Edit
ToolStripMenuItem	Name	MnuCut
	Text	Cut
ToolStripMenuItem	Name	MnuCopy
	Text	Copy
ToolStripMenuItem	Name	MnuPaste
	Text	Paste
ToolStripMenuItem	Name	MnuFormat
	Text	Format
ToolStripMenuItem	Name	MnuFont
	Text	Font
Color ToolStripMenuItem		
ToolStripMenuItem	Name	MnuBackcolor
	Text	Backcolor
ToolStripMenuItem	Name	MnuForeColor
	Text	ForeColor

ToolStripMenuItem	Name	MnuPrint
	Text	Print
ToolStripMenuItem	Name	MnuPrintPreview
	Text	Print Preview
ToolStripMenuItem	Name	MnuPagesetup
	Text	Page setup
PrintDocument1	Name	PrintDocument1
PageSetupDialog1	Name	PageSetupDialog1
	Document	PrintDocument1
PrintDialog1	Name	PrintDialog1
	Document	PrintDocument1
	AllowSelection	True
	AllowSomePages	True
PrintPreviewDialog1	Name	PrintPreviewDialog1
	Document	PrintDocument1
RichTextBox1	Name	RT1
FontDialog1	Name	FontDialog1
OpenFileDialog1	Name	OpenFileDialog1
SaveFileDialog1	Name	SaveFileDialog1
ColorDialog1	Name	ColorDialog1

Coding

```
Public Class Form1
    Dim s As String
      Private Sub NewToolStripMenuItem_Click(ByVal sender As System.Object, ByVal e As System.EventArgs) Handles Newmenu.Click
        RT1.Show()
        RT1.Text = ""
    End Sub
    Private Sub Openmnu_Click(ByVal sender As System.Object, ByVal e As System.EventArgs) Handles Openmnu.Click
        OpenFileDialog1.ShowDialog()
        RT1.LoadFile(OpenFileDialog1.FileName)
    End Sub
```

```
    Private Sub Savemnu_Click(ByVal sender As System.Object, ByVal
e As System.EventArgs) Handles Savemnu.Click
            SaveFileDialog1.ShowDialog()
            RT1.SaveFile(SaveFileDialog1.FileName)
    End Sub

    Private Sub Closemnu_Click(ByVal sender As System.Object,
ByVal e As System.EventArgs) Handles Closemnu.Click
            RT1.Hide()
    End Sub

    Private Sub Exitmnu_Click(ByVal sender As System.Object, ByVal
e As System.EventArgs) Handles Exitmnu.Click
            End
    End Sub

    Private Sub Cutmnu_Click(ByVal sender As System.Object, ByVal
e As System.EventArgs) Handles Cutmnu.Click
            s = RT1.SelectedText
            RT1.SelectedText = ""
    End Sub

    Private Sub Copymnu_Click(ByVal sender As System.Object, ByVal
e As System.EventArgs) Handles Copymnu.Click
            s = RT1.SelectedText
    End Sub

    Private Sub Pastemnu_Click(ByVal sender As System.Object,
ByVal e As System.EventArgs) Handles Pastemnu.Click
            RT1.SelectedText = s
    End Sub

    Private Sub Fontmnu_Click(ByVal sender As System.Object, ByVal
e As System.EventArgs) Handles Fontmnu.Click
            FontDialog1.ShowDialog()
            RT1.Font = FontDialog1.Font
    End Sub
```

```
    Private Sub Forcolor_Click(ByVal sender As System.Object,
ByVal e As System.EventArgs) Handles Forcolor.Click
        ColorDialog1.ShowDialog()
        RT1.ForeColor = ColorDialog1.Color
    End Sub

    Private Sub Backcolor_Click(ByVal sender As System.Object,
ByVal e As System.EventArgs) Handles Backcolor.Click
        ColorDialog1.ShowDialog()
        RT1.BackColor = ColorDialog1.Color
    End Sub

    Private Sub MnuPrint_Click(ByVal sender As System.Object,
ByVal e As System.EventArgs) Handles MnuPrint.Click
        If PrintDialog1.ShowDialog = Windows.Forms.DialogResult.OK
Then
            'showDialog method makes the dialog box visible
at run time
            PrintDocument1.Print()
        End If

    End Sub

    Private Sub MnuPrintPreview_Click(ByVal sender As System.Object,
ByVal e As System.EventArgs) Handles MnuPrintPreview.Click

        'Print preview

        Try
            PrintPreviewDialog1.ShowDialog()
            PrintPreviewDialog1.Update()

        Catch es As Exception
            MessageBox.Show(es.Message)
        End Try

    End Sub
```

```
        Private Sub MnuPageSetup_Click(ByVal sender As System.Object,
ByVal e As System.EventArgs) Handles MnuPageSetup.Click

            'page setup
            With PageSetupDialog1
                .PageSettings = PrintDocument1.DefaultPageSettings
            End With
            Try
                        If PageSetupDialog1.ShowDialog =
Windows.Forms.DialogResult.OK Then
                            PrintDocument1.DefaultPageSettings =
PageSetupDialog1.PageSettings
                End If
            Catch es As Exception
                MessageBox.Show(es.Message)
            End Try
        End Sub

        Private Sub PrintDocument1_PrintPage(ByVal sender As Object,
ByVal e As System.Drawing.Printing.PrintPageEventArgs) Handles
PrintDocument1.PrintPage

            Static intCurrentChar As Int32       'to store the
position of the last printed char
            Dim font As New Font("Times New Roman", 16)        '
initializing the font to be used for printing
          Dim PrintAreaHeight, PrintAreaWidth, marginLeft, marginTop
As Int32

            'Default Page Settings
            With PrintDocument1.DefaultPageSettings
                ' initializing the bounds of the printing area
              PrintAreaHeight = .PaperSize.Height - .Margins.Top
- .Margins.Bottom
                PrintAreaWidth = .PaperSize.Width - .Margins.Left
- .Margins.Right
                ' initializing margin values
```

```
                marginLeft = .Margins.Left
                marginTop = .Margins.Top
            End With

            'if the selection is landscape mode, swap the printing
area height and width
            If PrintDocument1.DefaultPageSettings.Landscape Then
                Dim intTemp As Int32
                intTemp = PrintAreaHeight
                PrintAreaHeight = PrintAreaWidth
                PrintAreaWidth = intTemp
            End If

            'calculating the total number of lines
             Dim intLineCount As Int32 = CInt(PrintAreaHeight /
font.Height)

            'initializing the printing area
              Dim rectPrintingArea As New RectangleF(marginLeft,
marginTop, PrintAreaWidth, PrintAreaHeight)

            'instantiating the StringFormat class for text layout
information
           Dim fmt As New StringFormat(StringFormatFlags.LineLimit)

             'determine the number of characters in the printing
area rectangle
            Dim intLinesFilled, intCharsFitted As Int32
            e.Graphics.MeasureString(Mid(RT1.Text, intCurrentChar +
1), font, New SizeF(PrintAreaWidth, PrintAreaHeight), fmt, intCharsFitted,
intLinesFilled)

            'print the text to the page
           e.Graphics.DrawString(Mid(RT1.Text, intCurrentChar + 1),
font, Brushes.Black, rectPrintingArea, fmt)

        End Sub
    End Class
```

Output

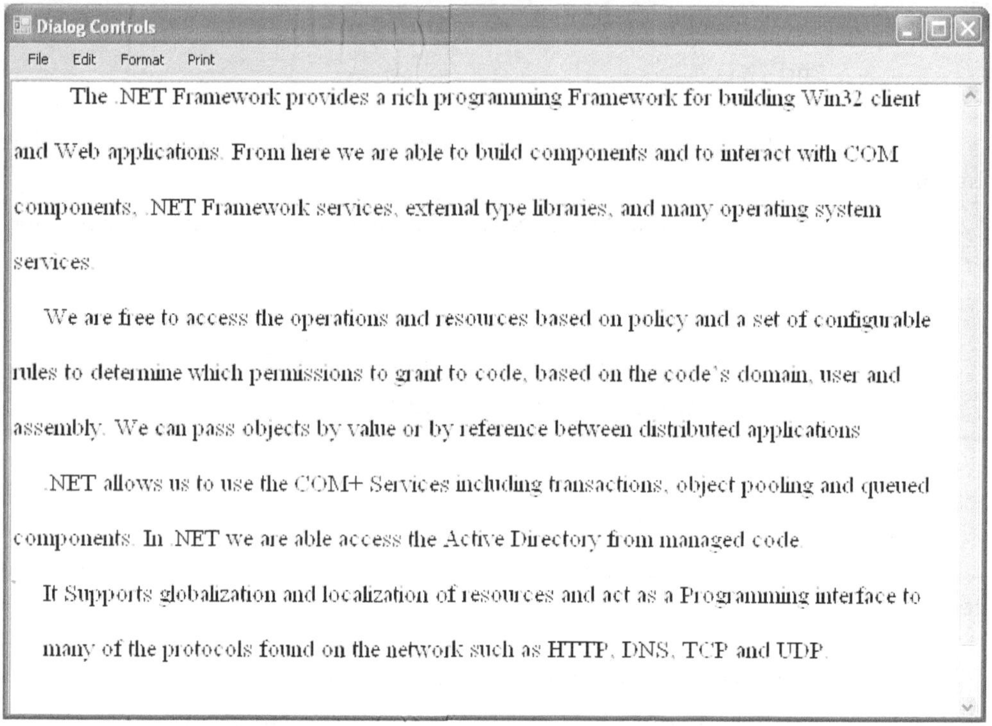
Dialog Controls
File Edit Format Print
The .NET Framework provides a rich programming Framework for building Win32 client and Web applications. From here we are able to build components and to interact with COM components, .NET Framework services, external type libraries, and many operating system services.
We are free to access the operations and resources based on policy and a set of configurable rules to determine which permissions to grant to code, based on the code's domain, user and assembly. We can pass objects by value or by reference between distributed applications
.NET allows us to use the COM+ Services including transactions, object pooling and queued components. In .NET we are able access the Active Directory from managed code.
It Supports globalization and localization of resources and act as a Programming interface to many of the protocols found on the network such as HTTP, DNS, TCP and UDP.

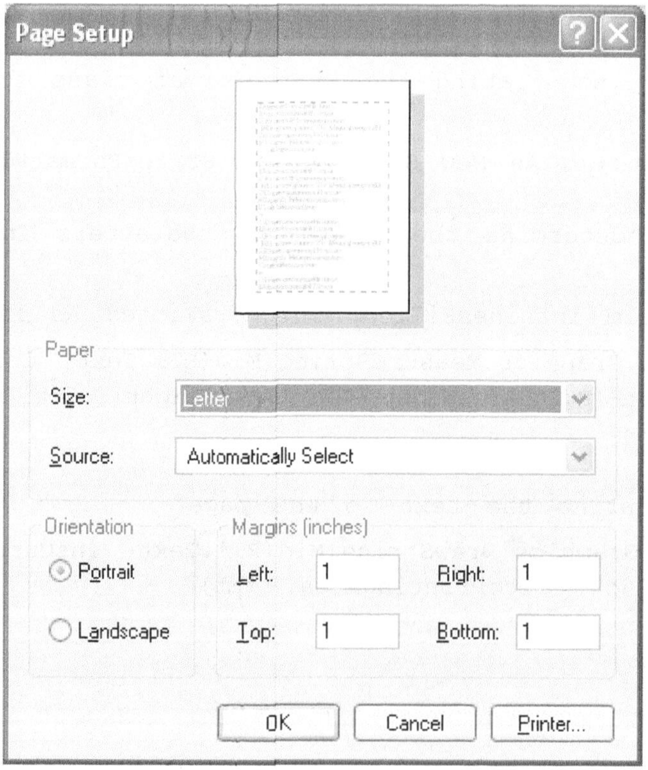
Page Setup
Paper
Size:
Letter
Source:
Automatically Select
Orientation
Portrait
Landscape
Margins (inches)
Left:
1
Right:
1
Top:
1
Bottom:
1
OK
Cancel
Printer...

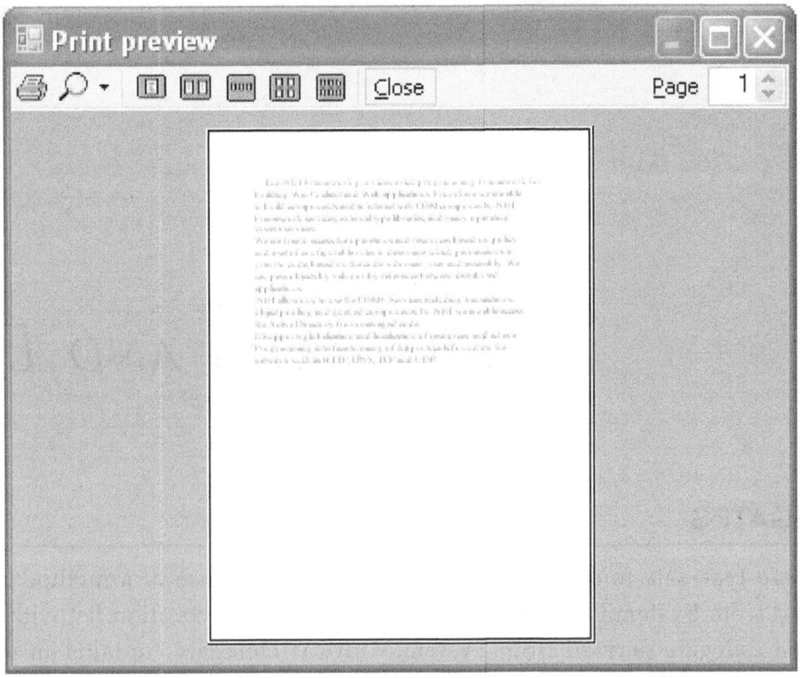
Print preview
Close
Page
1

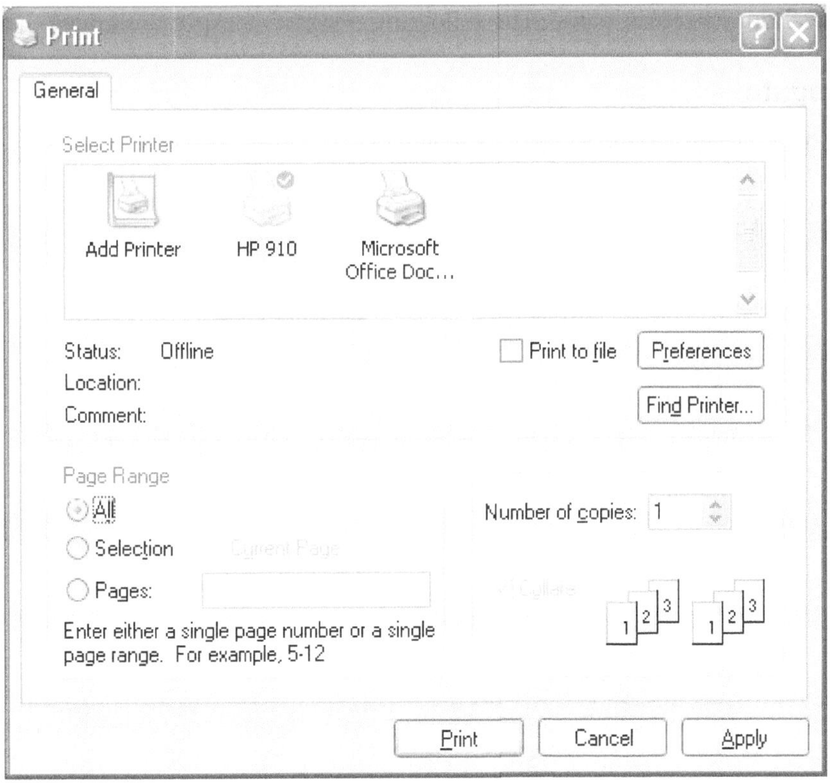
Print
General
Select Printer
Add Printer
HP 910
Microsoft Office Doc...
Status: Offline
Location:
Comment:
Print to file
Preferences
Find Printer...
Page Range
All
Selection
Pages:
Enter either a single page number or a single page range. For example, 5-12
Number of copies: 1
Print
Cancel
Apply

CHAPTER

19

DELEGATES AND EVENTS

19.1 DELEGATES

Delegates are type-safe function pointers that hold a reference of a method. A **Singlecast delegate** derived from **System.Delegate** class that contains an invocation list with one method. And a **Multicast delegate** derived from **System.MulticastDelegate** contains an invocation list with multiple methods. When we declare a delegate, we tell the compiler the type of each parameter and about its return value. The following program simply illustrates the delegates.

Simple Delegate

This simple program shows the use of delegate.

```
Imports System.Delegate
Module Module1
    Delegate Function Fun_delegate(ByVal Num As Integer)
'declaration of delegate
    Class Function_Pack
        Public Function Square(ByVal N As Integer)
            Return (N * N)
        End Function
        Public Function Cube(ByVal N As Integer)
            Return (N * N * N)
        End Function
        Public Function fact(ByVal N As Integer)
            Dim f As Integer = 1
            Dim i As Integer
            For i = 1 To N
```

```
                f = f * i
            Next
            Return f
        End Function
        Public Function Sqrt(ByVal N As Integer)
            Return (Math.Sqrt(N))
        End Function

    End Class
    Sub Main()
        Dim Deg1 As Fun_delegate
        Dim Deg2 As Fun_delegate
        Dim Deg3 As Fun_delegate
        Dim Deg4 As Fun_delegate

        Dim FP As New Function_Pack()

        Dim Num As Integer
        Console.WriteLine("Enter the Number : ")
        Num = Integer.Parse(Console.ReadLine())

       'Construct the delegat
        Deg1 = New Fun_delegate(AddressOf FP.Square)
        Deg2 = New Fun_delegate(AddressOf FP.Cube)
        Deg3 = New Fun_delegate(AddressOf FP.fact)
        Deg4 = New Fun_delegate(AddressOf FP.Sqrt)

  'call the method through delegate

Console.WriteLine("Square of {0} is {1} ", Num, Deg1.Invoke(Num))
Console.WriteLine("Cube of {0} is {1} ", Num, Deg2.Invoke(Num))
Console.WriteLine("Factorial of {0} is {1} ", Num, Deg3.Invoke(Num))
Console.WriteLine("Square Root of {0} is {1} ", Num, Deg4.Invoke(Num))
        Console.ReadLine()

    End Sub
```

```
End Module
```

Output

```
Enter the Number:
4
Square of 4 is 16
Cube of 4 is 64
Factorial of 4 is 24
Square Root of 4 is 2
```

19.2 EVENTS

An event is a signal that informs an application that something important has occurred. For example, when a user clicks a control on a form, the form can raise a **Click** event and call a procedure that handles the event. The Event Model of VB .NET based only on delegates. When we create an event in our application, the VB .NET compiler will create the delegate

Simple Event Generation

This program demonstrates the Event generation. It creates a button at run time and generates the **click** event associated with that button.

Form Designing

Table 19.1 Simple Event Generation

Control	*Property*	*Value*
Button1	Name	CmdDemo
	Text	EventDemo
Form1	Text	Event generation
	Name	Frmwelcome

Coding

```
Public Class Form1
Private Sub CmdDemo_Click(ByVal sender As System.Object, ByVal e As
System.EventArgs) Handles
                                        CmdDemo.Click
            Dim usrbut As New Button()
            usrbut.Text = "Click Here"
            Me.Controls.Add(usrbut)
```

```
        AddHandler usrbut.Click, AddressOf Me.Clickusrbut  'raise event

          End Sub
            Sub  Clickusrbut(ByVal  sender  As  Object,  ByVal  e  As
System.EventArgs)
                MsgBox("Keep your faith and a clear conscience")
          End Sub
    End Class
```

Output

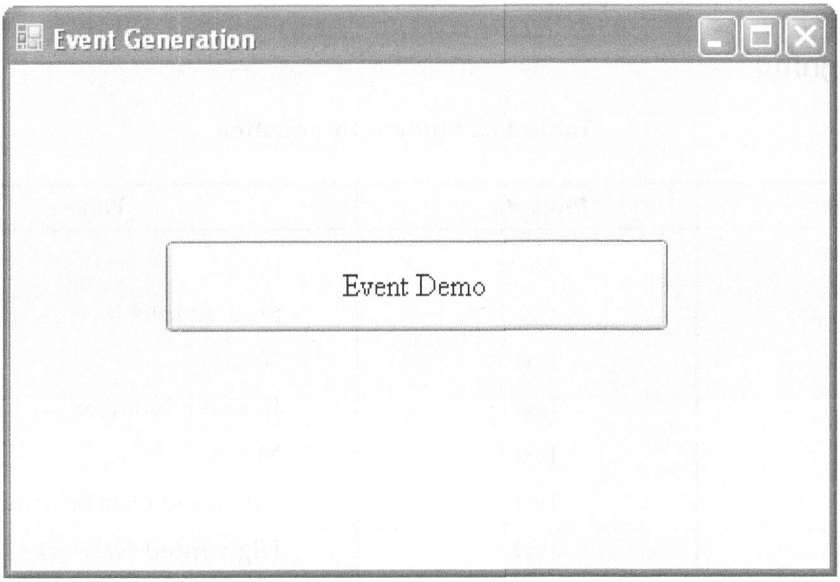

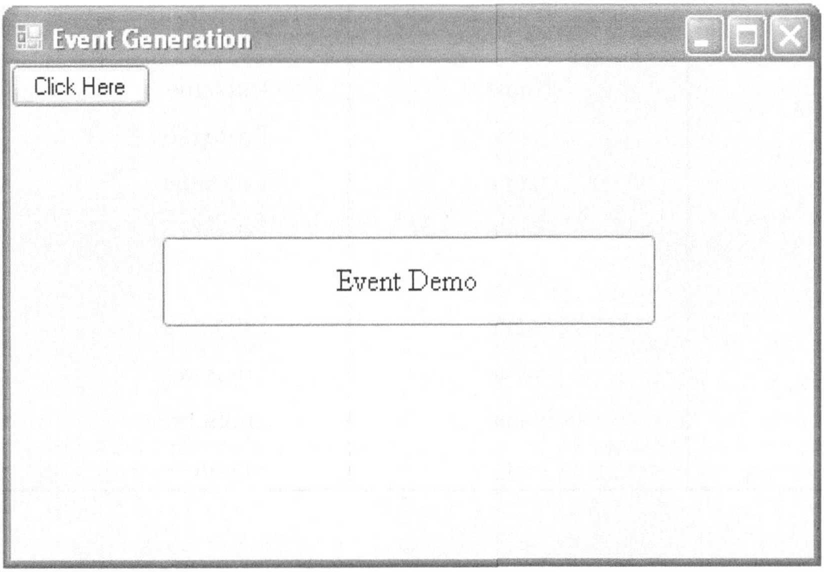

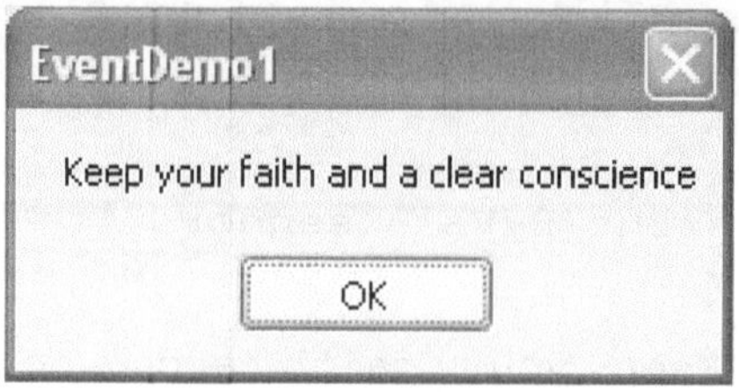

Student Information

This program deals the events with traditional Student information. It raises an event if the user going to enter the wrong input.

Form Designing

Table 19.2 Student Information

Control	*Property*	*Value*
Form1	Name	Form1
	Text	Student Info
Label1	Text	Name
Label2	Text	Register Number
Label3	Text	Maths
Label4	Text	Advanced Data Structure
Label5	Text	High Speed Networks
Label6	Text	Percentage
Label7	Text	Grade
TextBox1	Name	TxtName
TextBox2	Name	TxtRegno
Textbox3	Name	TxtMaths
TextBox4	Name	TxtADS
TextBox5	Name	TxtNW
TextBox6	Name	TxtPercent
TextBox7	Name	TxtGrade
Button1	Name	cmdSubmit
	Text	Submit

Coding

```
Public Class Form1
        Inherits System.Windows.Forms.Form

        Dim WithEvents obj As New Student_rec()

        Private Sub TxtName_Leave(ByVal sender As Object, ByVal e As
System.EventArgs) Handles TxtName.Leave
                obj.Sname = TxtName.Text
        End Sub
        Sub invalidname() Handles obj.invalidname
                MsgBox("Enter your Initial also", MsgBoxStyle.Critical,
"Invalid Input")
                TxtName.Focus()
                TxtName.Text = ""
        End Sub

        Private Sub TxtRegno _Leave(ByVal sender As Object, ByVal e
As System.EventArgs) Handles TxtRegno.Leave
                obj.Sid = Integer.Parse(TxtRegno.Text)
        End Sub
        Sub invalidid() Handles obj.invalidid
                    MsgBox("Register Number should be 10 in length",
MsgBoxStyle.Critical, "Invalid Input")
                TxtRegno.Focus()
                TxtRegno.Text = ""
        End Sub
        Private Sub TxtMaths _Leave(ByVal sender As Object, ByVal e
As System.EventArgs) Handles TxtMaths.Leave
                obj.M_mark = Integer.Parse(TxtMaths.Text)
        End Sub
        Sub invalidmarkM() Handles obj.invalidmarkM
              MsgBox("Mark does not exceed 100", MsgBoxStyle.Critical,
"Invalid Input")
                TxtMaths.Focus()
              TxtMaths.Text = ""
        End Sub
```

```
        Private Sub TxtADS _Leave(ByVal sender As Object, ByVal e As
System.EventArgs) Handles TxtADS.Leave
                obj.ADS_mark = Integer.Parse(TxtADS.Text)
        End Sub
        Sub invalidmarkADS() Handles obj.invalidmarkADS
            MsgBox("Mark does not exceed 100", MsgBoxStyle.Critical,
"Invalid Input")
                TxtADS.Focus()
            TxtADS.Text = ""

        End Sub
        Private Sub TxtNW_Leave(ByVal sender As Object, ByVal e As
System.EventArgs) Handles TxtNW.Leave
                obj.HSN_mark = Integer.Parse(TxtNW.Text)
        End Sub
        Sub invalidmarkHSN() Handles obj.invalidmarkHSN
            MsgBox("Mark does not exceed 100", MsgBoxStyle.Critical,
"Invalid Input")
                TxtNW.Focus()
                TxtNW.Text = ""
        End Sub

        Private Sub CmdSubmit_Click(ByVal sender As System.Object,
ByVal e As System.EventArgs) Handles CmdSubmit.Click
                TxtPercent.Text = obj.Spercentage
                TxtGrade.Text = obj.Sgrade
        End Sub
    End Class

    Class Student_rec
        Dim id As Integer
        Dim name As String
        Dim M, ADS, HSN As Integer
        Dim percentage As Decimal
        Dim grade As Char
        Public Event invalidname()
        Public Event invalidid()
```

```
Public Event invalidmarkM()
Public Event invalidmarkADS()
Public Event invalidmarkHSN()

Public Property Sname() As String
      Get
            Return name

      End Get
      Set(ByVal value As String)
            If (value.Contains(".")) Then
                  name = value
            Else
                  RaiseEvent invalidname()
            End If

      End Set
End Property
Public Property Sid() As Integer
      Get
            Return id
      End Get
      Set(ByVal value As Integer)
            Dim s As String = value.ToString()
            If (s.Length <> 10) Then
                  RaiseEvent invalidid()
            End If
            id = value
      End Set
End Property
Public Property M_mark() As Integer
      Get
            Return M
      End Get
      Set(ByVal value As Integer)
            If (value <= 100) Then
```

```
                    M = value
                Else
                    RaiseEvent invalidmarkM()
                End If
            End Set
        End Property
        Public Property ADS_mark() As Integer
            Get
                Return ADS
            End Get
            Set(ByVal value As Integer)
                If (value <= 100) Then
                    ADS = value
                Else
                    RaiseEvent invalidmarkADS()
                End If
            End Set
        End Property
        Public Property HSN_mark() As Integer
            Get
                Return HSN
            End Get
            Set(ByVal value As Integer)
                If (value <= 100) Then
                    HSN = value
                Else
                    RaiseEvent invalidmarkHSN()
                End If
            End Set
        End Property
        Function Spercentage()
            percentage = (M + ADS + HSN) / 3
            Return percentage
        End Function
        Function Sgrade()
            If percentage = 100 Then
                grade = "S"
```

```
        ElseIf percentage >= 95 Then
            grade = "A"
        ElseIf percentage >= 80 Then
            grade = "B"
        ElseIf percentage >= 75 Then
            grade = "C"
        ElseIf percentage >= 60 Then
            grade = "D"
        Else
            grade = "F"
        End If
        Return grade
    End Function
End Class
```

Output

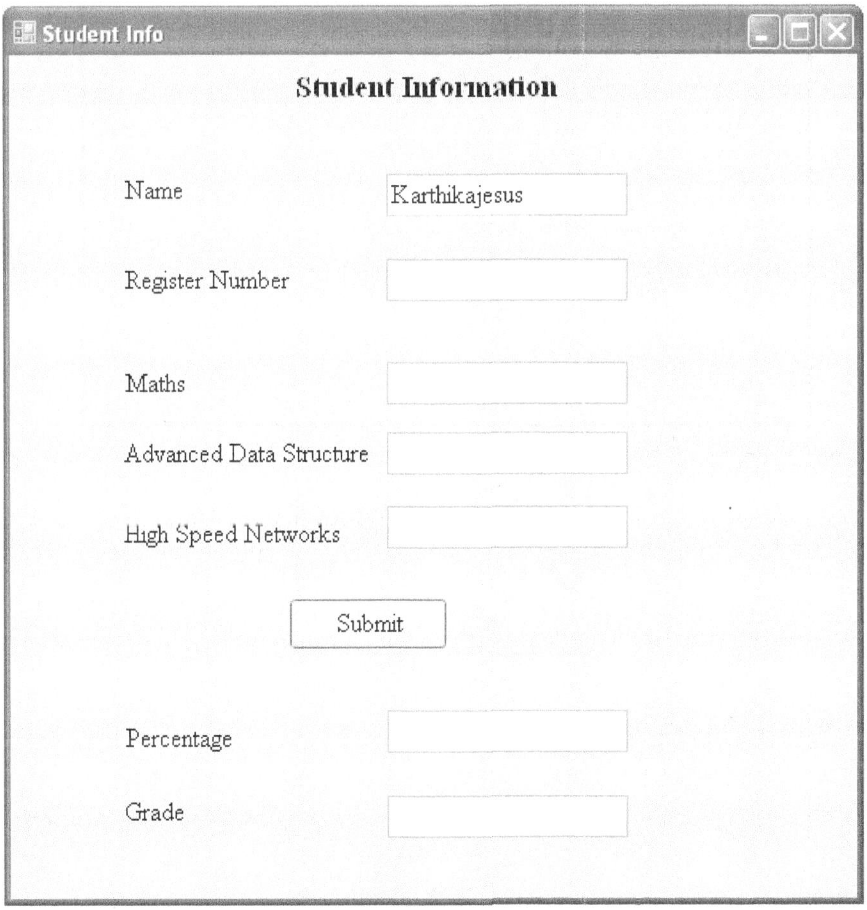

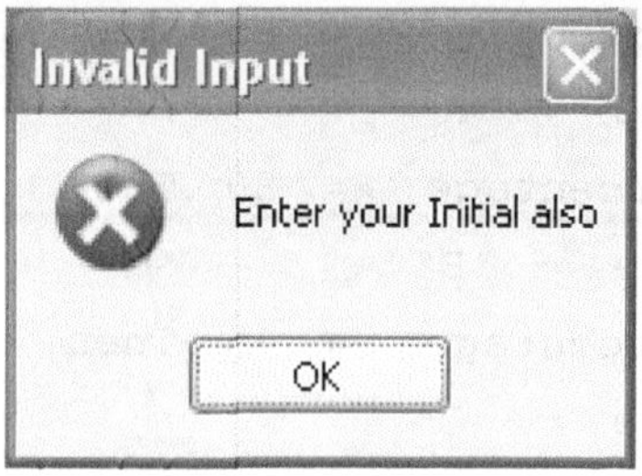
Invalid Input
Enter your Initial also
OK

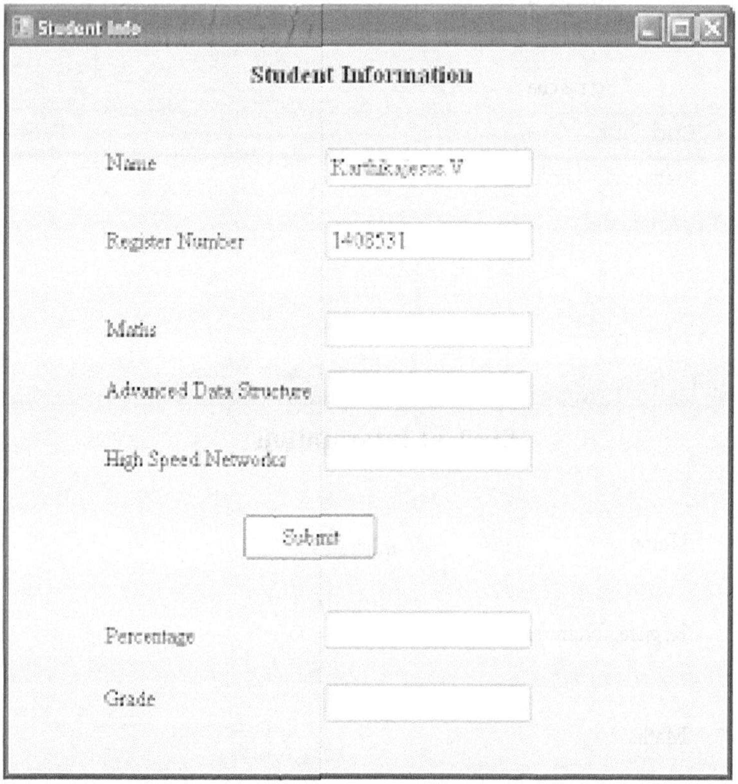
Student Info
Student Information
Name
Karthikayesan V
Register Number
1408531
Maths
Advanced Data Structure
High Speed Networks
Submit
Percentage
Grade

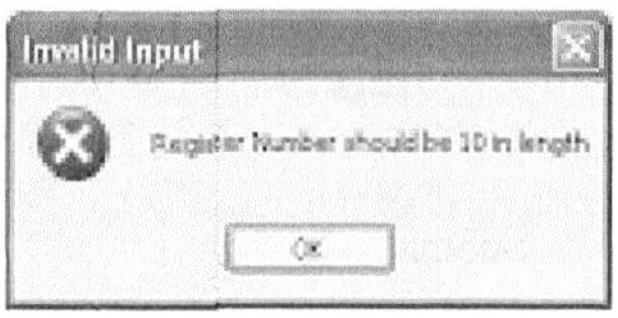
Invalid Input
Register Number should be 10 in length
OK

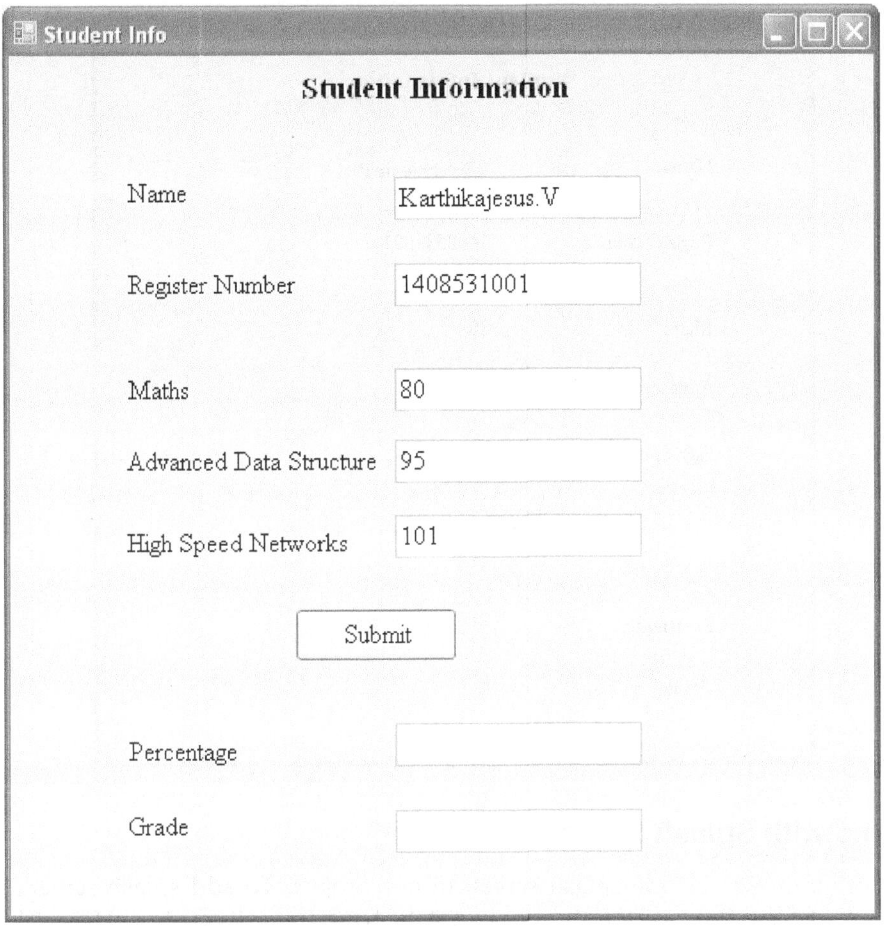
Student Info
Student Information
Name
Karthikajesus.V
Register Number
1408531001
Maths
80
Advanced Data Structure
95
High Speed Networks
101
Submit
Percentage
Grade

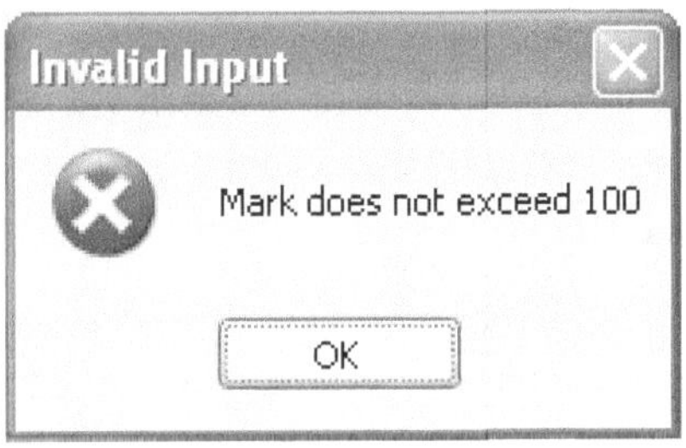
Invalid Input
Mark does not exceed 100
OK

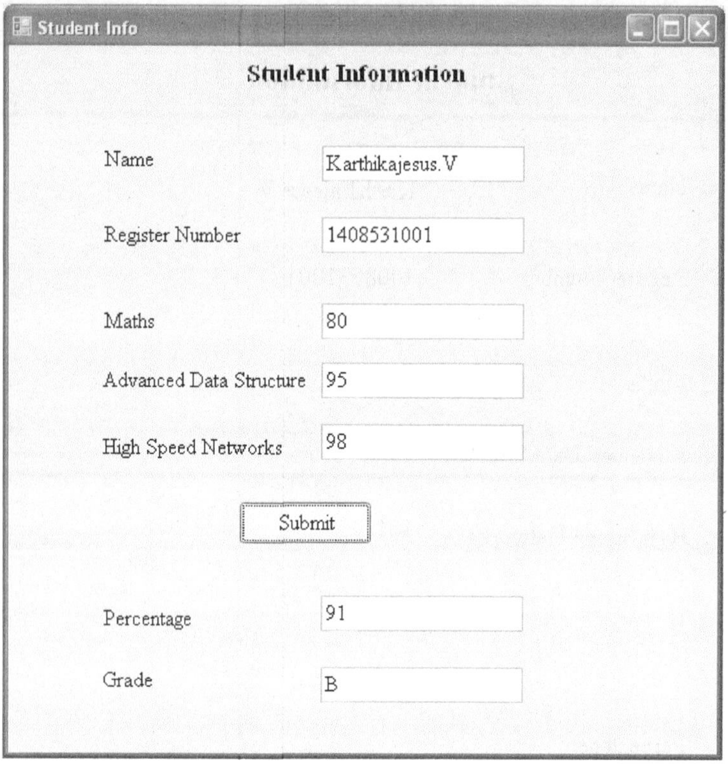

Event Demo with Splash Screen

In this program we include splash screen in our project. To add splash screen, in project menu, select **Add New Item** option. It opens an **Add New Item** dialog box. Here select **Splash Screen** as in Fig. 19.1

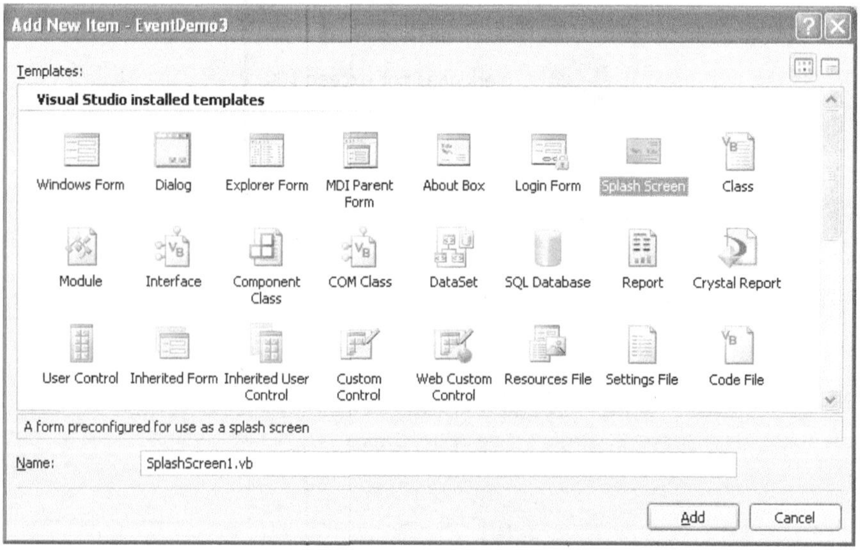

Fig. 19.1 *Add New Item Dialog Box*

Whatever is typed on the **TextBox** will be the name of the splash Screen. Here we give **welcome** as the name

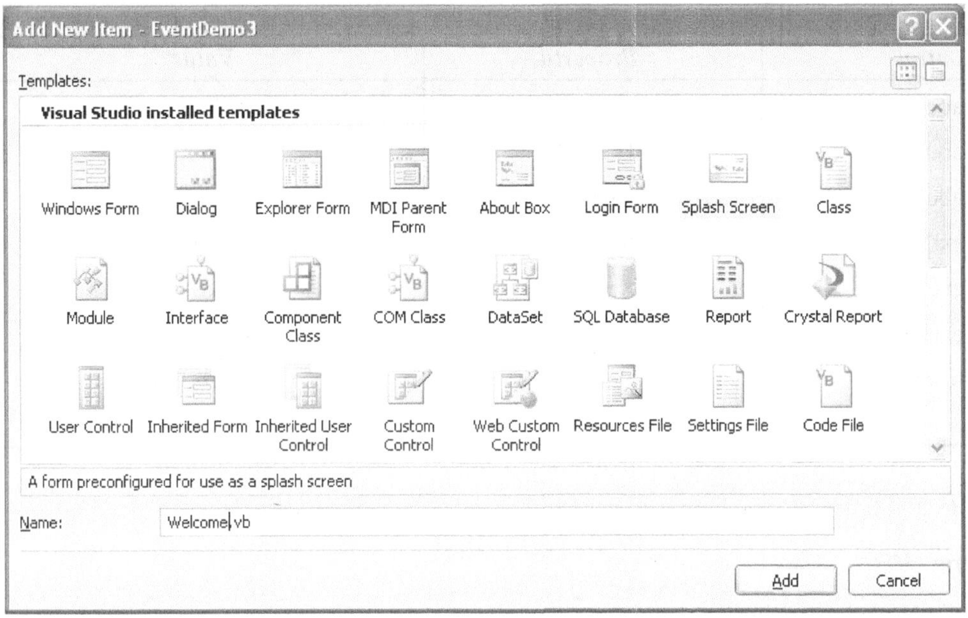

Form Designing

Welcome .VB [Design]

Table 19.3 Welcome .VB

Control	*Property*	*Value*
MainLayoutPanel	Name	MainLayoutPanel
DetailsLayoutPanel	Name	DetailsLayoutPanel
Version	Name	Version
	Text	U want to register your name
	Font	Times New Roman, 12pt
ApplicationTitle	Name	ApplicationTitle
	Text	Visu International
	Font	Times New Roman, 24pt, style=Bold
LinkLabel1	Name	LinkLabel1
	LinkColor	0, 0, 255
	Font	Microsoft Sans Serif, 12pt
	VisitedLinkColor	128, 0, 128
	ActiveLinkColor	Red

Form1 .VB [Design]

Table 19.4 Form1 .VB

Control	*Property*	*Value*
Label1	Text	Name
Label2	Text	Area
Label3	Text	Password
TextBox1	Name	TxtName
TextBox2	Name	TxtArea
TextBox3	Name	TxtPwd
Button1	Name	CmdSubmit
	Text	Submit

Coding

Welcome .VB

```
Public NotInheritable Class welcome
    'TODO: This form can easily be set as the splash screen for the application by going to the "Application" tab
    '  of the Project Designer ("Properties" under the "Project" menu).
    Private Sub welcome_Load(ByVal sender As Object, ByVal e As System.EventArgs) Handles Me.Load
        'Set up the dialog text at runtime according to the application's assembly information.
        'TODO: Customize the application's assembly information in the "Application" pane of the project
        '  properties dialog (under the "Project" menu).
        'Application title
        If My.Application.Info.Title <> "" Then
            ApplicationTitle.Text = "Visu International"
        Else
            'If the application title is missing, use the application name, without the extension
            ApplicationTitle.Text = System.IO.Path.GetFileNameWithoutExtension(My.Application.Info.AssemblyName)
        End If
```

```
            'Format the version information using the text set into the Version control at design time as the
            '  formatting string.  This allows for effective localization if desired.
            ' Build and revision information could be included by using the following code and changing the
            '  Version control's designtime text to "Version {0}.{1:00}.{2}.{3}" or something similar.  See
            '  String.Format() in Help for more information.
            '
            '     Version.Text = System.String.Format(Version.Text, My.Application.Info.Version.Major, My.Application.Info.Version.Minor, My.Application.Info.Version.Build, My.Application.Info.Version.Revision)

            Version.Text = System.String.Format(Version.Text, My.Application.Info.Version.Major, My.Application.Info.Version.Minor)

            'Copyright info
            'Copyright.Text = My.Application.Info.Copyright
        End Sub

    Private Sub LinkLabel1_LinkClicked(ByVal sender As System.Object, ByVal e As System.Windows.Forms.LinkLabelLinkClickedEventArgs) Handles LinkLabel1.LinkClicked
            Dim f As New Form1
            f.Show()
        End Sub

    Private Sub MainLayoutPanel_Paint(ByVal sender As System.Object, ByVal e As System.Windows.Forms.PaintEventArgs) Handles MainLayoutPanel.Paint

        End Sub

    Private Sub ApplicationTitle_Click(ByVal sender As System.Object, ByVal e As System.EventArgs) Handles ApplicationTitle.Click

        End Sub
  End Class
```

Form .VB

```
Public Class Form1
        Inherits System.Windows.Forms.Form
        Dim WithEvents obj As New Validate()
        Sub invalidinput() Handles obj.invalidinput
                MsgBox("Password required minimum 6 characters")
              TxtPwd.Focus()
              TxtPwd.Text = ""
        End Sub
       Private Sub TxtPwd _Leave(ByVal sender As Object, ByVal e As
System.EventArgs) Handles TxtPwd.Leave
                obj.getvalue = TxtPwd.Text
        End Sub
         Private Sub CmdSubmit_Click(ByVal sender As System.Object,
ByVal e As System.EventArgs) Handles CmdSubmit.Click
                MsgBox("You are Registered")
                End
        End Sub

End Class

Class Validate
        Dim pwd As String
        Public Event invalidinput()
        Public Property getvalue() As String
                Get

                        Return pwd

                End Get
                Set(ByVal value As String)
                        If (value.Length < 6) Then
                                RaiseEvent invalidinput()
                        End If
                        pwd - value
                End Set
        End Property
End Class
```

Output

Visu
International
U want to register your name
Sign Up

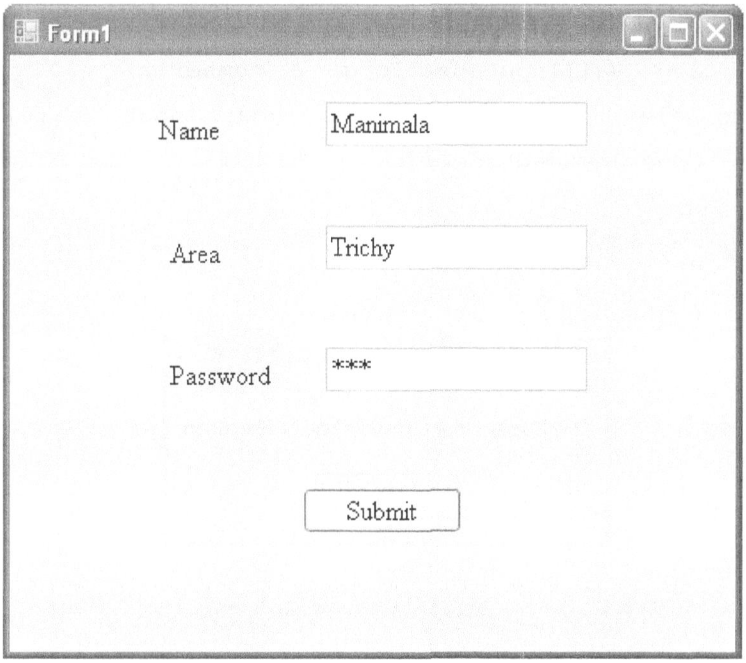
Form1
Name
Manimala
Area
Trichy
Password
***
Submit

Invalid Password
Password required minimum 6 characters
OK

19.3 DIFFERENT KIND OF EXECUTION

This program leads you for a different kind of execution.

```
Coding
Module Module1
      Sub Main()
            MsgBox("Welcome to our Different kind of execution")
            Dim a As Integer
            a = Val(InputBox("Enter a number"))
         Console.WriteLine("Square of your input is {0} ", a * a)
            Console.ReadLine()
      End Sub
End Module
```

Output

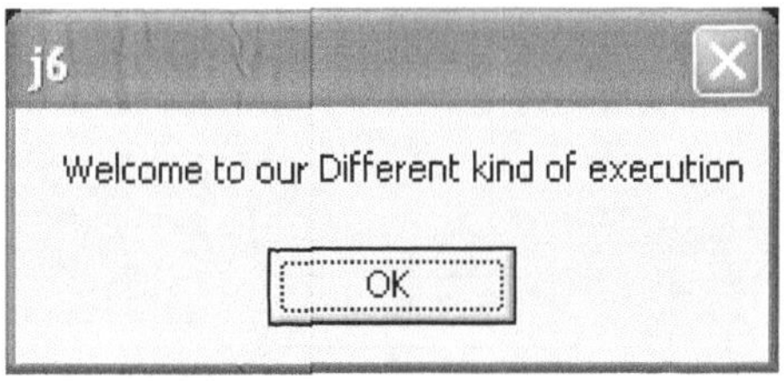

Square of your input is 16.

PART IV
CLASS LIBRARY

The .NET Framework class library is a library of classes, interfaces, and value types that are included in the Microsoft .NET Framework SDK. This library provides access to system functionality and is designed to be the foundation on which .NET Framework applications, components, and controls are built. Class libraries are equivalent to ActiveX DLL and ActiveX EXE project types of Visual Basic. We can create a class or a reusable component that exposes some functionality that can be used in various projects. These classes are created by activating **Class Library** template from the **New Project** window.

CHAPTER

20

CREATING OUR OWN CLASS LIBRARY

20.1 CREATION OF CLASS LIBRARY AND USING THEM IN AN APPLICATION

Here we create a class library and use it on our application. To create a class library, open a **New Project** and select **Class Library** template as in Fig. 20.1.

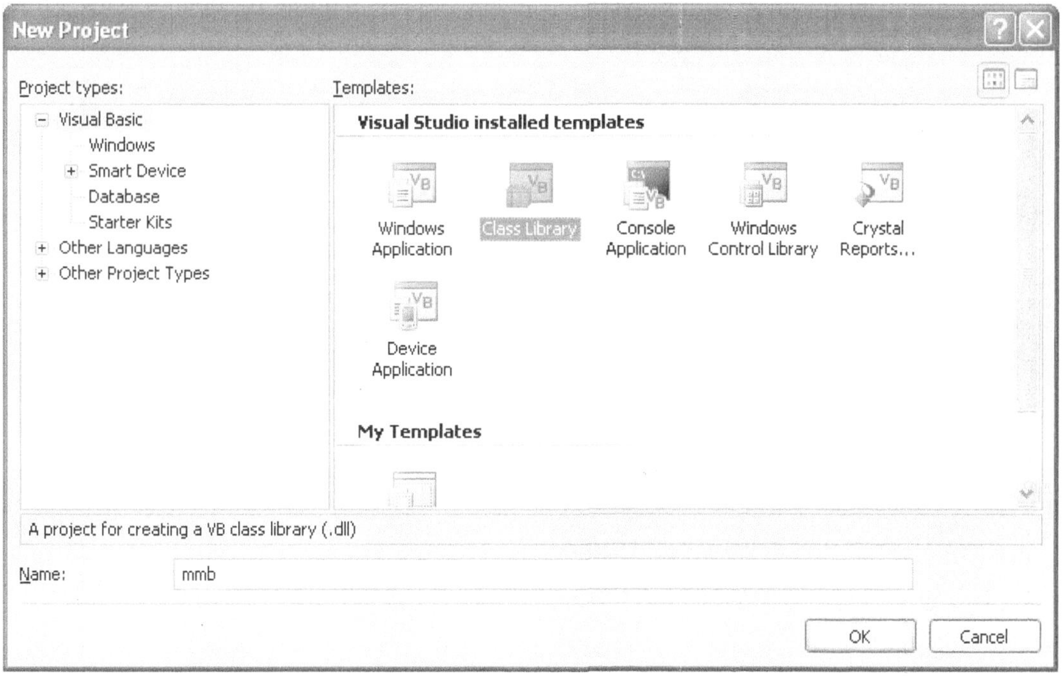

Fig. 20.1 *New Project Window for Selecting a Class Library*

Selection of **OK** button will opens the code window. Here we can create our own classes as in Fig. 20.2

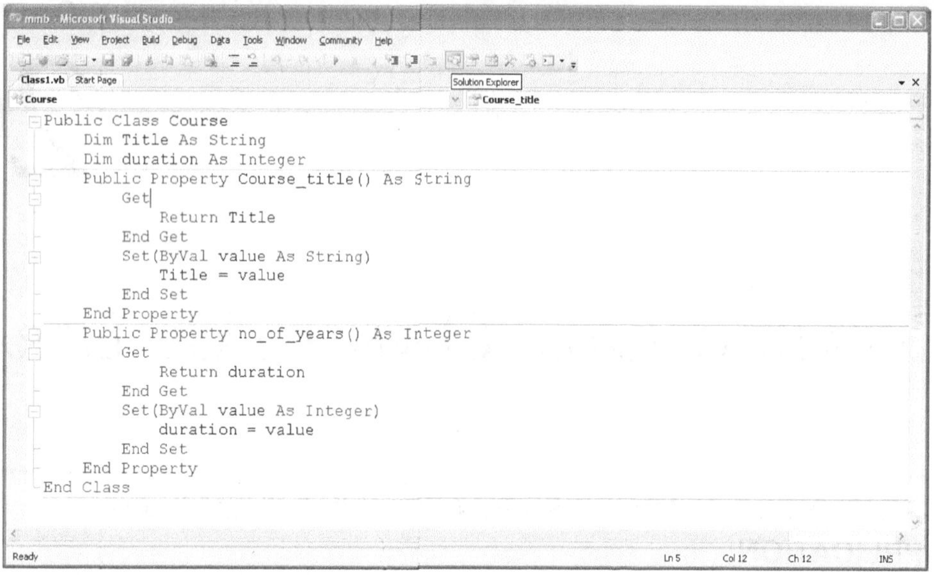

Fig. 20.2 *Code Window*

In the above window, class **Course** with two fields **Title** and **duration** is created .This class can be used in our applications. Now we use the above class **Course** by open a **New Project** window.

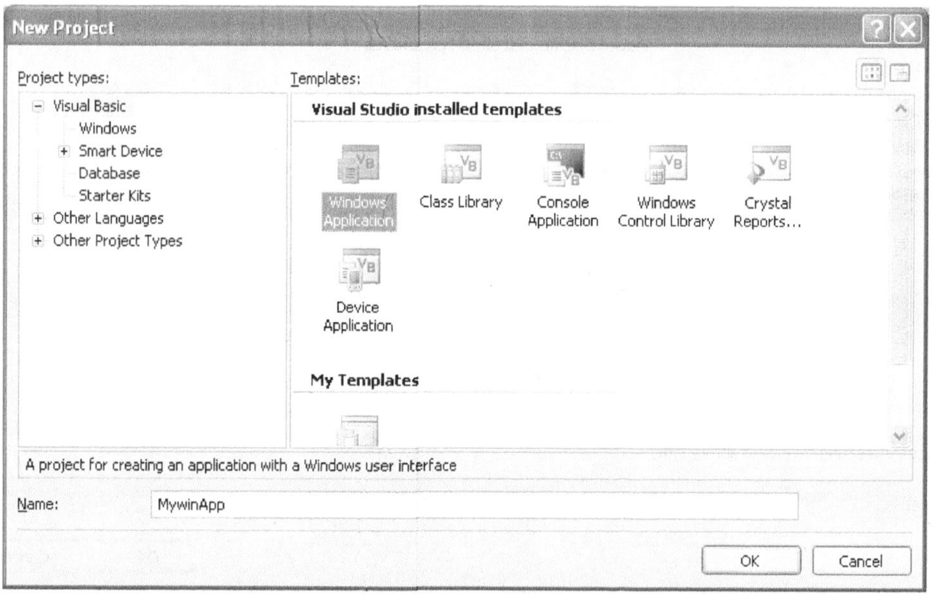

Fig. 20.3 *New Project Window for Selecting a Windows Application*

In this Windows Application, we import the class **Course**. This is done through the **Reference** folder in the **Solution Explorer**.

The Solution Explorer of the **MyWinApp** is shown below in the Fig. 20.4.

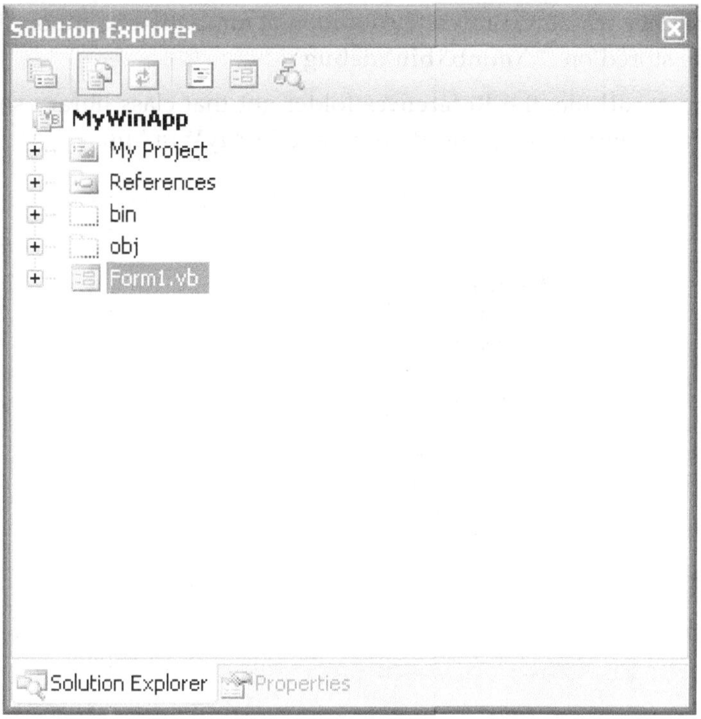

Fig. 20.4 *Solution Explorer*

In this **Solution Explorer** window, right click the **References** and select **Add Reference,** it opens the **Add Reference** window as in Fig. 20.5

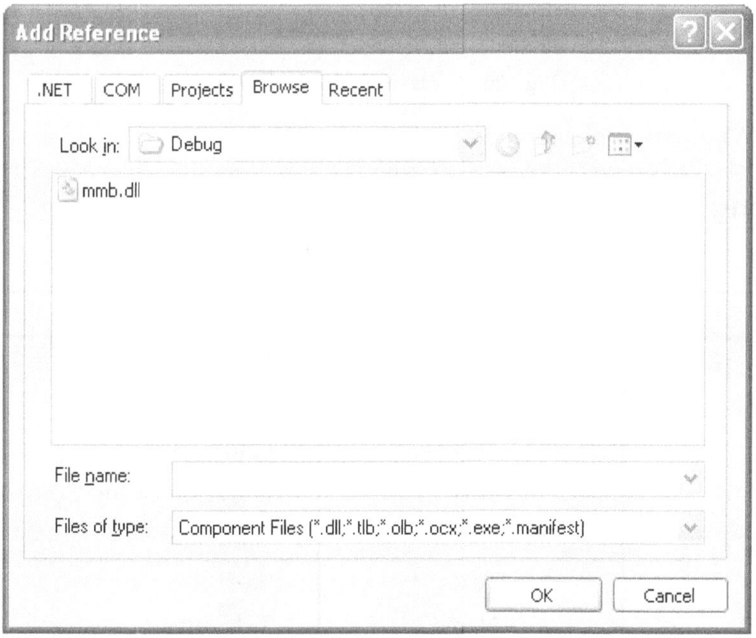

Fig. 20.5 *Add Reference Window*

In the **Add Reference** window, Browse the location of **mmb.dll** and import that in application. The **mmb.dll** will be stored on **...\mmb\bin\debug**

After importing of **.dll** file, the **References** folder got that class library shown in Fig. 20.6. Now this Library class **Course** can be used anywhere in **MyWinApp**.

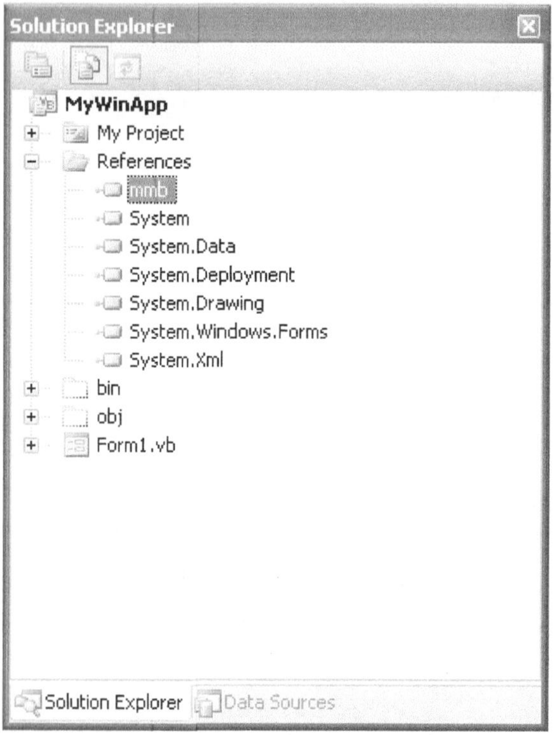

Fig. 20.6 *Class Library Included*

Design the Windows application as in the table 20.1

Form Designing

Table 20.1

Control	*Property*	*Value*
Form1	Name	Form1
	Text	Admission Form
Label1	Text	Course Title
Label2	Text	Duration of the Course (in year)
Button1	Name	CmdStore
	Text	Store
TextBox1	Name	TxtCourse
TextBox2	Name	TxtYear

Coding

```
Imports mmb                              'imports the Library
Public Class Form1
        Private Sub CmdStore_Click(ByVal sender As System.Object,
ByVal e As System.EventArgs) Handles CmdStore.Click
              Dim C As New Course
              C.Course_title = TxtCourse.Text
              C.no_of_years =Integer.parse( TxtYear.Text)
              MsgBox("Information Stored")
        End Sub
End Class
```

Output

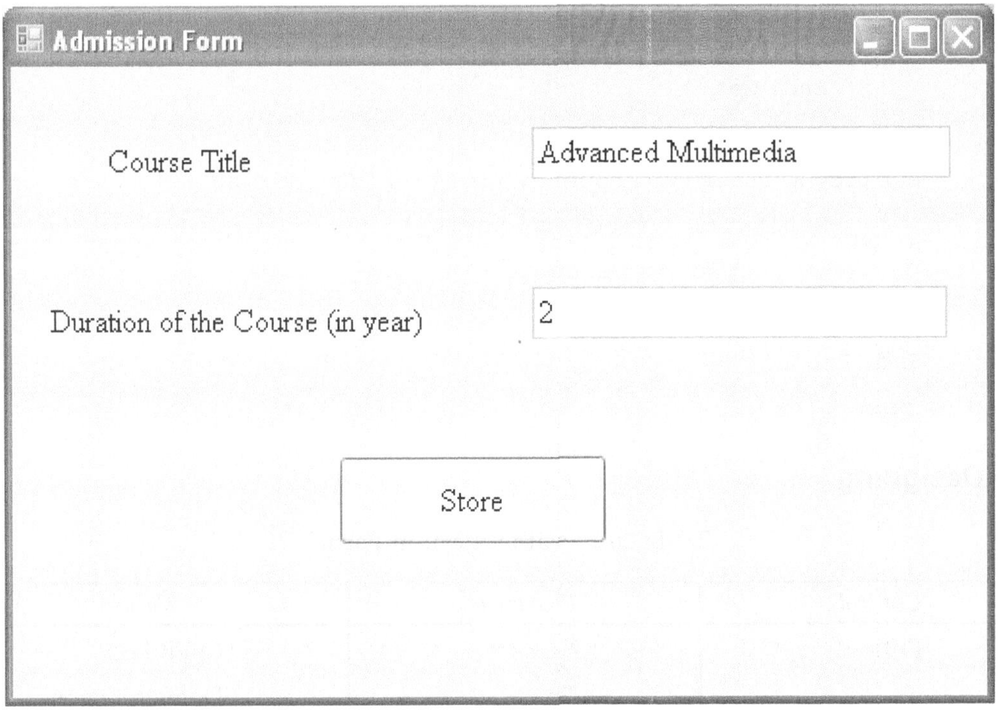

20.2 AUTHENTICATION FORM

This program illustrates that the class library which subjects to authentication. Here we imports the class **Password** that resides in the class library **MyLibrary.**

Library Class Password Stored in the MyLibrary

```
Public Class Password
      Dim pwd As String
      Public ReadOnly Property authen() As Boolean
            Get
                  If pwd = "Jesus" Then
                        Return True
                  Else
                        Return False
                  End If
            End Get
      End Property
      Public WriteOnly Property login() As String
            Set(ByVal value As String)
                  pwd = value
            End Set
      End Property
End Class
```

Form Designing

Table 20.2 Authentication Form

Control	*Property*	*Value*
Button1	Name	CmdCheck
	Text	Domain Logon
TextBox1	Name	Txtuser
	Text	Administrator
TextBox2	Name	Txtpwd
Label1	Text	User Name
Label2	Text	Password

Coding

```
Imports MyLibrary
Public Class Form1
    Private Sub CmdCheck_Click(ByVal sender As System.Object,
ByVal e As System.EventArgs) Handles CmdCheck.Click

        Dim PO As Password = New Password()
        PO.login = Txtpwd.Text
        If (PO.authen) Then
            MsgBox("Welcome to Domain")
        Else
            MsgBox("Access Denied")
        End If
    End Sub
End Class
```

Output

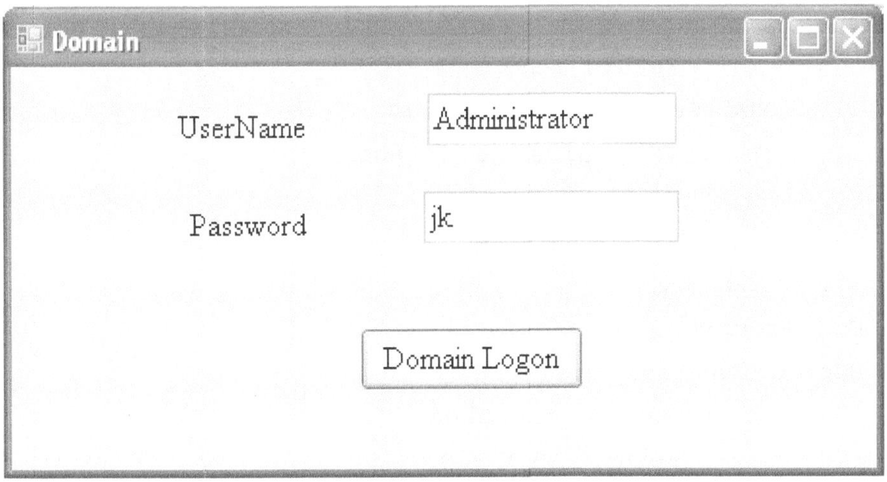

20.3 STUDENT MARK

This program illustrates that the class library which deals the mark processing. Here we imports the class **StudentMark** that resides in the class library **Student.**

Class StudentMark is Stored in the Student Class Library

```
Public Class StudentMark
       Dim name As String
       Dim mark As Integer
       Public Property sname()
              Get
                     Return name
              End Get
              Set(ByVal value)
                     name = value
              End Set
       End Property
       Public Property smark() As Integer
              Get
                     Return mark
              End Get
              Set(ByVal value As Integer)
                     mark = value

              End Set
       End Property
       Public Function grade() As Char
              If (mark >= 95) Then
                     Return "S"
              ElseIf (mark >= 90) Then
                     Return "A"
              ElseIf (mark >= 85) Then
                     Return "B"
              ElseIf (mark >= 80) Then
                     Return "C"
              ElseIf (mark >= 60) Then
                     Return "D"
```

```
        ElseIf (mark >= 50) Then
            Return "E"
        Else
            Return "F"
        End If
    End Function
End Class
```

Form Designing

Table 20.3 Student Mark

Control	*Property*	*Value*
Button1	Name	CmdStu
	Text	Student Grade
Label1	Text	Student Name
Label2	Text	Mark
Label3	Text	Student Name
Label4	Text	Grade
TextBox1	Name	TxtName
TextBox2	Name	TxtMark
TextBox3	Name	TxtDisp
TextBox4	Name	TxtGrade

Coding

Class Library Student Imported on the Application

```
Imports Student
Public Class Form1

    Private Sub CmdStu_Click(ByVal sender As System.Object, ByVal
e As System.EventArgs) Handles CmdStu.Click
        Dim Stuobj As StudentMark = New StudentMark()
        Stuobj.sname = TxtName.Text
        Stuobj.smark = Integer.Parse(TxtMark.Text)
        TxtDisp.Text = Stuobj.sname
        TxtGrade.Text = Stuobj.grade()
    End Sub
End Class
```

Output

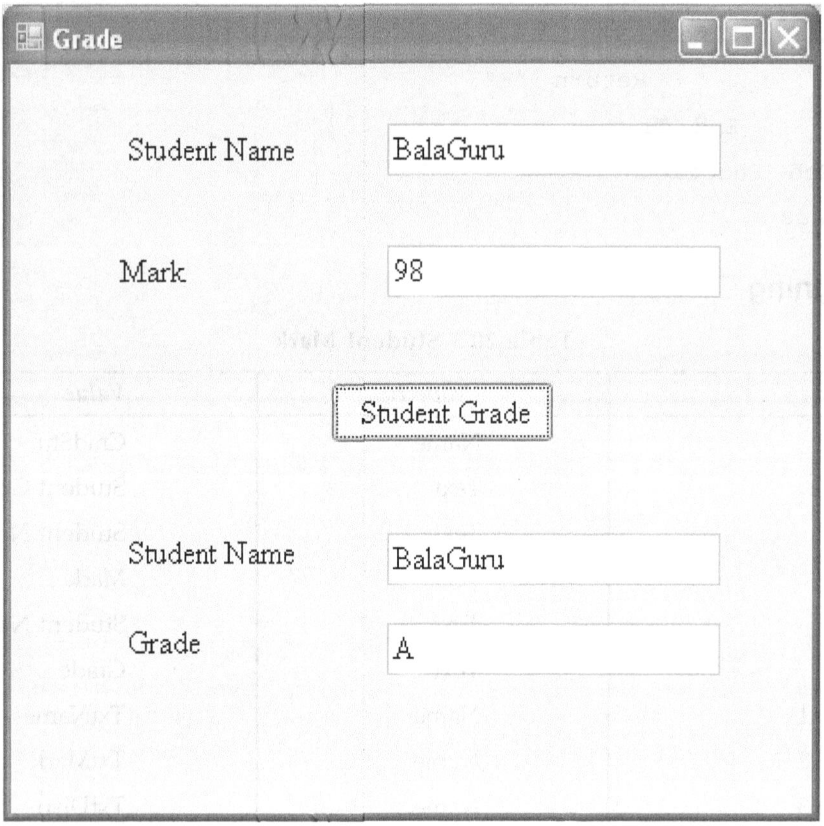
Grade
Student Name
BalaGuru
Mark
98
Student Grade
Student Name
BalaGuru
Grade
A

CHAPTER

21

OOP CONCEPTS IN LIBRARY

21.1 CONSTRUCTOR

Constructor is a special method which is used to give initial values to the class members. Constructor is called at time of object creation. In VB.NET Procedure New() act as a constructor.

This program illustrates that the class library constructor. Here we imports the class **Student** that is stored on the class Library **OOPLibrary.**

Class Student Stored on OOPLibrary

This program illustrates that the class library which deals the mark processing. Here we imports the class **StudentMark** that resides in the class library **Student.**

```
Public Class Student
    Dim name As String
    Sub New()
        name = "Muthulingam"
    End Sub
    Sub New(ByVal sname As String)
        name = sname
    End Sub
    Function getname() As String
        Return name
    End Function
End Class
```

Form Designing

Table 21.1 Constructor

Control	*Property*	*Value*
Button1	Name	CmdProcess
	Text	Process
Label1	Text	Student Name
Label2	Text	Student Name (constructor with out argument)
Label3	Text	Student Name (constructor with argument)
TextBox1	Name	TxtName
TextBox2	Name	TxtWOCons
TextBox3	Name	TxtWCons

Coding

```
Imports OOP_Library
Public Class Form1
    Private Sub CmdProcess_Click(ByVal sender As System.Object,
ByVal e As System.EventArgs) Handles CmdProcess.Click
        Dim na As String
        na = TxtName.Text
        Dim stuobj As Student = New Student
        TxtWOCons.Text = stuobj.getname
        Dim stuobj1 As Student = New Student(na)
        TxtWCons.Text = stuobj1.getname
    End Sub
End Class
```

Output

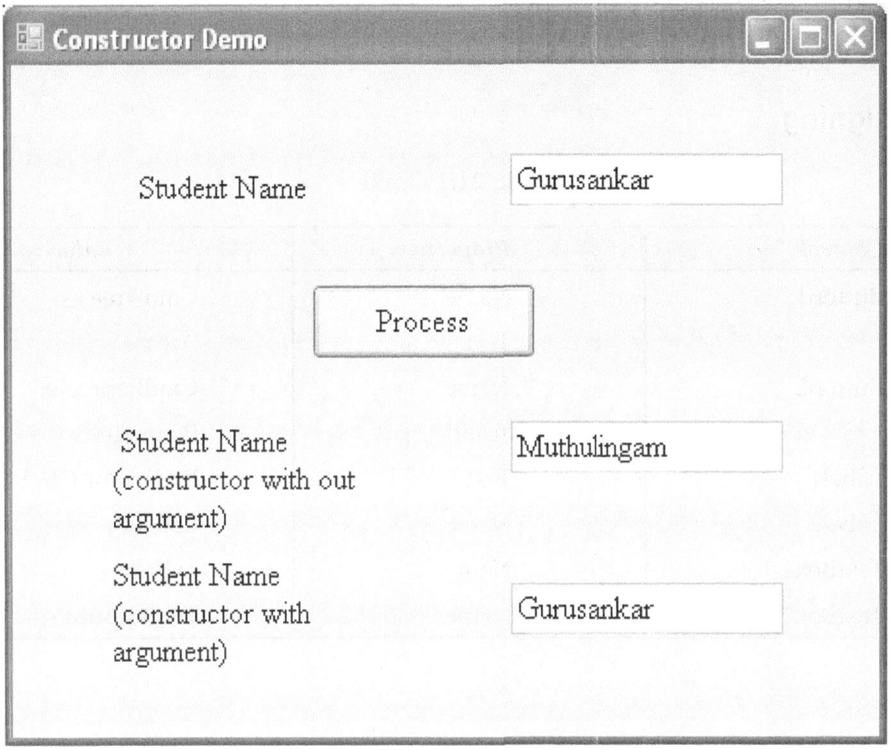

21.2 CIRCLE

Here we import the class **Circle** that stored in the class library **OOPLibrary.**

Class Circle Stored on OOPLibrary

```
Public Class Circle
    Dim r, A, P As Double
    Sub New(ByVal radius As Double)
        r = radius
    End Sub
    Public Function Area()
        A = Math.PI * Math.Pow(r, 2)
        Return A
    End Function
    Public Function Perimeter()
        P = 2 * Math.PI * r
```

```
            Return P
        End Function
    End Class
```

Form Designing

Table 21.2 Circle

Control	*Property*	*Value*
Button1	Name	CmdArea
	Text	Area
Button2	Name	CmdPerimeter
	Text	Perimeter
Label1	Text	Radius of Circle
Label2	Name	LblOut
TextBox1	Name	TxtInput
TextBox2	Name	TxtOutput

Coding

```
    Imports OOP_Library
    Public Class Form1

         Private Sub CmdArea _Click(ByVal sender As System.Object,
ByVal e As System.EventArgs) Handles CmdArea.Click
            Dim ra As Double
            ra = Double.Parse(TxtInput.Text)
            Dim C As Circle = New Circle(ra)
            LblOut.Text = "Area of Circle is"
            TxtOutput.Text = C.Area
        End Sub

        Private Sub CmdPerimeter _Click(ByVal sender As System.Object,
ByVal e As System.EventArgs) Handles CmdPerimeter.Click
            Dim ra As Double
            ra = Double.Parse(TxtInput.Text)
            Dim C As Circle = New Circle(ra)
            LblOut.Text = " Perimeter of Circle is"
            TxtOutput.Text = C.Perimeter
```

```
        End Sub
End Class
```

Output

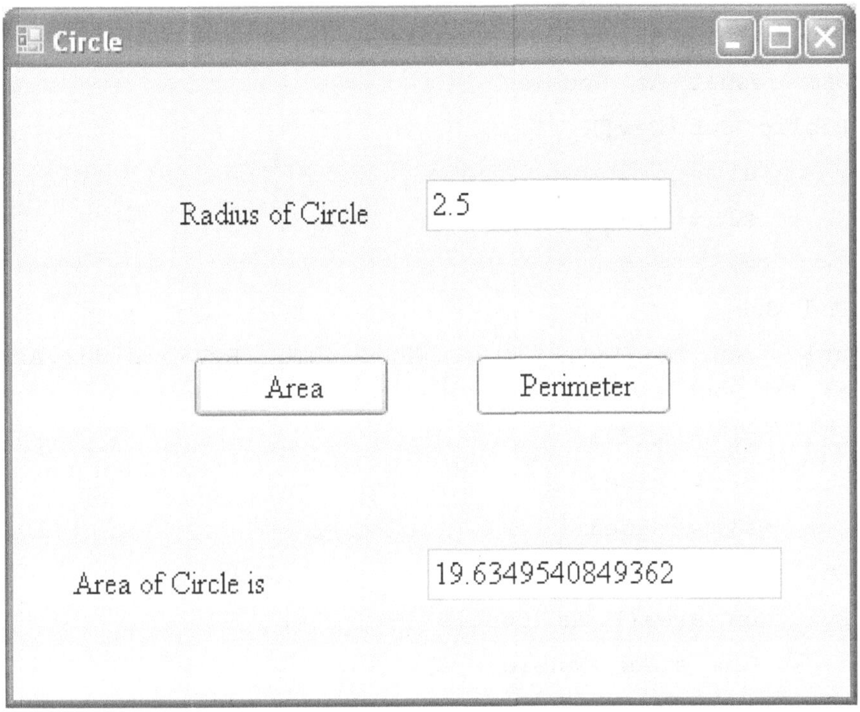

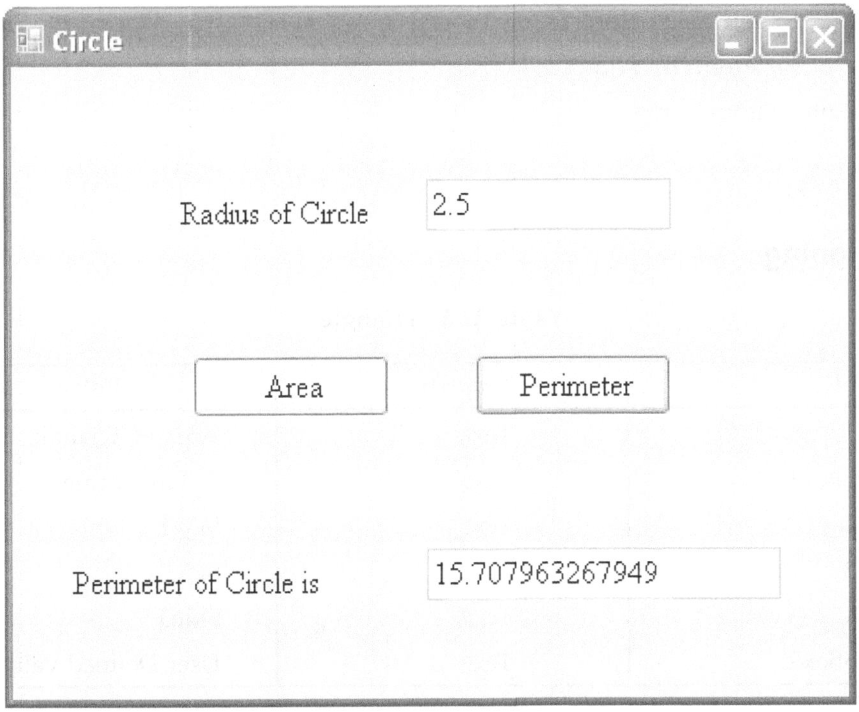

21.3 TRIANGLE

Here we imports the class **Shape** that stored in the class library **OOPLibrary**

```
Public Class Shape
Public s1, s2, s3 As Double
Dim result As Double
Public Sub New()
        s1 = 5.5
        s2 = 6.5
        s3 = 7.5
End Sub
    Public Sub New(ByVal side1 As Double, ByVal side2 As Double,
ByVal side3 As Double)
        s1 = side1
        s2 = side2
        s3 = side3
End Sub
Function area() As Double
        Dim s As Double
        s = (s1 + s2 + s3) / 2
      result = Math.Sqrt(s * (s - s1) * (s - s2) * (s - s3))
        Return result
End Function

End Class
```

Form Designing

Table 21.3 Triangle

Control	*Property*	*Value*
Label1	Text	Area of Triangle
GroupBox1	Text	Default values
Label2	Text	Side1
Label3	Text	Side2
Label4	Text	Side3
GroupBox2	Text	User Defined values

Label5	Text	Side1
Label6	Text	Side2
Label7	Text	Side3
Label8	Text	Area of Triangle
Button1	Name	CmdDefault
	Text	Default Values
Button2	Name	CmdUser
	Text	User Defined Values
TextBox1	Name	TxtDs1
TextBox2	Name	TxtDs2
TextBox3	Name	TxtDs3
TextBox4	Name	TxtUs1
TextBox5	Name	TxtUs2
TextBox6	Name	TxtUs3
TextBox7	Name	TxtResult

Coding

```
Imports OOPLibrary
Public Class Form1

        Private Sub Form1_Load(ByVal sender As System.Object, ByVal
e As System.EventArgs) Handles MyBase.Load
                GroupBox1.Enabled = False
                Dim S As Shape = New Shape()
                TxtDs1.Text = S.s1
                TxtDs2.Text = S.s2
                TxtDs3.Text = S.s3
        End Sub

        Private Sub CmdDefault _Click(ByVal sender As System.Object,
ByVal e As System.EventArgs) Handles CmdDefault.Click
                Dim S As Shape = New Shape() 'constructor with no
argument invoked
                TxtResult.Text = S.area()
```

```
        End Sub

         Private Sub CmdUser _Click(ByVal sender As System.Object,
ByVal e As System.EventArgs) Handles CmdUser.Click
             Dim a, b, c As Double
             a = Double.Parse(TxtUs1.Text)
             b = Double.Parse(TxtUs2.Text)
             c = Double.Parse(TxtUs3.Text)
             Dim Us As Shape = New Shape(a, b, c) 'Constructor
with argument is invoked
             TxtResult.Text = Us.area
        End Sub
    End Class
```

Output

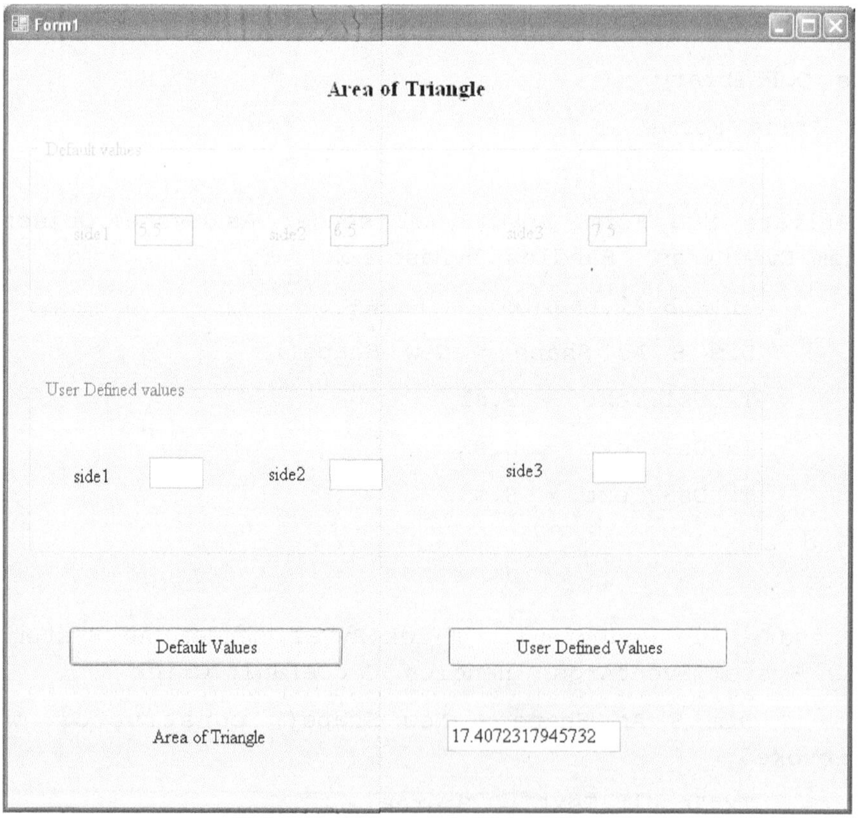

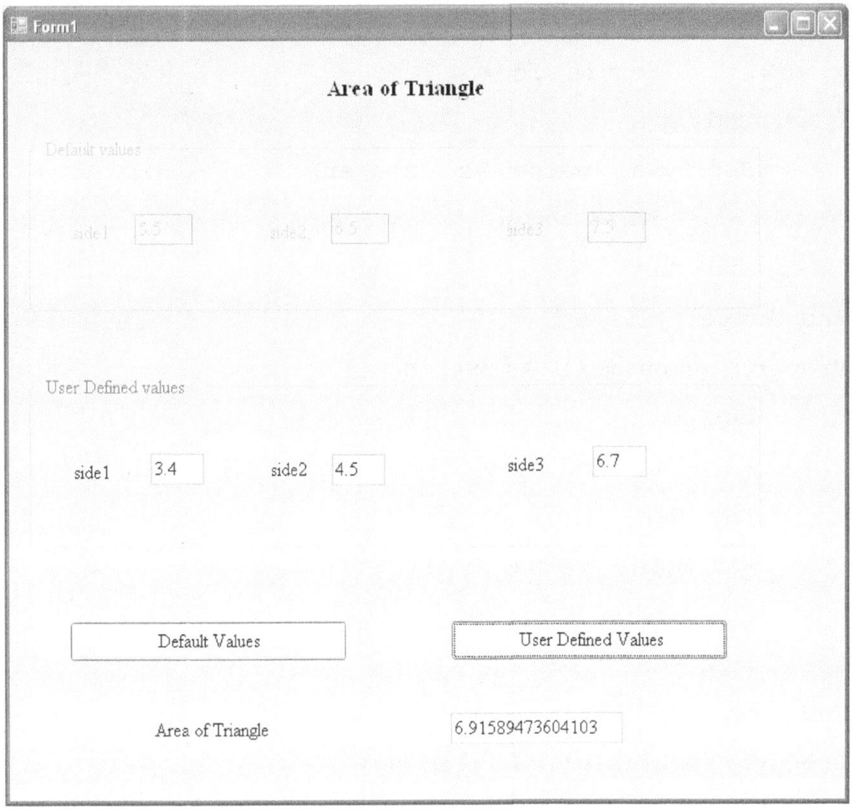

21.4 INHERITANCE IN EMPLOYEE RECORD

Inheritance is the process of creating new classes from the existing classes. The new classes are called sub class or derived class and the existing classes are called super class or base class.

Advantages

- New classes can be derived from the existing classes without modification
- It saves time and memory

In this program we import the derived class **Employee** that stored in the class library **OOP Library.** Note that class **Employee** is derived from base class **Employ**

```
'inheritence
Public Class Employ
      Dim id As Integer
      Dim name As String
      Dim desi As String
      Property empid() As Integer
```

```
            Get
                  Return id
            End Get
            Set(ByVal value As Integer)
                  id = value
            End Set
      End Property
      Property empname() As String
            Get
                  Return name
            End Get
            Set(ByVal value As String)
                  name = value
            End Set
      End Property
      Property empdesig() As String
            Get
                  Return desi
            End Get
            Set(ByVal value As String)
                  desi = value
            End Set
      End Property
End Class

Public Class Employee
      Inherits Employ
      Dim basicpay, Hra, DA As Decimal
      Property bp() As Decimal
            Get
                  Return basicpay
```

```
        End Get
        Set(ByVal value As Decimal)
            basicpay = value
        End Set
    End Property
    Property hr_allowance() As Decimal
        Get
            Return Hra
        End Get
        Set(ByVal value As Decimal)
            Hra = value
        End Set
    End Property
    Property D_allowance() As Decimal
        Get
            Return DA
        End Get
        Set(ByVal value As Decimal)
            DA = value
        End Set
    End Property
    Public Function grosspay() As Decimal
        Return (bp() + D_allowance() + hr_allowance())
    End Function
End Class
```

Form Designing

Table 21.4 Inheritance in Employee Record

Control	*Property*	*Value*
Form1	Text	Employee Record
Label1	Text	Employee ID
Label2	Text	Employee Name

Label3	Text	Designation
Label4	Text	Basic Pay
Label5	Text	HRA
Label6	Text	DA
Label7	Text	Gross Pay
Button1	Name	CmdProcess
	Text	Process
TextBox1	Name	TxtID
TextBox2	Name	TxtName
TextBox3	Name	TxtDesi
TextBox4	Name	TxtBP
TextBox5	Name	TxtHRA
TextBox6	Name	TxtDA
TextBox7	Name	TxtGP

Coding

```
Imports OOPLibrary
Public Class Form1

    Private Sub CmdProcess _Click(ByVal sender As System.Object,
ByVal e As System.EventArgs) Handles CmdProcess.Click
        Dim Emp As Employee = New Employee
        Emp.empid = Integer.Parse(TxtID.Text)
        Emp.empname = TxtName.Text
        Emp.empdesig = TxtDesi.Text
        Emp.bp = Decimal.Parse(TxtBP.Text)
        Emp.hr_allowance = Decimal.Parse(TxtHRA.Text)
        Emp.D_allowance = Decimal.Parse(TxtDA.Text)
        TxtGP.Text = Emp.grosspay()

    End Sub
End Class
```

Output

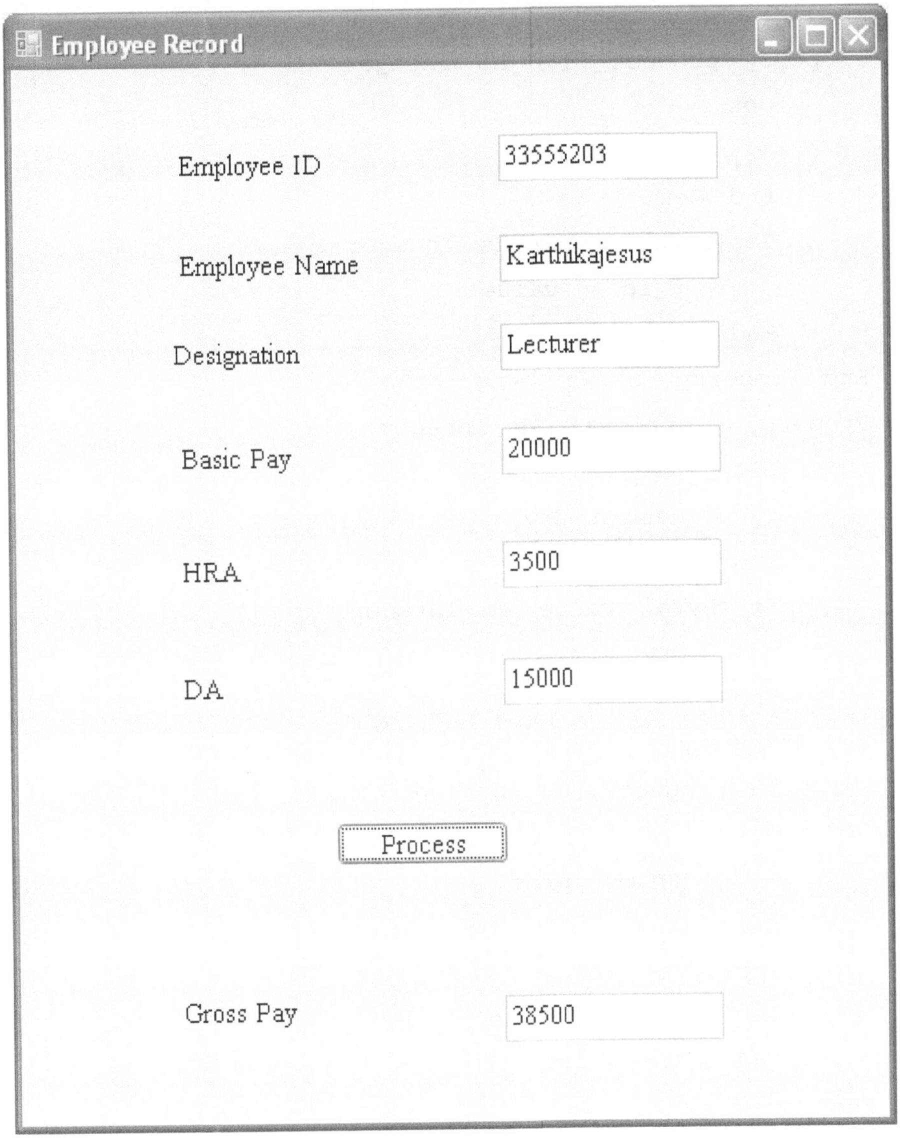

21.5 SALES AND SERVICING

This program demonstrates the sales and servicing for a particular product. For this, in this program we imports the derived class **Service** that stored in the class library **Ad_OOP.** Note that the class **Service** is derived from the class **Sales**

```
Public Class Sales
        Dim p_id, Qty As Integer
        Dim prod As String
```

```
Dim rate As Decimal

Property product_id() As Integer
      Get
            Return p_id
      End Get
      Set(ByVal value As Integer)
            p_id = value
      End Set
End Property
Property quantity() As Integer
      Get
            Return Qty
      End Get
      Set(ByVal value As Integer)
            Qty = value
      End Set
End Property
Property product() As String
      Get
            Return prod
      End Get
      Set(ByVal value As String)
            prod = value
      End Set
End Property
Property amount() As Decimal
      Get
            Return rate
      End Get
      Set(ByVal value As Decimal)
            rate = value
      End Set
End Property
```

```
        Overridable Function display()
            Return (Qty * rate)
        End Function

    End Class
    Public Class Service
        Inherits Sales
        Dim max As Integer
        Dim pay As Decimal
        Property max_delivery_day() As Integer
            Get
                Return max
            End Get
            Set(ByVal value As Integer)
                max = value
            End Set
        End Property
        Property payment() As Decimal
            Get
                Return pay
            End Get
            Set(ByVal value As Decimal)
                pay = value
            End Set
        End Property
        Overrides Function display()
            If (max > 30) Then
        Return (pay + 1000)    'after 30 days ,1000 will be charged
            Else
                Return (pay + 1500)    ' before 30 days, 1500 will
be charged
            End If
        End Function
    End Class
```

Form Designing

Table 21.5 Sales and Servicing

Control	*Property*	*Value*
GroupBox1	Text	Sales
GroupBox2	Text	Service
Label1	Text	ProductID
Label2	Text	Product
Label3	Text	Quantity
Label4	Text	Rate
Label5	Text	Total Amount
Label6	Text	ProductID
Label7	Text	Product
Label8	Text	Payment
Label9	Text	Days Avail
Label10	Text	Amount
TextBox1	Name	TxtSalesID
TextBox2	Name	TxtSalesProd
TextBox3	Name	TxtSalesQty
TextBox4	Name	TxtSalesRate
TextBox5	Name	TxtSalesAmount
TextBox6	Name	TxtServiceID
TextBox7	Name	TxtServiceProd
TextBox8	Name	TxtServicePayment
TextBox9	Name	TxtServiceDaysAvail
TextBox10	Name	TxtServiceAmount
Button1	Name	CmdSales
	Text	Sales
Button2	Name	CmdService
	Text	Service

Coding

```
Imports Ad_OOP
Public Class Form1
        Private Sub Form1_Load(ByVal sender As System.Object, ByVal
e As System.EventArgs) Handles MyBase.Load
        End Sub
    Private Sub CmdSales _Click(ByVal sender As System.Object, ByVal e
As System.EventArgs) Handles CmdSales.Click
                Dim S As Sales = New Sales()
                S.product_id = Integer.Parse(TxtSalesID.Text)
                S.product = TxtSalesProd.Text
                S.quantity = Integer.Parse(TxtSalesQty.Text)
                S.amount = Decimal.Parse(TxtSalesRate.Text)
                TxtSalesAmount.Text = S.display()
        End Sub

    Private Sub CmdService _Click(ByVal sender As System.Object, ByVal
e As System.EventArgs) Handles CmdService.Click
        Dim Se As Service = New Service()
        Se.product_id = Integer.Parse(TxtServiceID.Text)
            Se.product = TxtServiceProd.Text
            Se.payment = Decimal.Parse(TxtServicePayment.Text)
    Se.max_delivery_day = Integer.Parse(TxtServiceDaysAvail.Text)
    TxtServiceAmount.Text = Se.display()

        End Sub
    End Class
```

Output

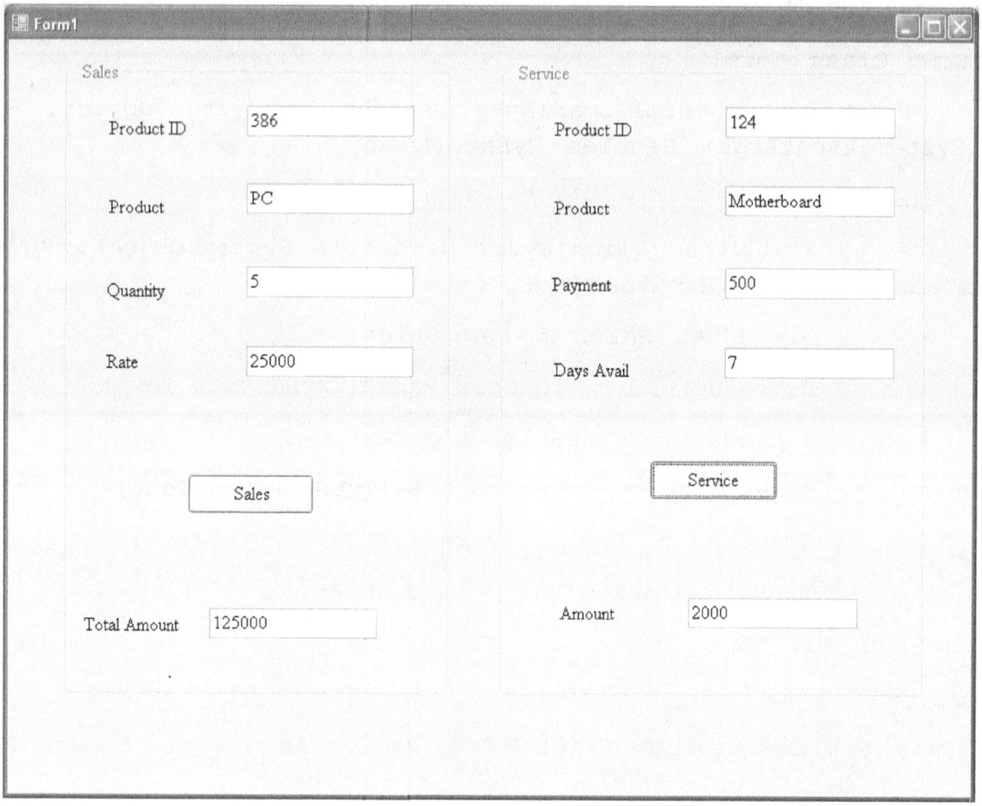
Form1
Sales
Product ID
386
Product
PC
Quantity
5
Rate
25000
Sales
Total Amount
125000
Service
Product ID
124
Product
Motherboard
Payment
500
Days Avail
7
Service
Amount
2000

PART V

WINDOWS CONTROL LIBRARY

The Windows Control Library project template is used to create custom controls to use on Windows Forms. It is an effective option to create custom control that can be included to the user interface. A Windows control or simply control such as a **TextBox** or **Button,** is a basic element of the user interface which provide the functionality that are predefined. Here we can build our own custom controls for very specific operations to simplify the development of large applications in a team environment.

CHAPTER

22

CREATING OUR OWN WINDOWS LIBRARY

22.1 CREATION OF WINDOWS CONTROL LIBRARY AND USE THEM AS AN APPLICATION

To create the Windows Library select **Windows Control Library** template from the **New Project** as in Fig. 22.1

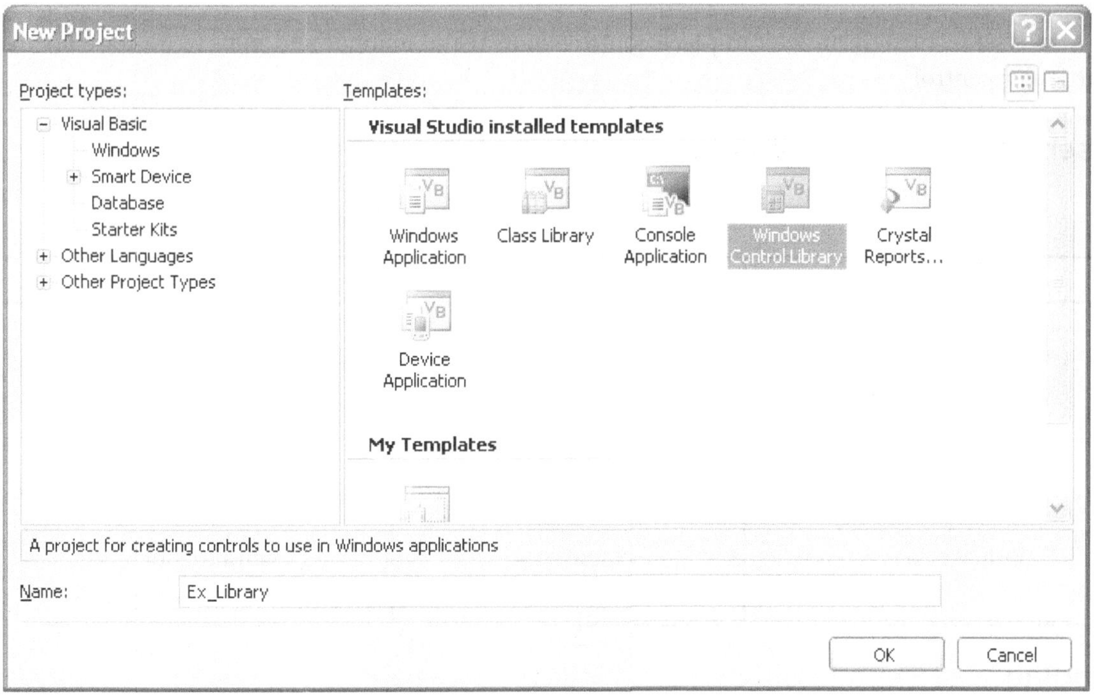

Fig. 22.1 *New Project Window*

Whatever typed on the Textbox will be the name of the windows Control Library. Select **OK** button which opens the following user control form as in Fig. 22.2

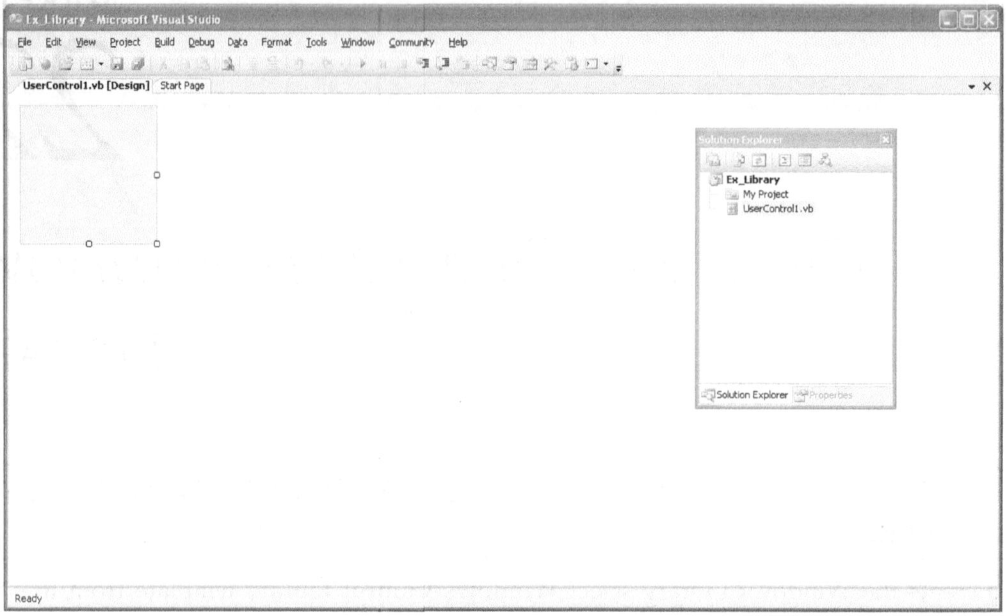

Fig. 22.2 *User Control Form*

In User Control form we can place controls in as usual manner and may write code for the particular control

User Control Form Designing

Table 22.1 User Control Form Designing

Control	*Property*	*Value*
UserControl1	Name	UserControl1
Label1	Text	UserName
Label2	Text	Password
TextBox1	Name	TxtUser
TextBox2	Name	TxtPwd
Button1	Name	CmdLogon
	Text	Log on

Coding

```
Public Class UserControl1

        Private Sub CmdLogon_Click(ByVal sender As System.Object,
ByVal e As System.EventArgs) Handles CmdLogon.Click
```

```
        If  TxtUser.Text = "admin" And TxtPwd.Text = "compuserv" Then
          MsgBox("Welcome", MsgBoxStyle.Exclamation, "User Control")
              Else
                 MsgBox("Access denied", MsgBoxStyle.Critical, "User
Control")
              End If
         End Sub
    End Class
```

This code can be tested by selecting **Start Debugging** option from **Debug** menu or press **F5.** User Control Test container test our user control as in Fig. 22.3

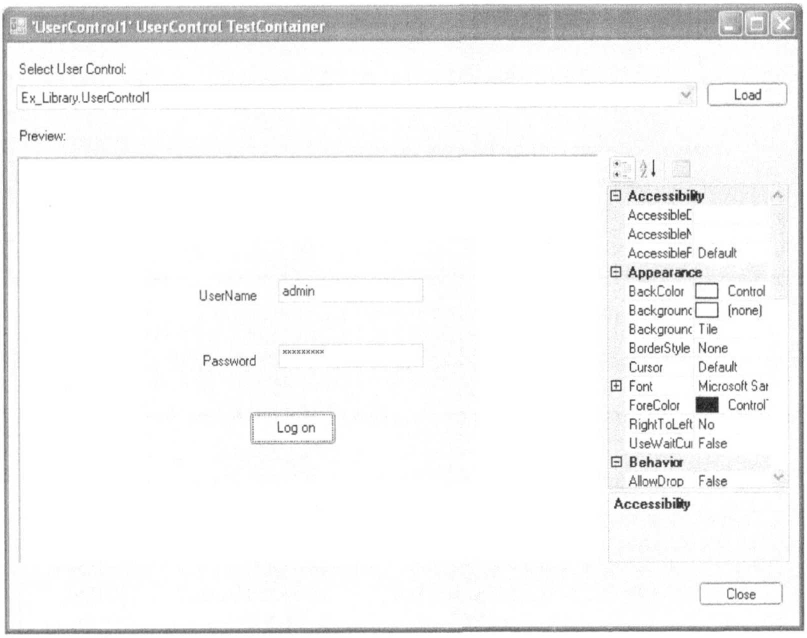

Fig. 22.3 *Test Container for User Control*

After the successful testing of a **UserControl,** it is included in the toolbox. The following steps done to execute this function.

Step 1:

Right click the tool box and select **Choose Items...** option

Step 2:

The **Choose Toolbox Items** dialogbox will appear as in Fig. 22.4

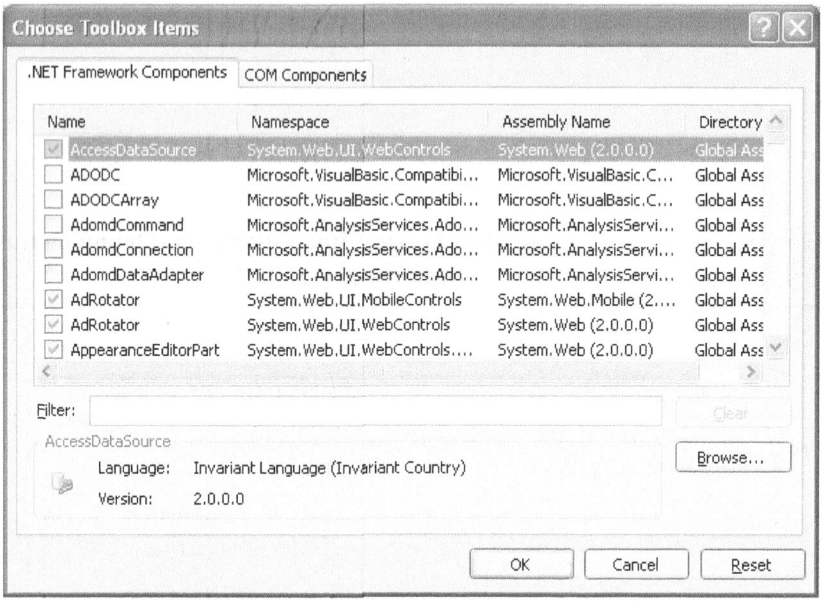

Fig. 22.4 *Choose Toolbox Items Appears*

Step 3:

Browse the **Ex_Library.dll** file from .../Ex_Library/Bin/Debug/ as in Fig. 22.5

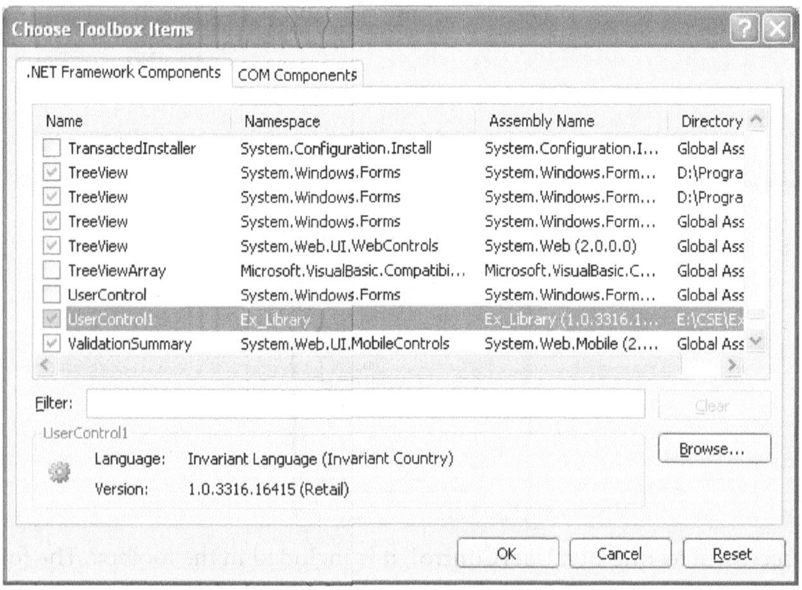

Fig. 22.5 *Browse the File Ex_Library.dll*

Press **Ok** Button will load the **userControl1** to the toolbox as in the following Fig. 22.6

Fig. 22.6 *Toolbox*

This user control can be placed in our form and can be used as required

Form Designing

Table 22.2 Windows Form Designing

Control	*Property*	*Value*
UserControl1	Name	UserControl1
Form1	Text	UserControl Demo

We may place other controls on the form and include code for the same as required.

Coding

```
Public Class Form1
    Private Sub Form1_Load(ByVal sender As System.Object, ByVal
e As System.EventArgs) Handles MyBase.Load
        MsgBox("This is UserControl Demo")
    End Sub
End Class
```

Output

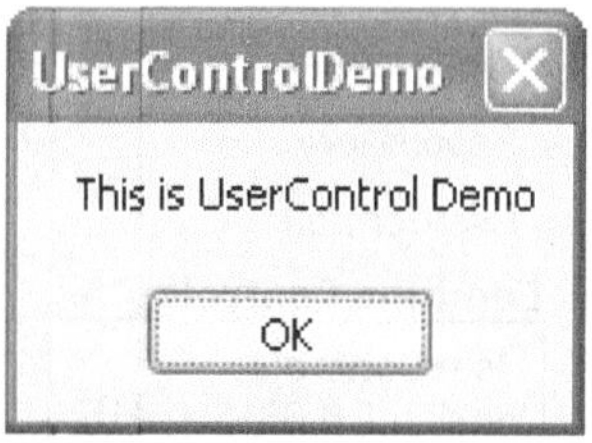

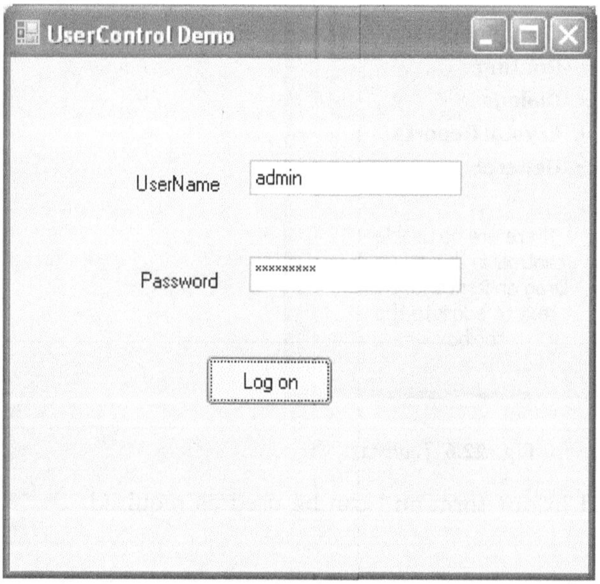

PART VI

DATABASE, REPORTS AND GRAPHICS

This part deals the concept of database, Report generation and Graphic Applications. Here the MS SQL is used for our Database connection. To run these programs the user must install MS SQL 2000 or Later. And the Reports are generated with the help of Crystal Reports. The Graphics chapter deals the some of graphics methods in VB.Net.

CHAPTER

23

EXCEL APPLICATION IN VB .NET

23.1 EXCEL IN VB .NET

In this chapter we brought the Excel application in our project. Here Excel application is activated from our coding module.

Form Designing

Table 23.1 Excel in VB .NET

Control	*Property*	*Value*
Button1	Name	CmdExcel
	Text	Excel

Coding

```
Public Class Form1
        Private Sub CmdExcel_Click(ByVal sender As System.Object,
ByVal e As System.EventArgs) Handles CmdExcel.Click
        Dim obj As New Excel.Application ' create reference to excel
              obj.Visible = True ' excel applicaiton displayed
              obj.Workbooks.Add()                'Adding work book
        End Sub
End Class
```

Output

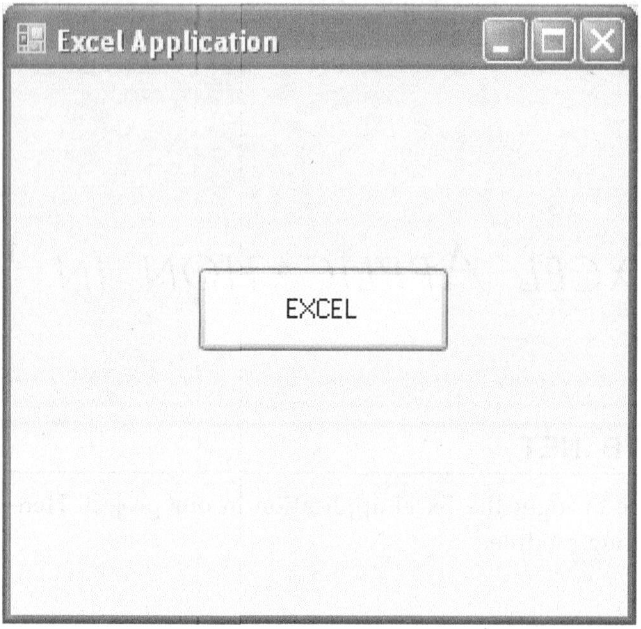

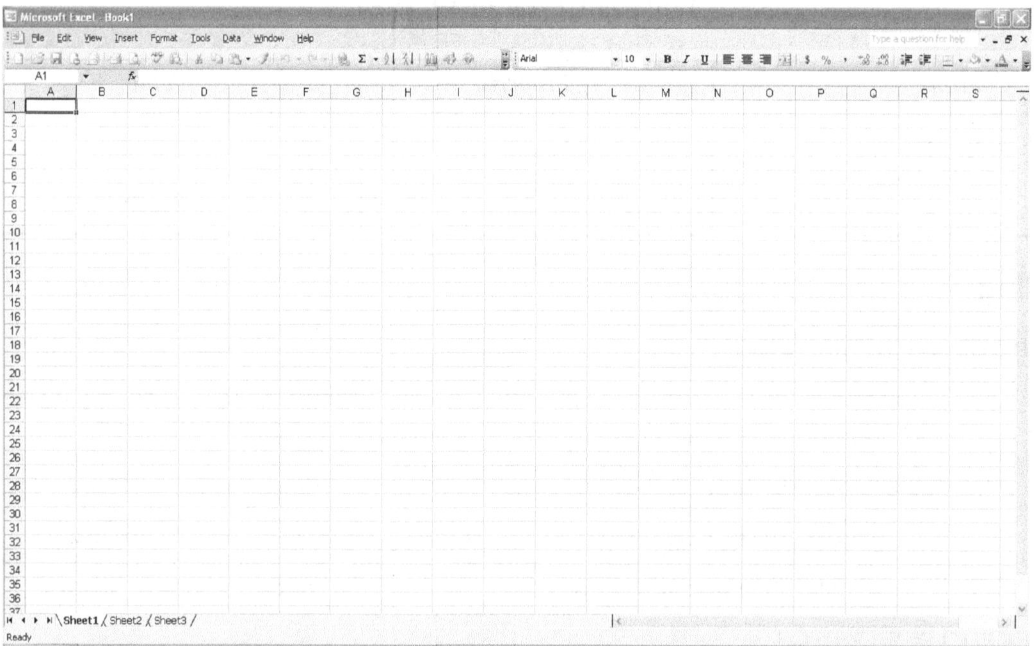

23.2 MARKSHEET

Here Excel application is activated with some data from our coding module.

Form Designing

Table 23.2 Marksheet

Control	*Property*	*Value*
Button1	Name	CmdMark
	Text	MarkSheet

Coding

```
Public Class Form1
    Private Sub CmdMark_Click(ByVal sender As System.Object, ByVal
e As System.EventArgs) Handles CmdMark.Click
    Dim obj As New Excel.Application'create reference to excel
        obj.Visible = True           'excel applicaiton displayed
        obj.Workbooks.Add()              'Adding work book
        obj.Range("A1").Select()
        obj.ActiveCell.FormulaR1C1 = "Name"
        obj.Range("B1").Select()              'select the cell B1
        obj.ActiveCell.FormulaR1C1 = "Maths" 'place the text on
                                              the cell B1
        obj.Range("C1").Select()
        obj.ActiveCell.FormulaR1C1 = "Science"
        obj.Range("D1").Select()
        obj.ActiveCell.FormulaR1C1 = "GK"
        obj.Range("E1").Select()
        obj.ActiveCell.FormulaR1C1 = "Total"

        obj.Range("A2").Select()
        obj.ActiveCell.FormulaR1C1 = "Bala"
        obj.Range("A3").Select()
        obj.ActiveCell.FormulaR1C1 = "Akash"
        obj.Range("A4").Select()
        obj.ActiveCell.FormulaR1C1 = "Wisva"
```

```
            obj.Range("B2").Select()
            obj.ActiveCell.FormulaR1C1 = "98"
            obj.Range("B3").Select()
            obj.ActiveCell.FormulaR1C1 = "95"
            obj.Range("B4").Select()
            obj.ActiveCell.FormulaR1C1 = "94"

            obj.Range("C2").Select()
            obj.ActiveCell.FormulaR1C1 = "95"
            obj.Range("C3").Select()
            obj.ActiveCell.FormulaR1C1 = "93"
            obj.Range("C4").Select()
            obj.ActiveCell.FormulaR1C1 = "98"

            obj.Range("D2").Select()
            obj.ActiveCell.FormulaR1C1 = "92"
            obj.Range("D3").Select()
            obj.ActiveCell.FormulaR1C1 = "98"
            obj.Range("D4").Select()
            obj.ActiveCell.FormulaR1C1 = "95"

            obj.Range("E2").Select()
            obj.ActiveCell.FormulaR1C1 = "=sum(Rc[-4]:Rc[-1])"
                                                          'apply the
formula among cells
            obj.Range("E3").Select()
            obj.ActiveCell.FormulaR1C1 = "=sum(Rc[-4]:Rc[-1])"
              obj.Range("E4").Select()
              obj.ActiveCell.FormulaR1C1 = "=sum(Rc[-4]:Rc[-1])"

        End Sub
    End Class
```

Output

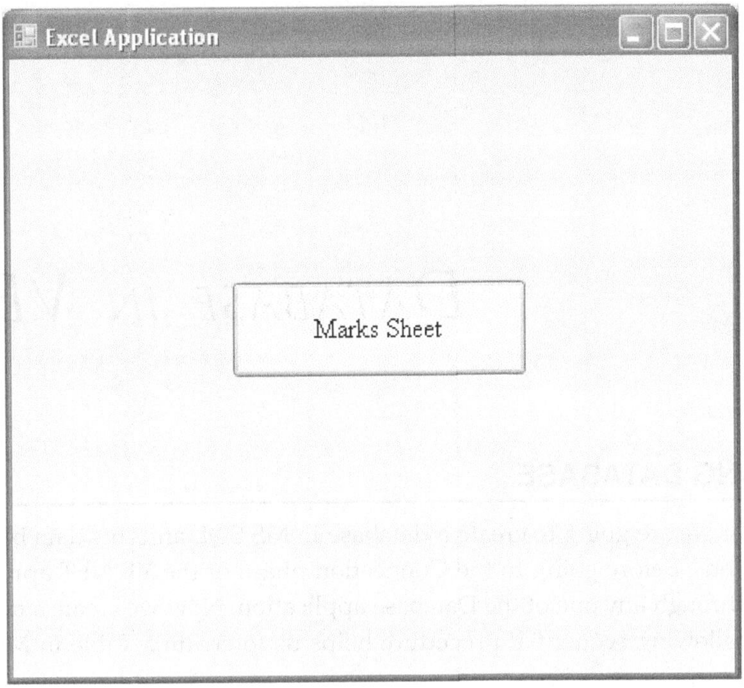
Excel Application
Marks Sheet

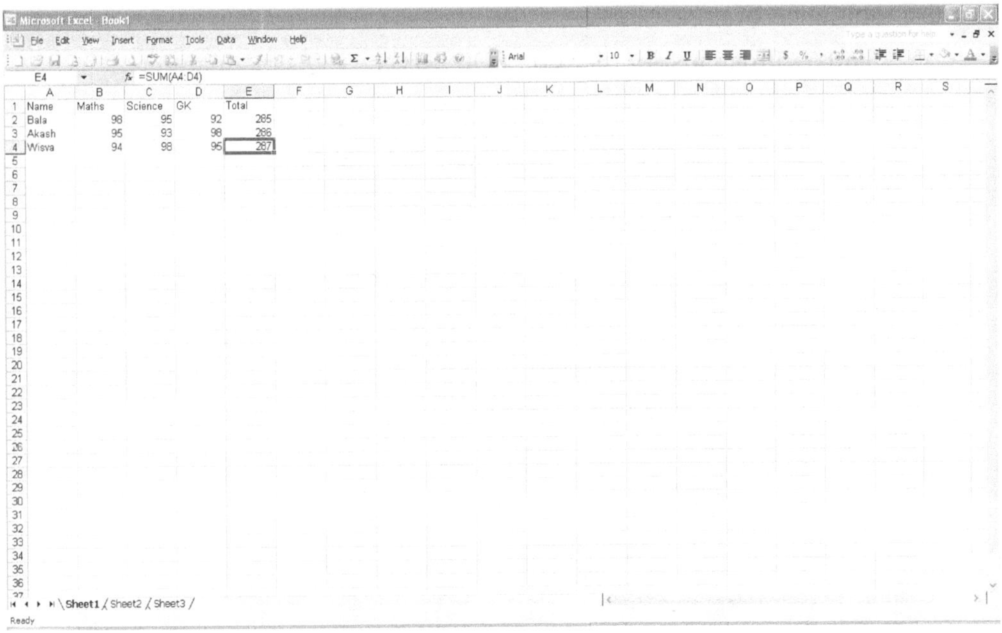
Microsoft Excel - Book1
E4
=SUM(A4:D4)
Name Maths Science GK Total
Bala 98 95 92 285
Akash 95 93 98 286
Wisva 94 98 95 287
Sheet1 Sheet2 Sheet3
Ready

CHAPTER

24

DATABASE IN VB .NET

24.1 CREATING DATABASE

In this chapter we are going to create a database in MS SQL and this data base is connected with our applications. Before going to the Connection phase of the VB.NET application first we create a database through any one of the Database application. Now we create a table in Microsoft SQL server. The following sequential procedure helps us to create a Table in Microsoft SQL.

Step (*i*): Enter into SQL Server

Open the application by

Start → Programs → Microsoft SQL Server → Query Analyzer

This will open ***Connect to SQL Server*** window as in Fig. 24.1

Fig. 24.1 *Connect to SQL Server*

In the SQL Server combo box select the Host in which we are going to store the database, if you are in network. Specifying (dot symbol) will lead you to store the database in local machine. Logon using the Login name **sa** (system administrator) and the password as you mentioned during the installation of SQL Server.

When you logged on to the **SQL Query Analyzer**, it displays the query window with default selection of **master** database as in Fig. 24.2

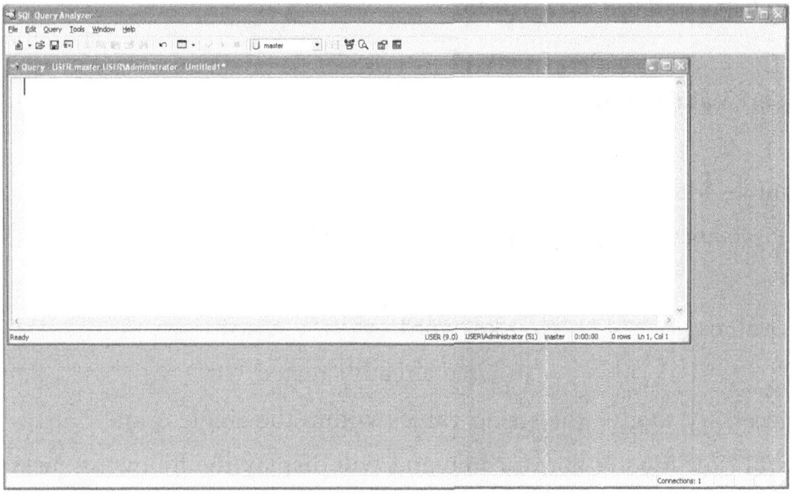

Fig. 24.2 *Query Window*

Step (*ii*): Table Creation

Now we give query to create a Table

create table products (sno int,pid varchar(10),pro_name varchar(20),Qty int)

where

create , table	→	Keyword
products	→	Table name
sno,pid, pro_name, Qty	→	Fields of the table products
int	→	integer data type
varchar	→	string datatype

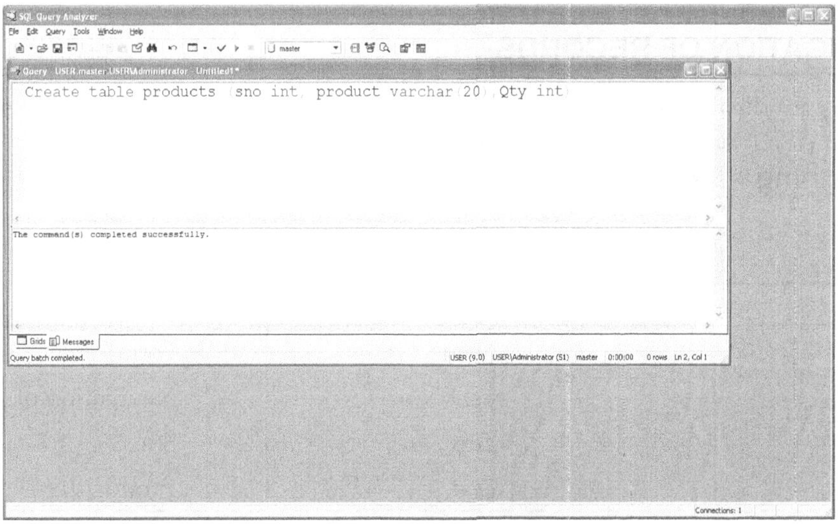

Execute the above query by selecting **Execute** option from **Query** menu or by hit **F5**
The successful execution of above command will display the following message
The command(s) completed successfully.

Step *iii*: Insert Values into the Table

Insert the values into the table by using the following query
insert into products values(1,'KX01', 'Keyboard',100)
where
insert, into, values → keyword
products → table already created
Here it is necessary to give the string values within the single quote.
The successful execution of above command will display the following message
(1 row(s) affected)
Insert some more records to the table as required.

Step *iv*: Display the Records
The following query will display all the records.
select * from products
select, from → keyword
products → table name
* represents that this query displays all the records
Now we have the table **products** in the **master** database

24.2 NAVIGATION OF RECORDS

This program displays the records in the form. For this open a new **windows Application**

Form Designing

Table 24.1 Navigation of Records

Control	*Property*	*Value*
Form1	Name	Form1
	Text	Navigation of Record
Label1	Text	Sno
Labe2	Text	Product ID

Label3	Text	Product Name
Label4	Text	Quantity
TextBox1	Name	TxtSno
TextBox2	Name	TxtProductID
TextBox3	Name	TxtProduct
TextBox4	Name	TxtQuantity
Button1	Name	CmdFirst
	Text	<<
Button2	Name	CmdPrevious
	Text	<
Button3	Name	CmdNext
	Text	>
Button4	Name	TxtLast
	Text	>>

Coding

```
Imports System.Data
Imports System.Data.SqlClient
Public Class Form1
      Dim con As SqlConnection
      Dim adap As SqlDataAdapter
      Dim ds As DataSet
      Dim dt As DataTable
      Dim r, c As Int16
      Shared p As Integer
Private Sub Form1_Load(ByVal sender As System.Object, ByVal e As System.EventArgs) Handles MyBase.Load
            ‘request for connection by specifying server, database, username and password
              con = New SqlConnection(“server=.;database=master;user id =sa;pwd=praise”)
              con.Open()  ‘Establish the connection’
               adap = New SqlDataAdapter(“Select * from products”, con)
              ds = New DataSet()
              adap.Fill(ds, “products”)
```

```
            dt = ds.Tables(0)
            r = dt.Rows.Count
            c = dt.Columns.Count
            p = 0
            assign()
        End Sub

       Private Sub CmdNext_Click(ByVal sender As System.Object, ByVal
e As System.EventArgs) Handles CmdNext.Click
            'next
            If p < r - 1 Then
               p = p + 1
                  assign()
            Else
                  MsgBox("End of record")
            End If
        End Sub

       Private Sub CmdLast_Click(ByVal sender As System.Object, ByVal
e As System.EventArgs) Handles CmdLast.Click
            ' last
            p = r - 1
            assign()
        End Sub
        Sub assign()
            TxtSno.Text = dt.Rows(p)(0)
            TxtProductID.Text = dt.Rows(p)(1)
           TxtProduct.Text = dt.Rows(p)(2)
            TxtQuantity.Text = dt.Rows(p)(3)

        End Sub

         Private Sub CmdFirst_Click(ByVal sender As System.Object,
ByVal e As System.EventArgs) Handles CmdFirst.Click
            'first
```

```
            p = 0
            assign()

        End Sub

        Private Sub CmdPrevious_Click(ByVal sender As System.Object,
ByVal e As System.EventArgs) Handles CmdPrevious.Click
            'previous
            If p > 0 Then
                p = p - 1
                assign()
            Else
                MsgBox("First Record")
            End If
        End Sub
    End Class
```

Output

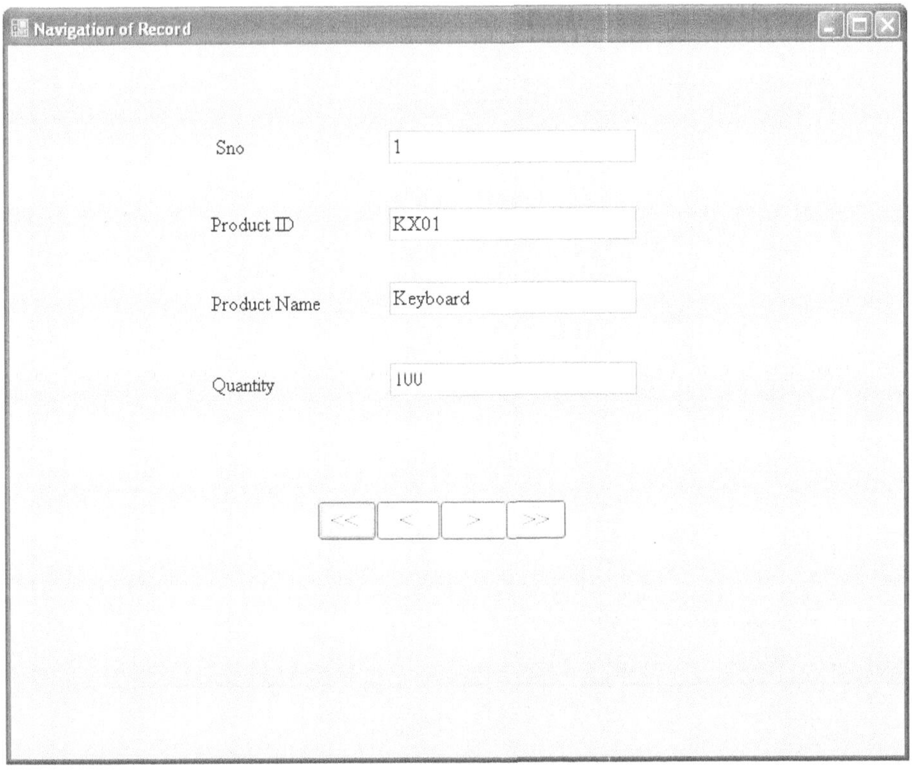

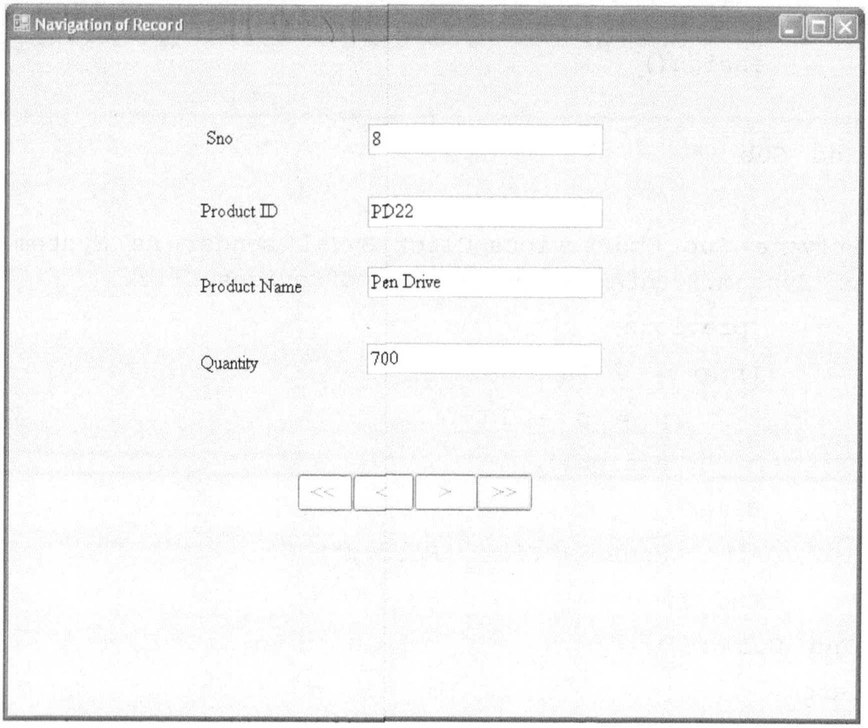
Navigation of Record
Sno
8
Product ID
PD22
Product Name
Pen Drive
Quantity
700
<<
<
>
>>

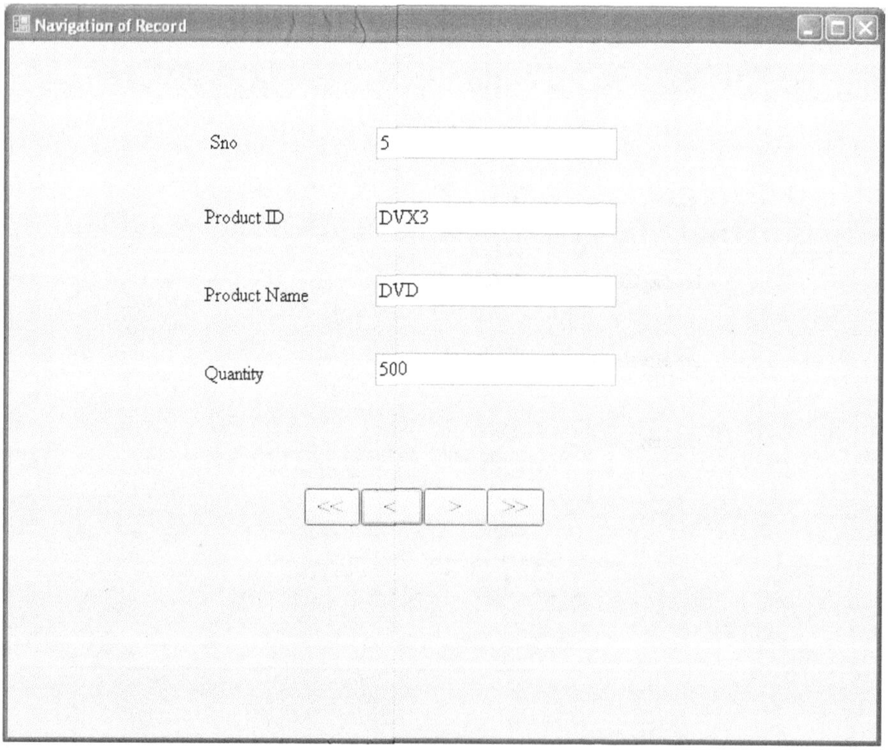
Navigation of Record
Sno
5
Product ID
DVX3
Product Name
DVD
Quantity
500
<<
<
>
>>

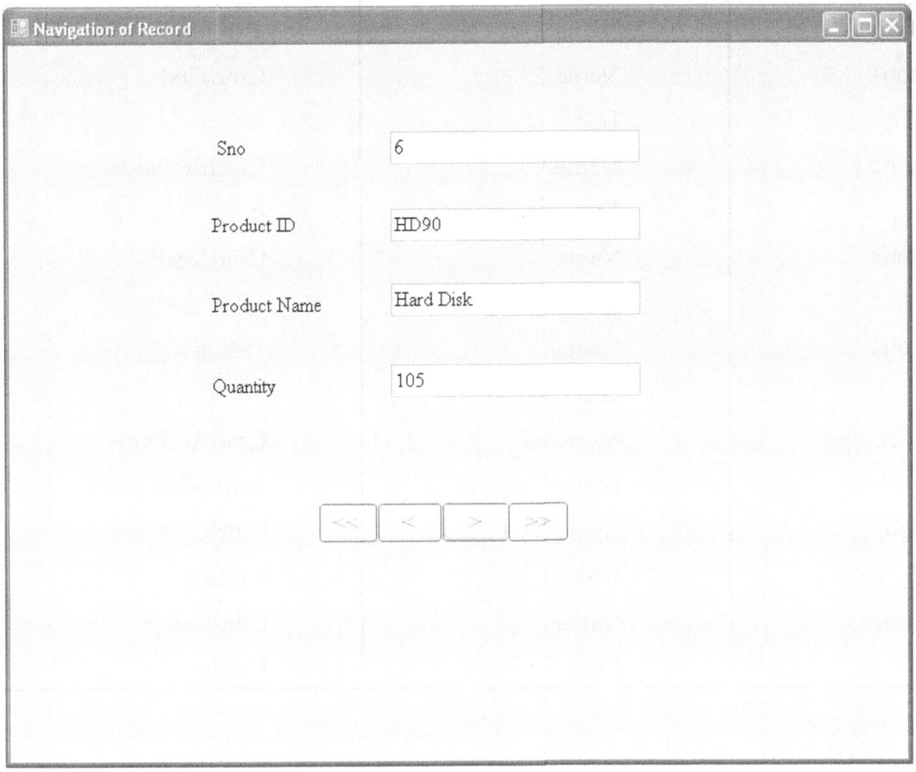

24.3 ELEMENTARY OPERATIONS OF DATABASE

In this program we can insert records in to the table and delete a particular record from the running Form.

Form Designing

Table 24.2 Elementry Operations of Database

Control	*Property*	*Value*
Form1	Name	Form1
	Text	Record Manipulation
Label1	Text	Sno
Labe2	Text	Product ID
Label3	Text	Product Name
Label4	Text	Quantity
TextBox1	Name	TxtSno
TextBox2	Name	TxtProductID

TextBox3	Name	TxtProduct
TextBox4	Name	TxtQuantity
Button1	Name	CmdFirst
	Text	<<
Button2	Name	CmdPrevious
	Text	<
Button3	Name	CmdNext
	Text	>
Button4	Name	TxtLast
	Text	>>
Button5	Name	CmdAddNew
	Text	Add New
Button6	Name	CmdUpdate
	Text	Update
Button7	Name	CmdDelete
	Text	Delete

Coding

```
Imports System.Data
Imports System.Data.SqlClient
Public Class Form1
      Dim con As SqlConnection
      Dim adap As SqlDataAdapter
      Dim ds As DataSet
      Dim dt As DataTable
      Dim r, c As Int16
      Shared p As Integer
      Private Sub Form1_Load(ByVal sender As System.Object, ByVal
e As System.EventArgs) Handles MyBase.Load
            con = New SqlConnection("server=.;database=master;user
id =sa;pwd=praise;")
            con.Open()
         adap = New SqlDataAdapter("Select * from products", con)
          ds = New DataSet()
            adap.Fill(ds, "products")
```

```
            dt = ds.Tables(0)
            r = dt.Rows.Count
            c = dt.Columns.Count
            p = 0
            assign()
        End Sub

    Private Sub CmdNext_Click(ByVal sender As System.Object, ByVal
e As System.EventArgs) Handles CmdNext.Click
            'next
            If p < r - 1 Then
                p = p + 1
                assign()
            Else
                MsgBox("End of record")
            End If
        End Sub

    Private Sub CmdLast_Click(ByVal sender As System.Object, ByVal
e As System.EventArgs) Handles CmdLast.Click
            ' last
            p = r - 1
            assign()
        End Sub
        Sub assign()
            TxtSno.Text = dt.Rows(p)(0)
            TxtProductID.Text = dt.Rows(p)(1)
           TxtProduct.Text = dt.Rows(p)(2)
            TxtQuantity.Text = dt.Rows(p)(3)

        End Sub

      Private Sub CmdFirst_Click(ByVal sender As System.Object,
ByVal e As System.EventArgs) Handles CmdFirst.Click
            'first
            p = 0
            assign()
```

```
        End Sub

        Private Sub CmdPrevious_Click(ByVal sender As System.Object,
ByVal e As System.EventArgs) Handles CmdPrevious.Click
            'previous
            If p > 0 Then
                p = p - 1
                assign()
            Else
                MsgBox("First Record")
            End If
        End Sub

    Private Sub CmdDelete_Click(ByVal sender As System.Object, ByVal e
As System.EventArgs) Handles CmdDelete.Click
            'Delete
            Dim a As Integer
            con = New SqlConnection("Server=.;database=master;user
id=sa;pwd=;")
            ds1 = New DataSet()
            a = Integer.Parse(TextBox1.Text)
            MsgBox(a)
            MsgBox("Delete permanently?")
            adap1 = New SqlDataAdapter("delete from products where
sno=" & a & "", con)
            adap1.Fill(ds1, "products")
            MsgBox("Record Deleted Permenetly!")
        End Sub

        Private Sub CmdUpdate_Click(ByVal sender As System.Object,
ByVal e As System.EventArgs) Handles CmdUpdate.Click
            'update
            Dim sno, qty As Integer
            Dim Pid, pname As String
            sno = Integer.Parse(Txtsno.Text)
            Pid = TxtProductid.Text
```

```
            pname = TextBox3.Text
            qty = Integer.Parse(TextBox4.Text)
            ds = New DataSet()
            con = New SqlConnection("server=.;database=master;user
id =sa;pwd=praise;")
            adap = New SqlDataAdapter("insert into products values
(" & sno & ", & Pid & ",'" & pname & "'," & qty & ")", con)
            adap.Fill(ds, "products")
            MsgBox("Record inserted")
        End Sub

        Private Sub CmdNew_Click(ByVal sender As System.Object, ByVal
e As System.EventArgs) Handles CmdNew.Click
                            TxtSno.Text = ""
    TxtProductID..Text = ""
            TxtProduct.Text = ""
             TextBox4.Text = ""
        End Sub
    End Class
```

Output

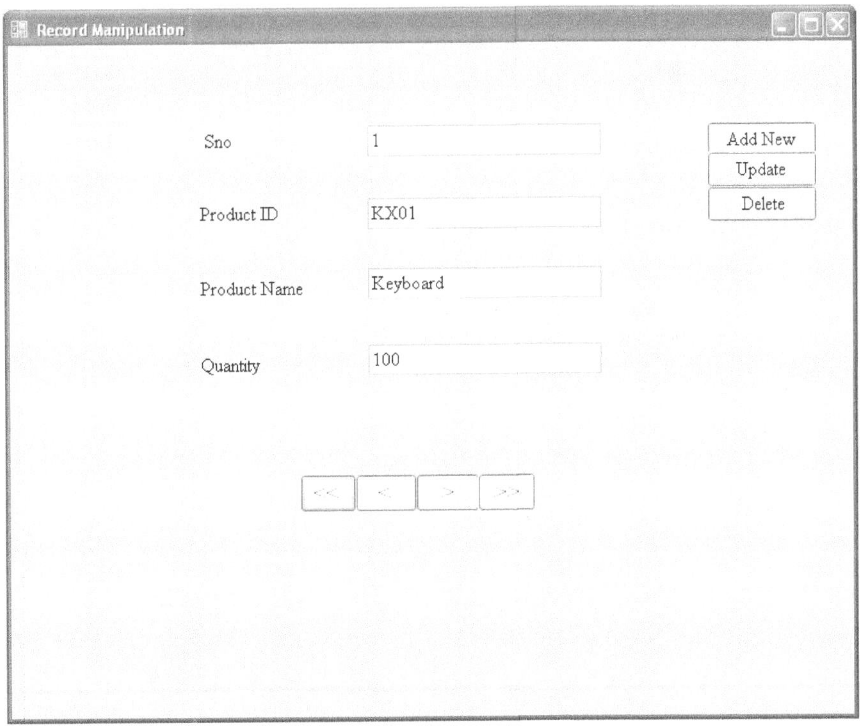

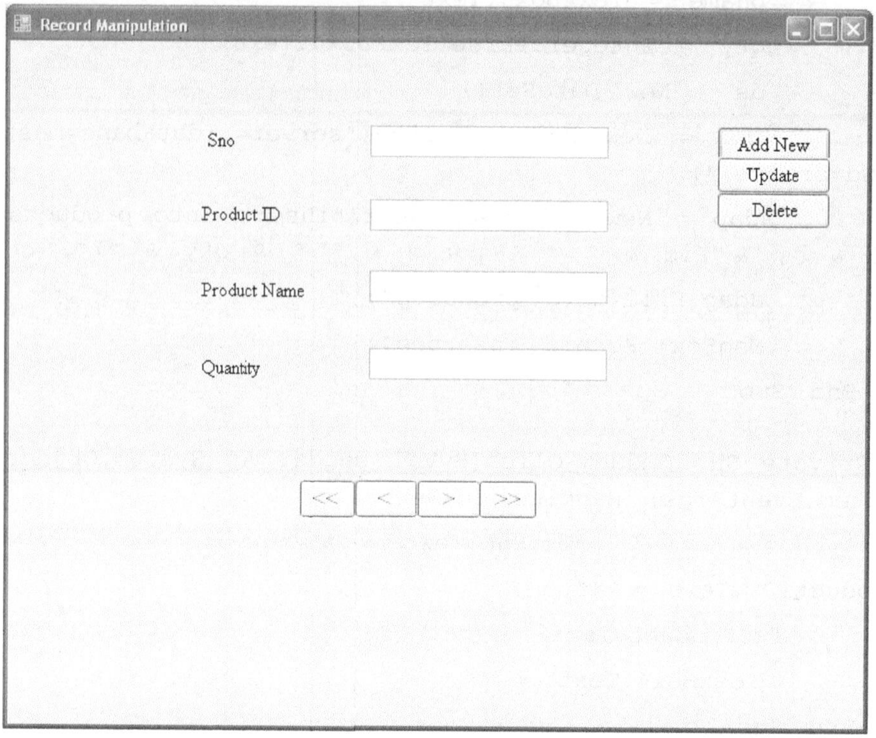
Record Manipulation
Sno
Product ID
Product Name
Quantity
Add New
Update
Delete
<<
<
>
>>

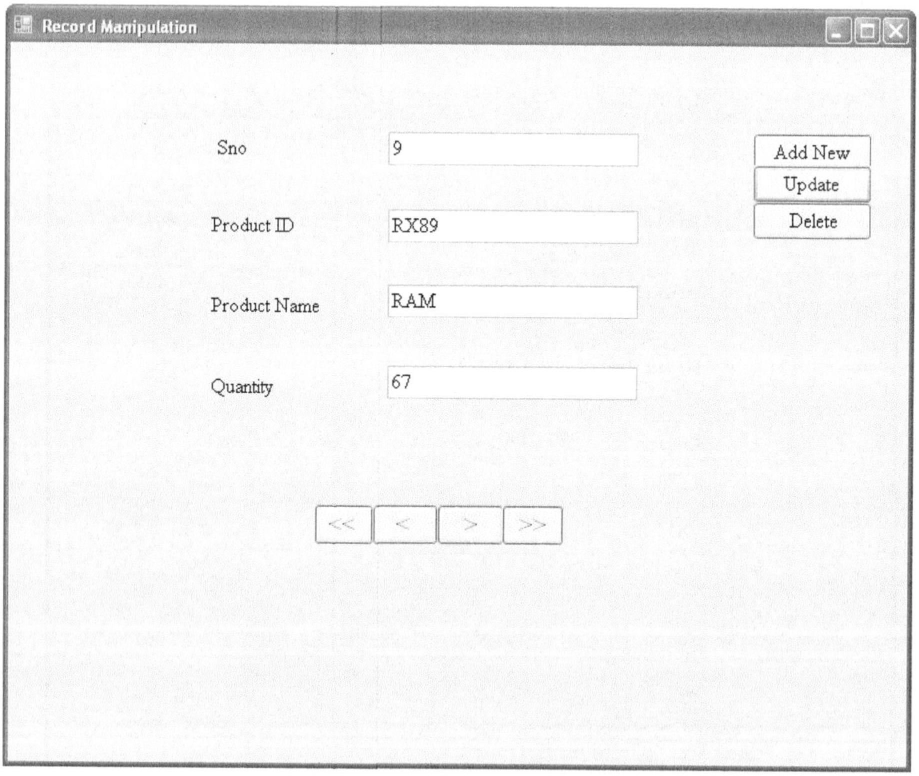
Record Manipulation
Sno
9
Product ID
RX89
Product Name
RAM
Quantity
67
Add New
Update
Delete
<<
<
>
>>

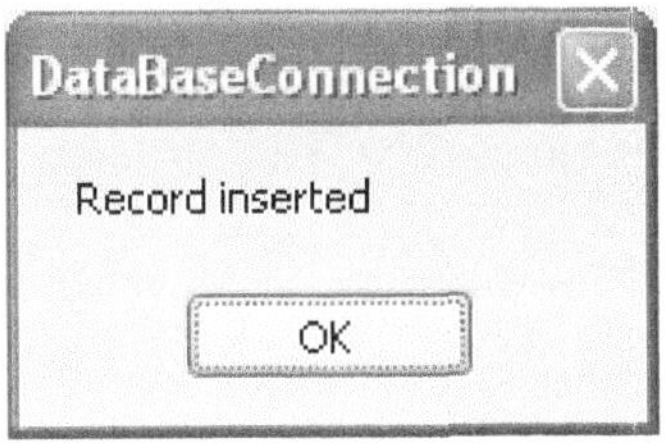
DataBaseConnection
Record inserted
OK

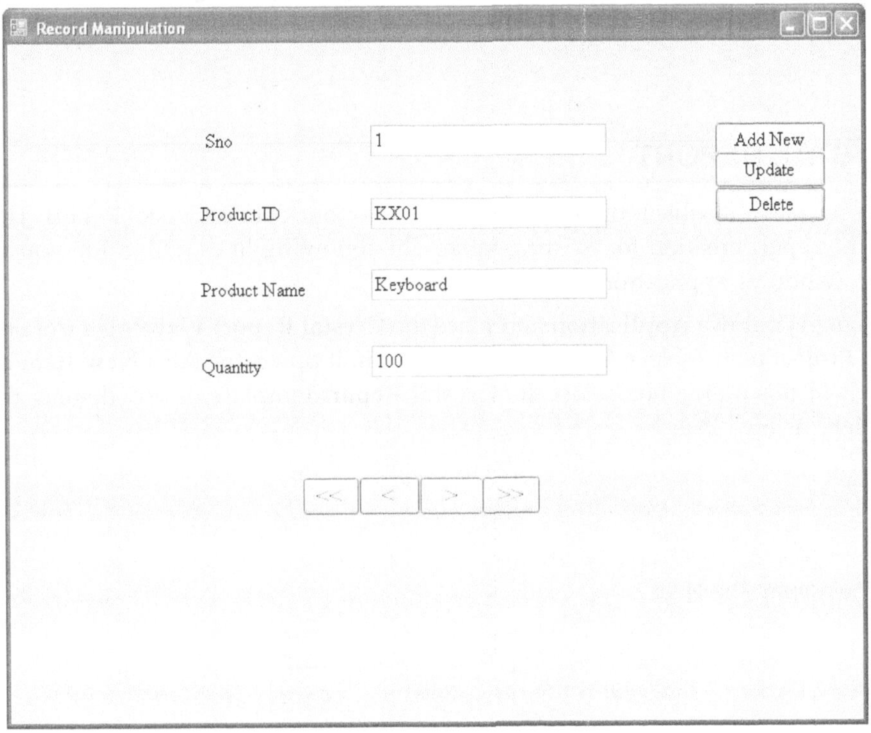
Record Manipulation
Sno
1
Product ID
KX01
Product Name
Keyboard
Quantity
100
Add New
Update
Delete
<<
<
>
>>

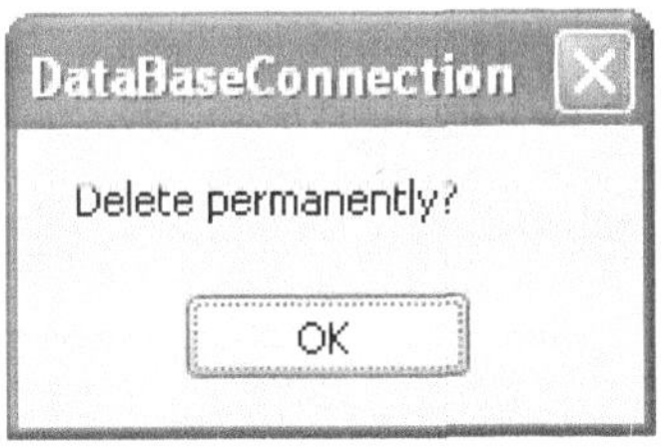
DataBaseConnection
Delete permanently?
OK

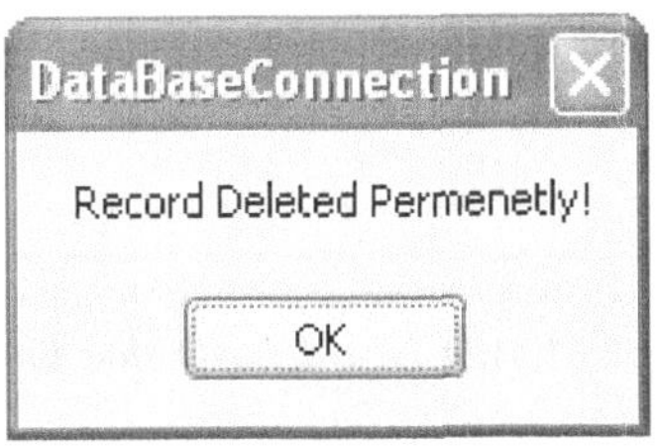
DataBaseConnection
Record Deleted Permenetly!
OK

CHAPTER

25

REPORT GENERATION

25.1 CRYSTAL REPORT

VB.Net provides a flexible tool to generate reports for our data is Crystal Report. This chapter deals about the report creation for existing table. The following lines will guide you to create a report on the windows application.

Open a new **Windows Application** and place the **Crystal Report Viewer** control on the form. For this, in a **Project** menu select **Add New Item** option, it opens the **Add New Item** dialog box as in Fig. 25.1. In this dialog box select the **Crystal Report** template. It will display the **Crystal Reports Gallery** as Fig. 25.2.

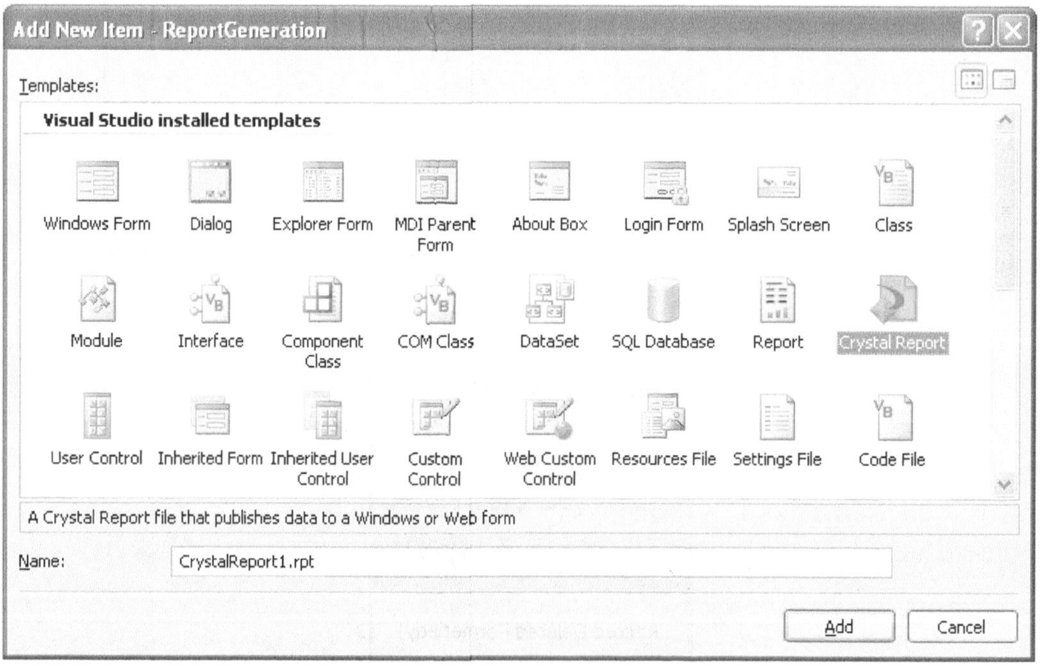

Fig. 25.1 *Add New Item Dialog Box*

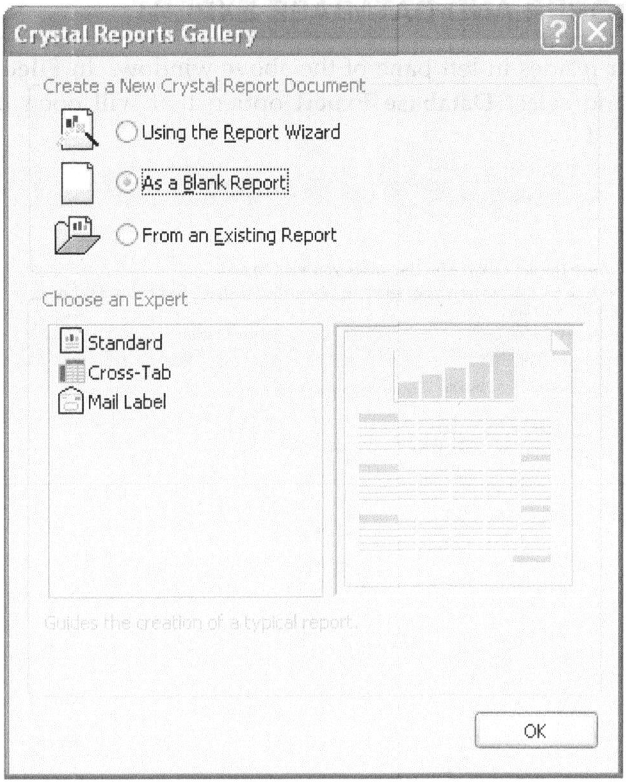

Fig. 25.2 *Crystal Reports Gallery*

In this dialog box, select the option **As a Blank Report.** Confirm the selection by **OK** button; it opens the blank report as in Fig. 25.3

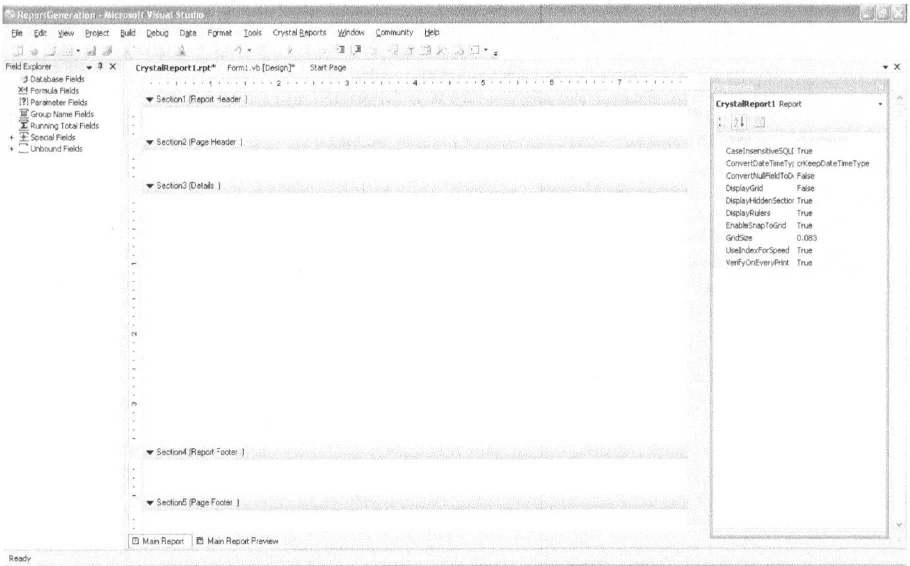

Fig. 25.3 *Blank Report*

25.2 FIELD EXPLORER AND DATABASE EXPERT

The **Field Explorer** resides in left pane of the above window. In **Filed Explorer** right click the **Database Fields**, and select **Database Expert** option that will open the **Database Expert** dialog box as in Fig. 25.4

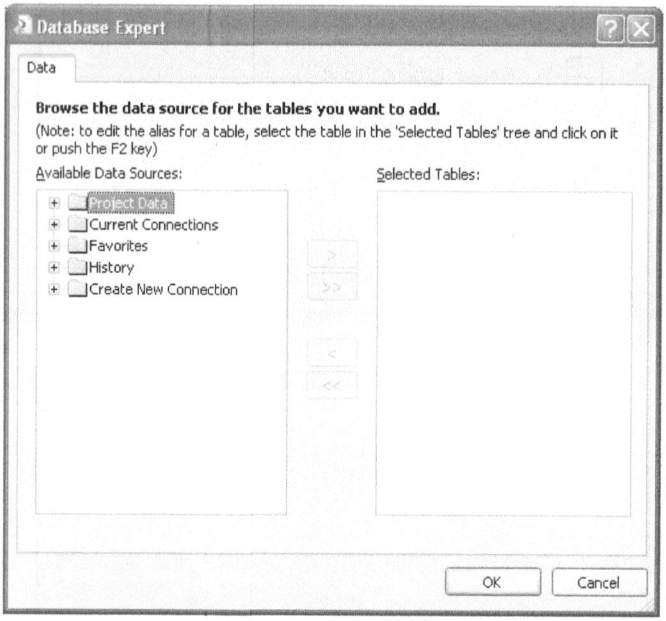

Fig. 25.4 *Database Expert Dialog Box*

In this Database Expert window Expand the **Create New Connection** and select **OLE DB (ADO)** as in Fig. 25.5 which opens the **OLE BD (ADO)** dialog box as in Fig. 25.6.

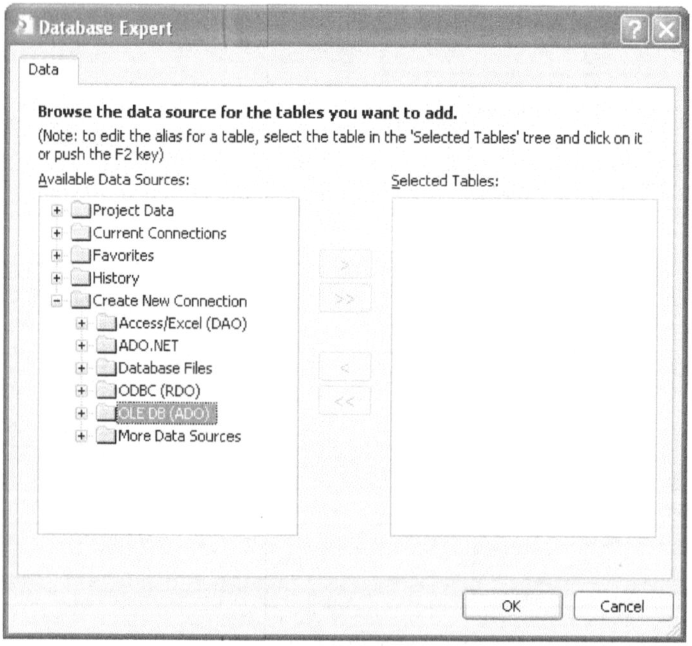

Fig. 25.5 *Selection of OLE BD (ADO)*

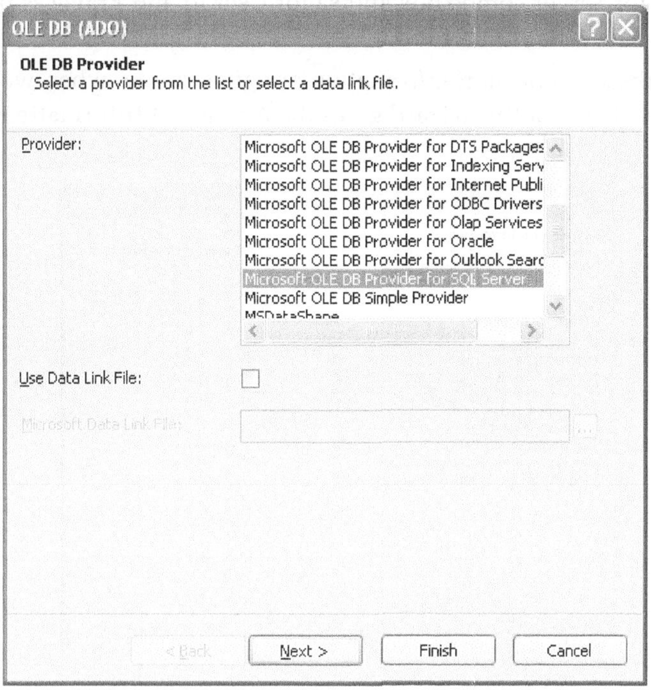

Fig. 25.6 *OLE BD (ADO) Dialog Box*

In the OLE DB (ADO) dialog box, select **Microsoft OLE DB Provider for SQL Server** option and go to the next step of the wizard by selecting the **Next >** button. It shows the connection information as shown in Fig. 25.7

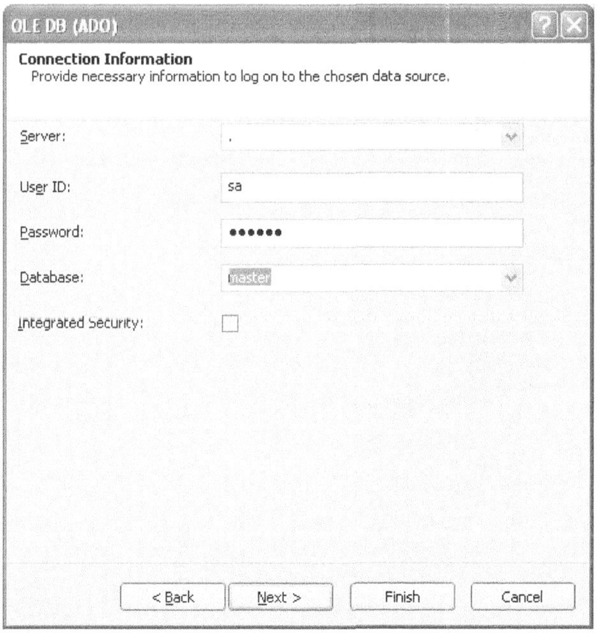

Fig. 25.7 *Connection Information*

Here give **.** (dot) for Server combo box and **sa** for User Id and **Praise** as password and select **master** database.

Remember that these connection information are given by us when we creating a table in Microsoft SQL. The Next step of this wizard gives the **Advanced Information** for our connection as in Fig. 25.8

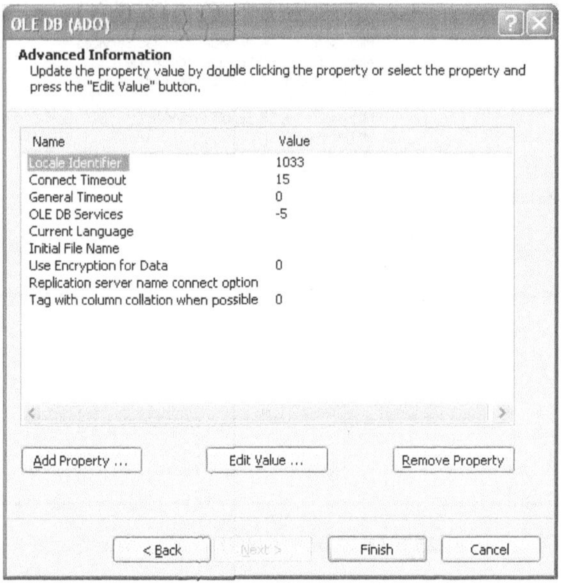

Fig. 25.8 *Advanced Information*

Finish the Wizard by selecting the **Finish** button. Now we return to the **Database Expert** dialog box and it is now shown as in Fig. 25.9

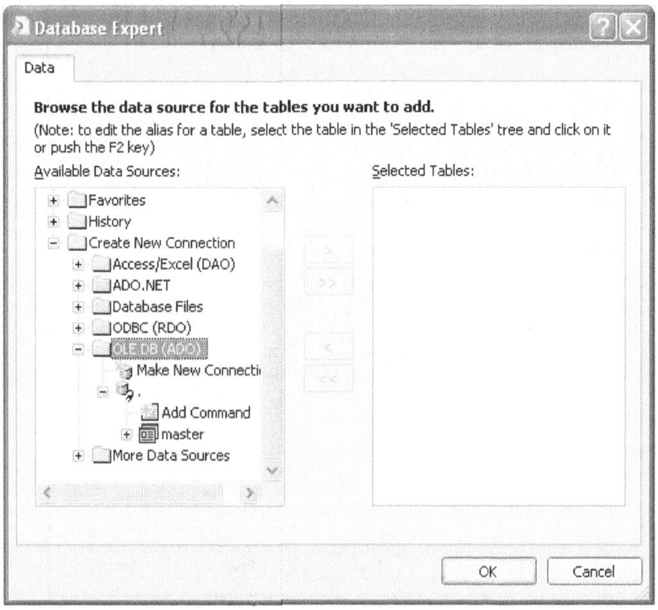

Fig. 25.9 *Return to the Database Expert Window*

From here we select the **master** database and our table **products** and assign the table to right pane as shown Figs. 25.10 and 25.11.

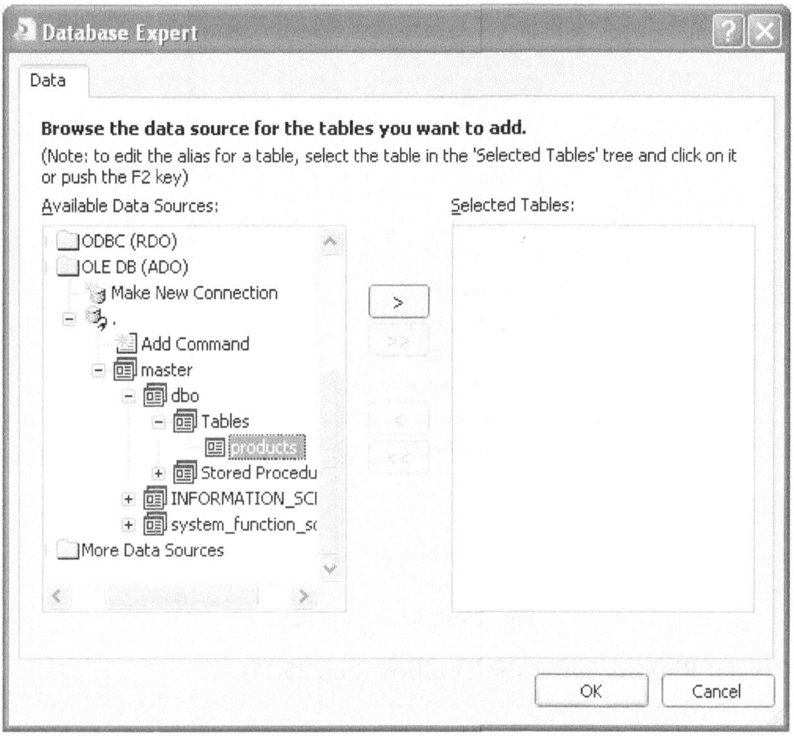

Fig. 25.10 *Selecting the Table Products*

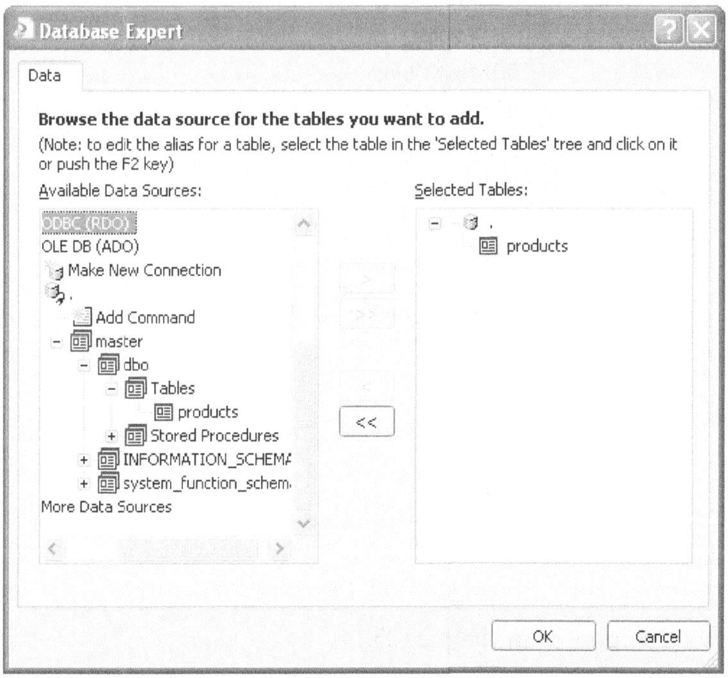

Fig. 25.11 *Assign the Table Products to Right Pane*

This will make the **Field Explorer** as shown below Fig. 25.12

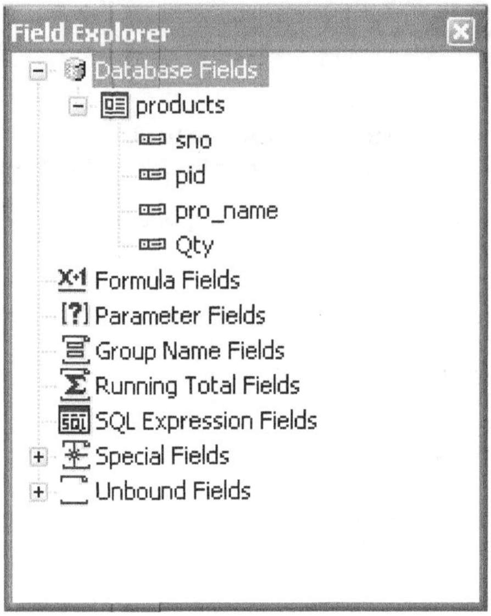

Fig. 25.12 *Field Explorer*

Select the **Crystal Reports** tab in the **Toolbox (Fig. 25.13)**

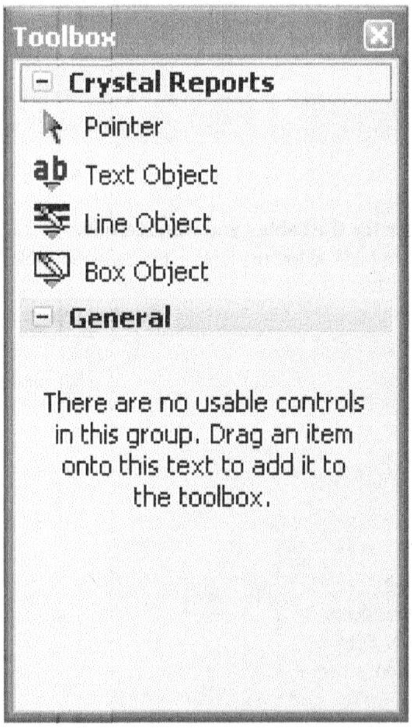

Fig. 25.13 *Toolbox*

Design the Crystal Report as in the Fig. 25.14

Form Desigring

Table 25.1 Crystal Report Designing

Control	*Property*	*Value*
CrystalReport1	Name	CrystalReport1
Text1	Name	Text1
	Text	Product List Report [Type directly on the control]
Textbox1	Font	Select font name and size from the dialog box

Output

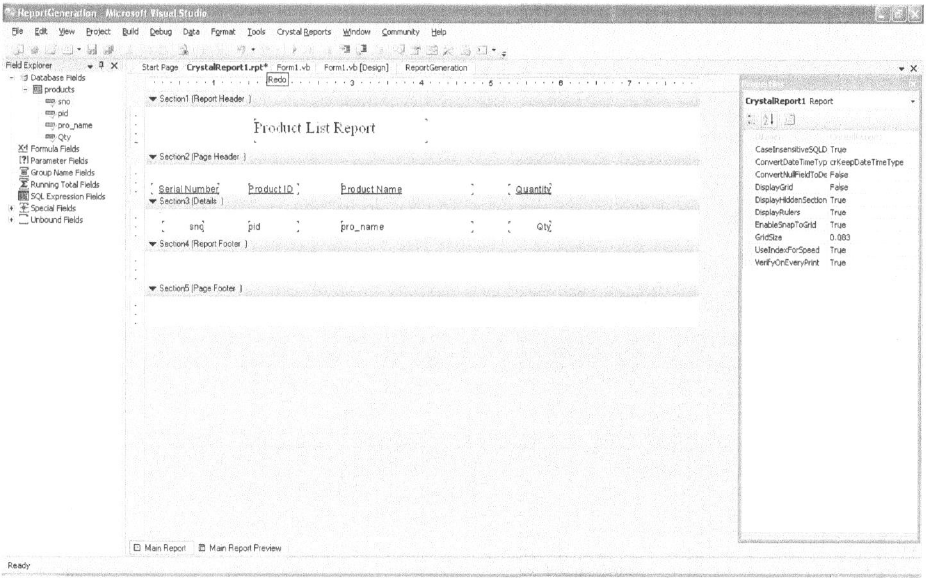

Fig. 25.14 *Crystal Report Designed*

To edit the Text control, Right click the **Text** controls and select **Edit Text Object** option in order to change the text displayed.

Form Designing

Table 25.2 Form Designing

Control	*Property*	*Value*
CrystalReportViewer1	Name	CrystalReportViewer1
	ReportSource	E:\ReportGeneration\CrystalReport1.rpt[Browse the CrystalReport1 stored on the Application Report Generation]
Form1	Text	Report Generation

Note: Before to change the CrystalReportViewer properties save the application in a required folder.

Coding

```
Public Class Form1

        Private Sub CrystalReportViewer1_Load(ByVal sender As System.Object, ByVal e As System.EventArgs) Handles CrystalReportViewer1.Load
            MsgBox("Crystal Report Viewer Loaded")
        End Sub
End Class
```

Run the application will yield the following output

Output

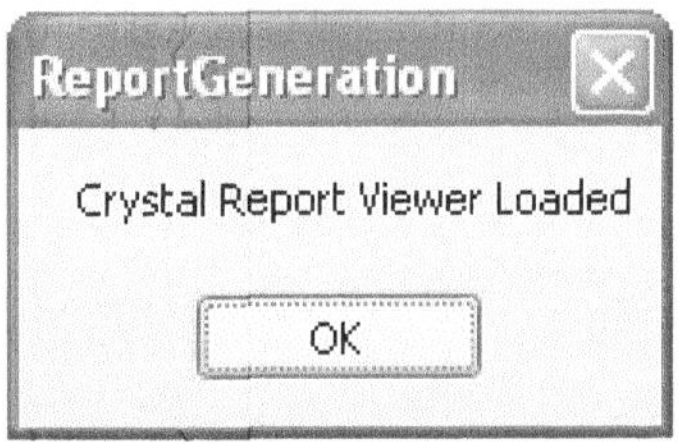

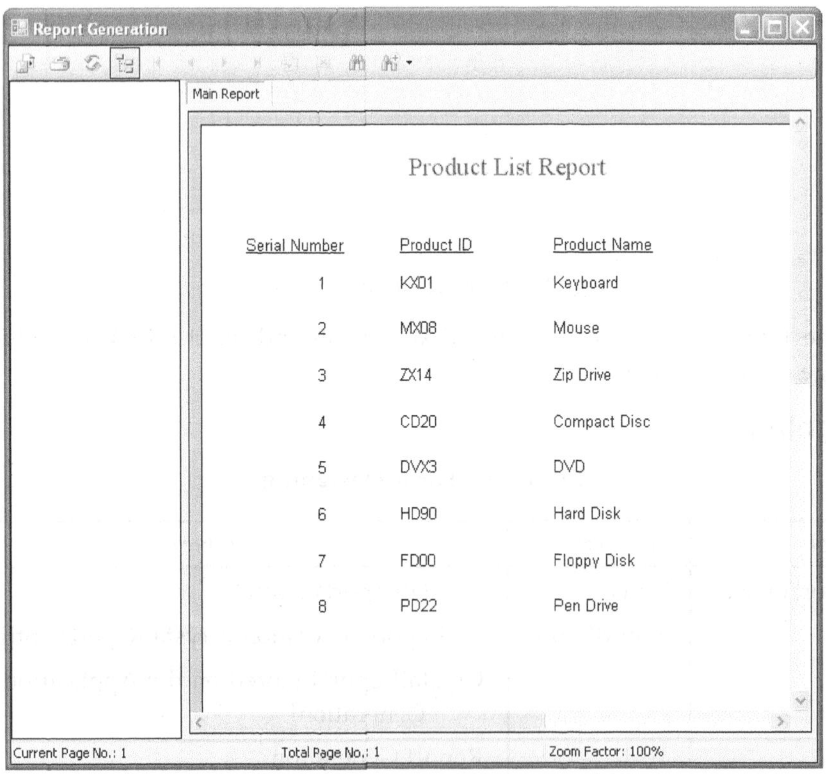

CHAPTER

26

GRAPHICS IN VB .NET

26.1 DISPLAYING A STRING

This program displays a string using **DrawString()** method.

Form Designing

Table 26.1 Displaying a String

Control	*Property*	*Value*
Form1	Name	Form1
	Text	Displaying a Text

Coding

```
Public Class Form1
    Protected Overrides Sub OnPaint(ByVal e As PaintEventArgs)
        Dim g As Graphics
        g = e.Graphics
        Dim myf As Font
        myf = New Font("Viner Hand ITC", 35, FontStyle.Bold)
        Dim myb As Brush
        myb = Brushes.MidnightBlue
        g.DrawString("Death and life are in the power of the
tongue", myf, myb, 0, 100)
    End Sub
End Class
```

Output

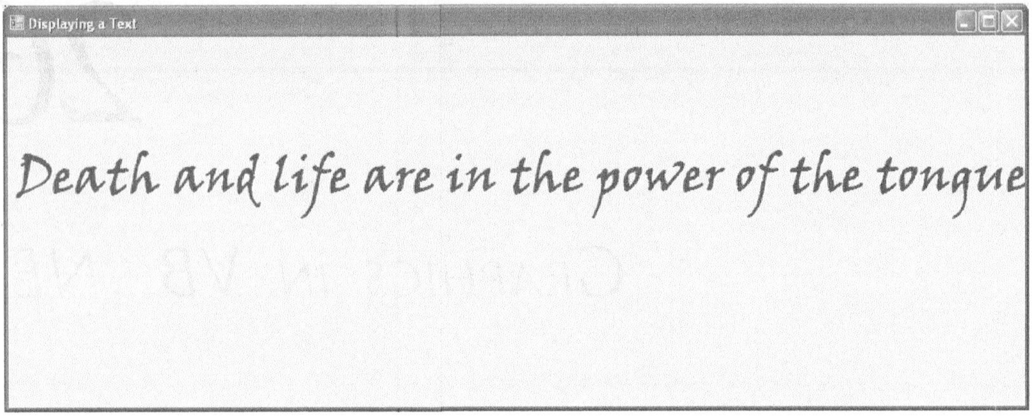

26.2 DISPLAYING A LINE

This program display a line using **DrawLine()**

Form Designing

Table 26.2 Displaying a Line

Control	*Property*	*Value*
Form1	Name	Form1
	Text	Line

Coding

```
Public Class Form1
    Protected Overrides Sub OnPaint(ByVal e As PaintEventArgs)

        Dim g As Graphics
        g = e.Graphics
        Dim mypen As Pen
mypen = New Pen(Color.DarkOliveGreen, 4)
        g.DrawLine(mypen, 40, 60, 156, 178)

   End Sub
End Class
```

Output

26.3 DISPLAYING LINES

This program displays lines which produces rectangle shape.

Form Designing

Table 26.3 Displaying Lines

Control	*Property*	*Value*
Form1	Name	Form1
	Text	Line

Coding

```
Public Class Form1
    Protected Overrides Sub OnPaint(ByVal e As PaintEventArgs)

        Dim g As Graphics
        g = e.Graphics
        Dim mypen As Pen
        mypen = New Pen(Color.DarkRed, 4)
        g.DrawLine(mypen, 240, 260, 540, 260)
```

```
            g.DrawLine(mypen, 240, 400, 540, 400)
            g.DrawLine(mypen, 240, 260, 240, 400)
            g.DrawLine(mypen, 540, 260, 540, 400)
            g.DrawLine(mypen, 240, 260, 540, 400)
            g.DrawLine(mypen, 540, 260, 240, 400)
        End Sub
    End Class
```

Output

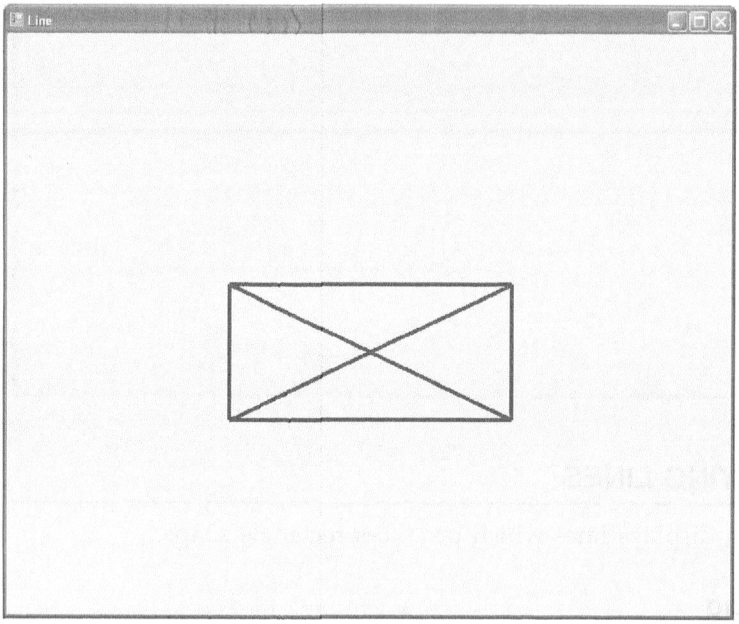

26.4 DISPLAYING A SQUARE

This program displays a square using **DrawRectangle()** method.

Form Designing

Table 26.4 Displaying a Square

Control	*Property*	*Value*
Form1	Name Text	Form1 Rectangle

```
Public Class Form1

    Protected Overrides Sub OnPaint(ByVal e As PaintEventArgs)
```

```
            Dim dc As Graphics
            dc = e.Graphics
            Dim mypen As Pen
            mypen = New Pen(Color.DarkOliveGreen, 4)
            dc.DrawRectangle(mypen, 40, 60, 50, 50)

        End Sub
    End Class
```

Output

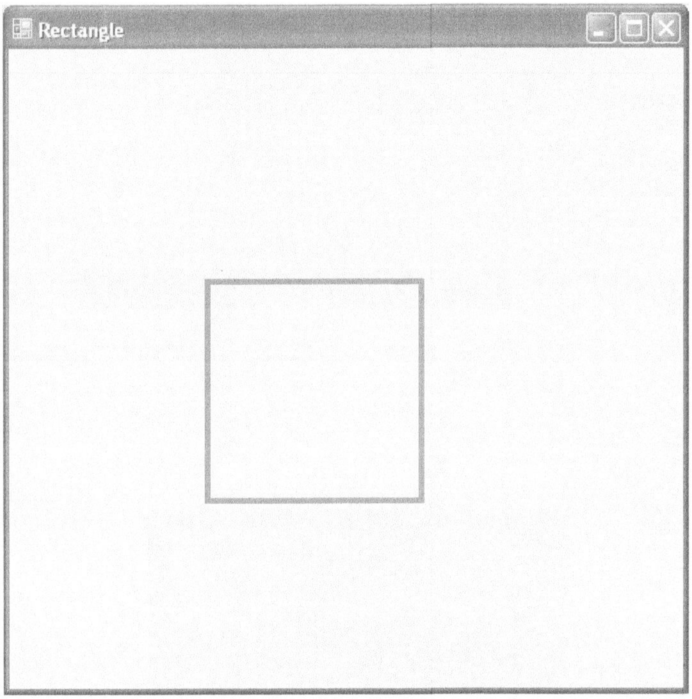

26.5 DISPLAYING A SOLID RECTANGLE

This program displays a solid rectangle.

Form Designing

Table 26.5 Displaying a Solid Rectangle

Control	*Property*	*Value*
Form1	Name	Form1
	Text	Displaying a solid rectangle

```
Public Class Form1
      Protected Overrides Sub OnPaint(ByVal e As PaintEventArgs)

            Dim g As Graphics
            g = e.Graphics
            Dim mypen As Pen
            mypen = New Pen(Color.DarkRed, 4)
            Dim mybrush As Brush
mybrush = New SolidBrush(Color.BlueViolet)
            g.FillRectangle(mybrush, 140, 160, 340, 260)

      End Sub

End Class
```

Output

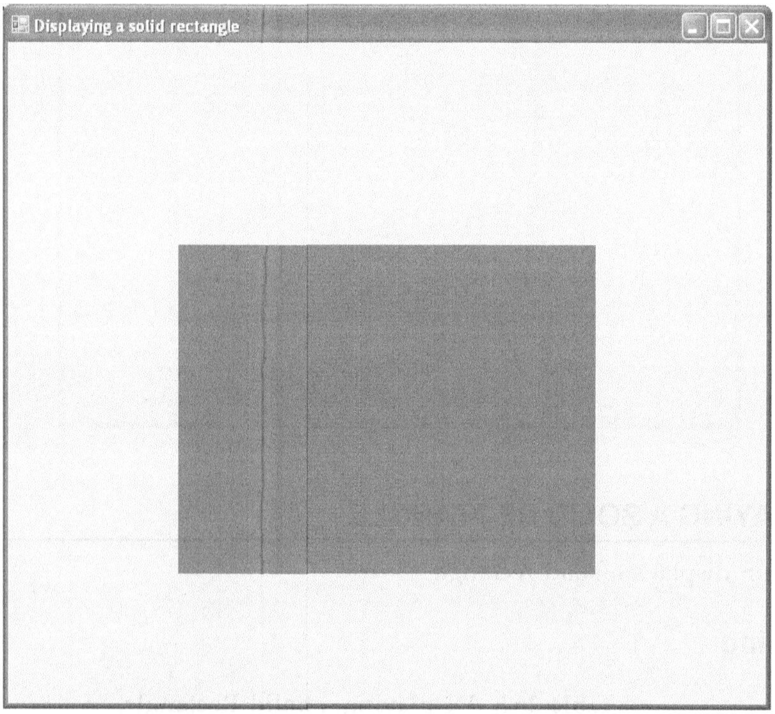

26.6 DISPLAYING AN IMAGE

This program displays an image.

Form Designing

Table 26.6 Displaying an Image

Control	*Property*	*Value*
Form1	Name	Form1
	Text	Displaying an Image

Coding

```
Public Class Form1
    Protected Overrides Sub OnPaint(ByVal e As PaintEventArgs)
        Dim g As Graphics
        g = e.Graphics
        Dim myimage As Image
        myimage = Image.FromFile("D:\karthikajesus\baby.jpg")
        g.DrawImage(myimage, 0, 0)
    End Sub
End Class
```

Output

INDEX

D

E

F

G

H

I

R

S

T

U

V

W